A Being More Intense

the art of six wood engravers

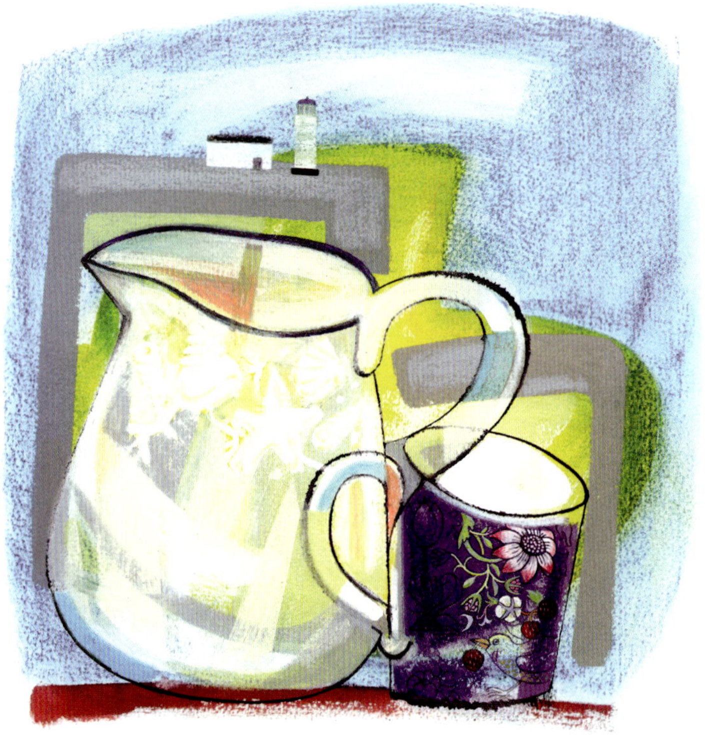

PETER LAWRENCE: *Quay 2, ink, pastel and gouache, 2004, 360 × 360 mm*

A Being More Intense

the art of six wood engravers

Jenny Pery

OBLONG

Published in 2009, on the occasion of the twenty-fifth anniversary of
the re-foundation of the Society of Wood Engravers in 1984,
by Oblong Creative Ltd
416B Thorp Arch Estate
Wetherby
West Yorkshire
LS23 7FG

ISBN 978 0 955 6576 1 0

Designed by Derek Brown at Oblong

Printed and bound by Henry Ling Ltd, The Dorset Press, Dorchester

Contents

1. Inner Worlds

The delicate crunch of the graver, the silky surface of the wood under the fingers, the control of the cut line, the gradual revealing of the image by banishing darkness and letting in the light, the tactile delight in printing from the smooth surface of the block, the range of silvery tones and the surprising authority of the printed image – all these things form part of the sensual and intellectual attractions of wood engraving. There is something about the medium, and the way in which the viewer peers at an engraved print, that is secretive, that invites the investigation of arcane ideas, that hovers on the edge of dreams. Many artists have worked out ideas and fantasies in wood engravings when other more confrontational mediums have seemed inappropriate. The small scale and exacting nature of the medium can liberate the imagination. Whole worlds can be suggested in tiny spaces.

Wood engraving depends upon drawing. The child's delight in drawing for its own sake, in manipulating lines and marks to express private ideas and loves, and the child's ability to live inside the developing drawing as if acting in a play, is an important motivating factor. Wood engravers have not lost the childhood compulsion to draw, and because drawing is translated into the much slower process of engraving, the pleasure of the mark-making is extended. A love and understanding of monochrome drawing comes with constant practice, and is essential for its reinvention into cut marks on the wood block. But it is the discovery of the special qualities of the incised mark that attracts engravers. The linear tracery that remains on the block after cutting is versatile enough to suggest a multitude of textures and densities very different from those that are drawn. The cut line, infinitely varied under different pressures with different tools, or side-cut to stand proud as a black line, has a crispness quite unlike the drawn line.

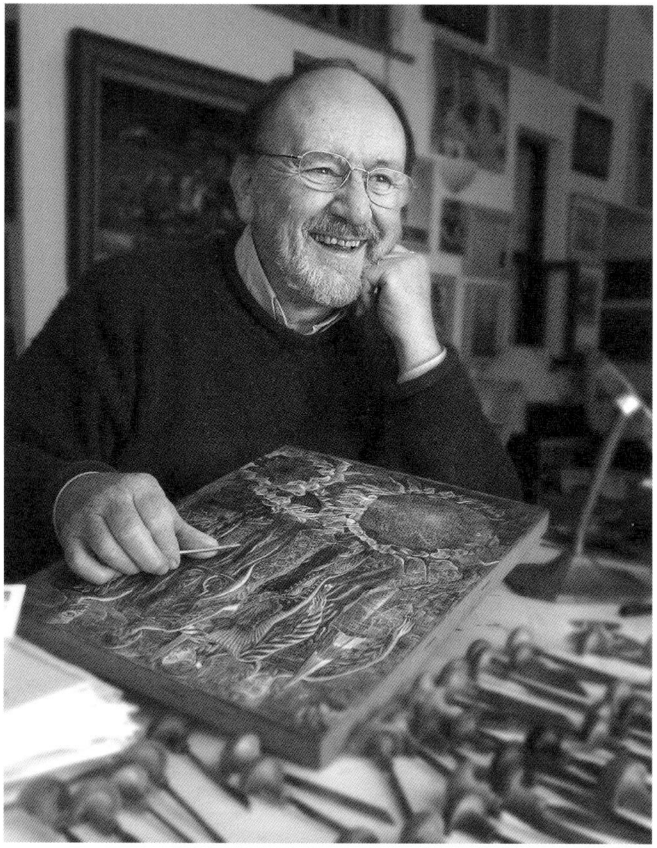

George Tute, photographed c. 2005 with the tools of the trade

For wood engravers a love of the material and the right use of tools is also a *sine qua non.* The hours of patient work required to complete a block necessitate positive enjoyment in handling tools and honing skills to perfection. It has recently been fashionable to dismiss manual dexterity as a barrier to the spontaneous expression now expected in art, but in the world of printmaking this is patently misguided. New ideas and new art do emerge from expertise or even depend on it, as William Blake believed: 'Innovation depends Altogether upon Execution or Organisation; as that is right or wrong so is the Invention perfect or imperfect. Whoever is set to Undermine the Execution of Art is set to destroy Art.'

Similar strictures have been applied to colour, or the lack of it. Since the explosion of colour caused by the mass of new pigments and media it has been fashionable to disregard monochrome work, which is not so insistent on the eye and can therefore have difficulty holding its own in mixed exhibitions. But monochrome work invites close scrutiny in a way that colour does not, and there is nothing better for revealing the thought processes of the artist. Wood engravings, traditionally printed in black and white, can play the tonal scale with a virtuosity that obviates the need for colour. The huge range of tones and textures achievable suggest colour, and viewers may provide their own optical colour by their knowledge of the subject depicted. The crepuscular delights of black, white and grey seem to fire the imagination and draw the viewer into the image. In wood engraving it is rare for added colour to improve on the intensity and sparkle of the blacks and whites.

The necessary limitation of size in wood engraving has the advantage of increasing the intensity of the image, thus involving the viewer. The compression of pictorial space, as well as the distinctive character of the mark-making, invites a different way of looking. The viewer not only 'reads' the engraved marks, feeling the human hand behind them, but also sympathetically shrinks, Alice-through-the-Looking-Glass-wise, to enter into the picture. The senses are activated. The fingertips respond to delicate, feathery marks and bold, bravura cutting, while the clarion counterpoint of black and white seems to ring in the ears.

This book celebrates the endurance of wood engraving as a serious artistic medium within the general flux of contemporary art. Disregarded and unfashionable for some years, wood engraving has been brought again to the forefront by the artists

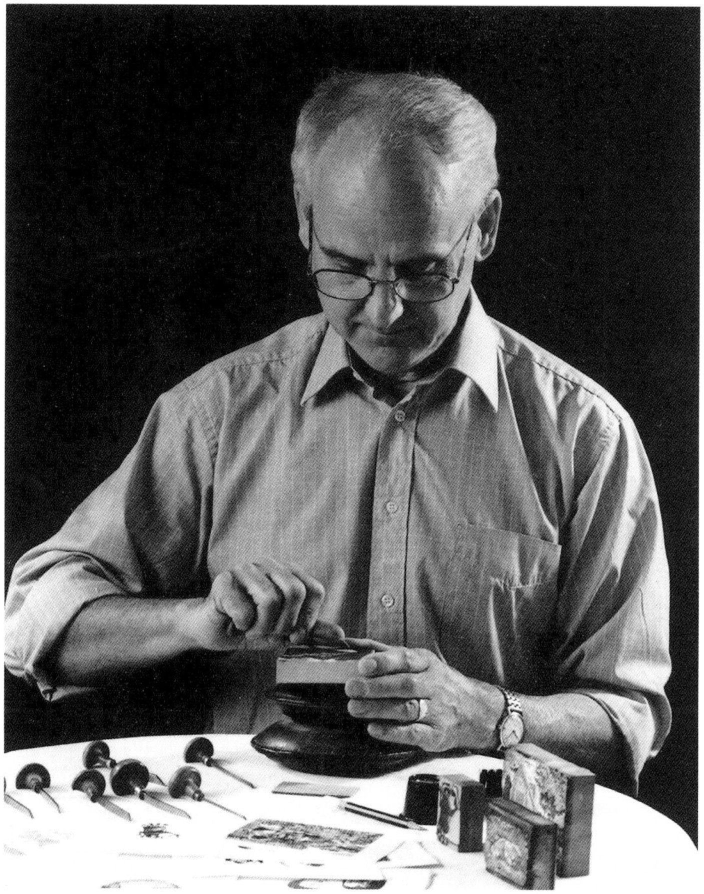

Ian Stephens, photographed in 2003 in engraving mode

who have persisted with it. It now holds its place happily in contemporary exhibitions alongside other forms of printmaking. Perhaps because engravings are small and affordable, they are popular with the public. They are also the *crème de la crème* of book illustration.

The essays in this book explore the formative years, and dip into the inner worlds, of six artists, to discover the roots of their art and their reasons for choosing this exacting medium. Different artistic backgrounds – painting, graphic design, illustration, sculpture – have formed them. But despite the differences in their personal backgrounds and their approaches to art, they have all come to share a fascination with the engraved line and the tonal range of which the medium is capable, as well as a liking for the patience and control required. Their work covers a wide range of subjects – landscape, townscape, still life, genre, history, mythology, fantasy, pure abstraction. All six, as masters of their medium, have exhibited their work widely in solo and mixed exhibitions, national and international, and have undertaken commercial work as well as making autographic prints. They have also been 'enablers', teaching or promoting the medium, especially through the Society of Wood Engravers. They have been instrumental in organising the Society's exhibitions to provide a showcase for wood engraving and a forum for the cross-fertilisation of ideas. Most importantly, they are in love with their medium, which has become a major part of their lives. Perhaps that is the point of artistic endeavour. As Byron put it:

> 'Tis to create, and in creating live
> A being more intense, that we endow
> With form our fancy, gaining as we give
> The life we image.

All quotations in the following chapters are taken from recorded conversations with Jenny Pery or from the artists' own writings. Where no size is stated, engravings are reproduced actual size.

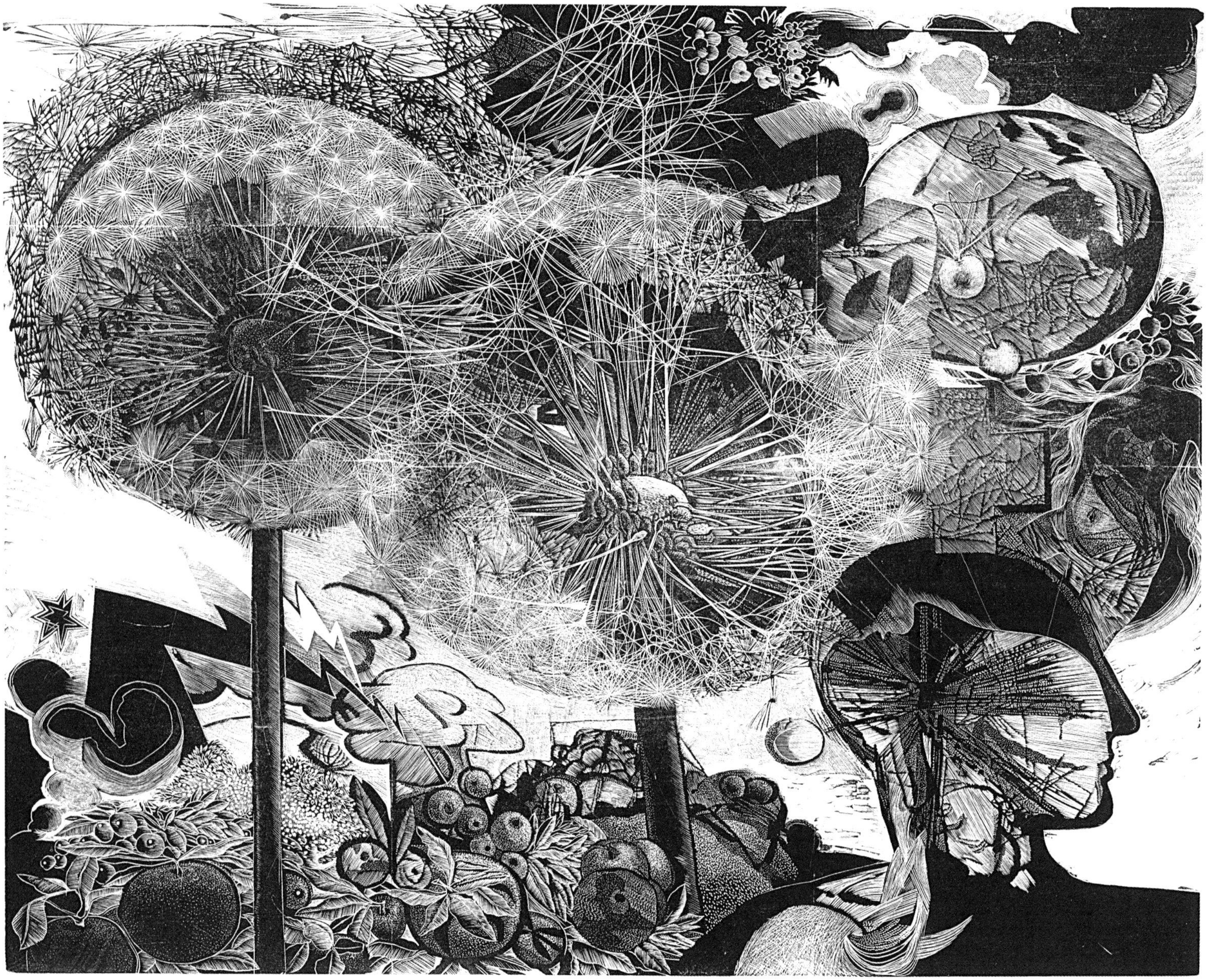

2. Layering Experience

George Tute

Chairman of the Society of Wood Engravers 1984–1986

Part fantasy, part fact, the world that appears in George Tute's paintings and prints teems with a richly bucolic mixture of people, animals and plants. Tute's romantic imagination fills to brimming point the large canvases and small woodblocks that he keeps on the go at the same time. Chance encounters recall previous experiences and set him dreaming, and the pictorial working-out of his dreams unfolds new layers of meaning and unexpected depths. As he asserts, the very different media complement each other. 'I have always painted at the same time as wood engraving; one technique gives you something that the other cannot. Painting is a much

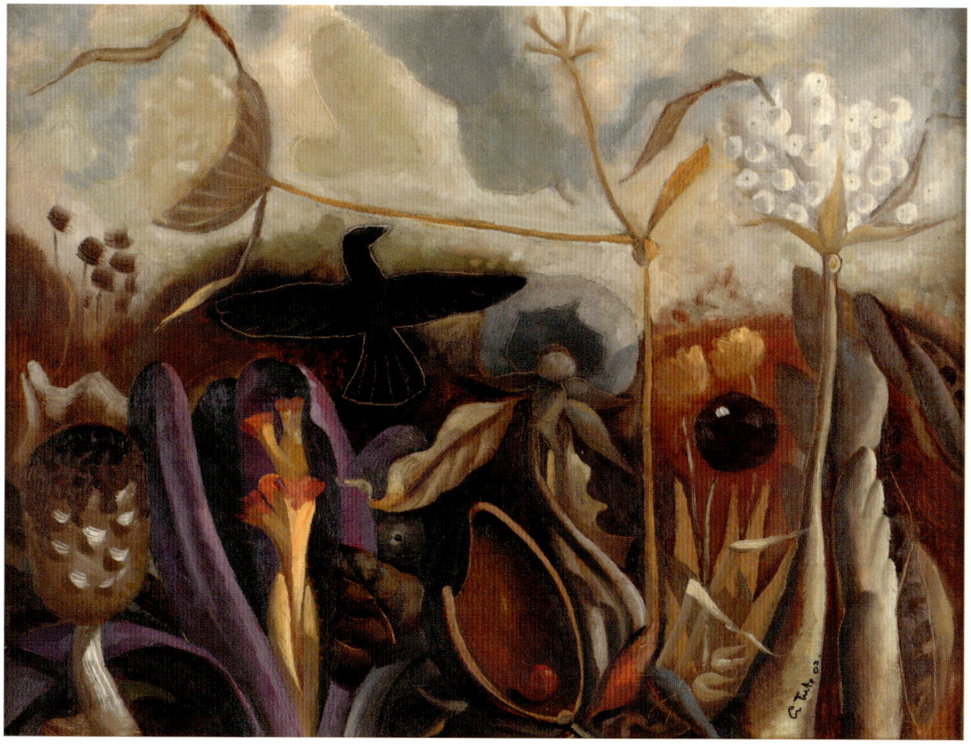

Opposite: Transition, c. 1970, 277 × 352 mm

This page: Blackbird, oil, 2002, 500 × 600 mm

GEORGE TUTE

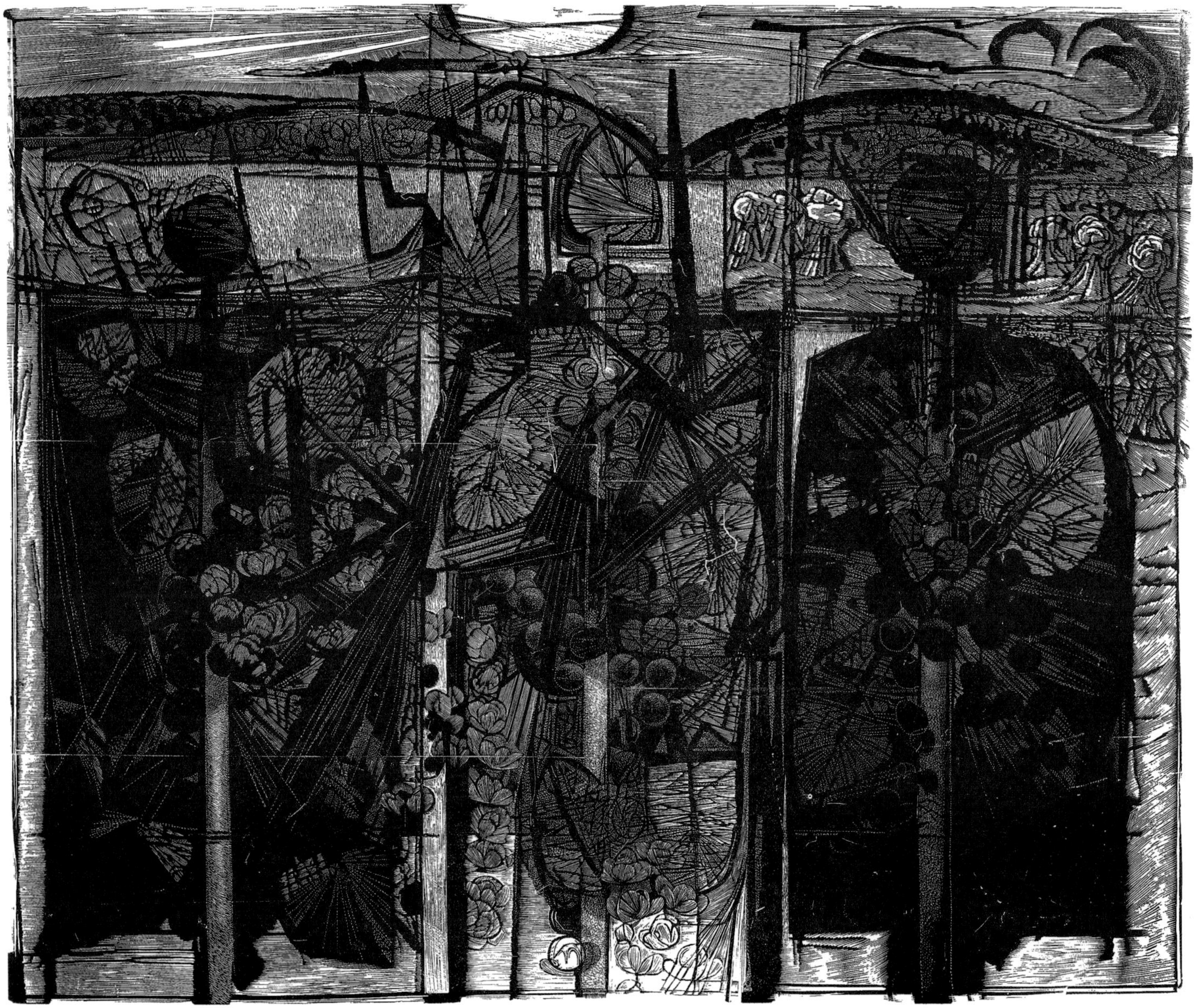

8

freer process, you can alter and use accident. The happy accident has to be seized and is then modified by feedback, judgement and experience. I start by tinting the canvas with burnt umber, using big brushes and lots of swirly turps. I don't overstress the meaning or force the images but allow them to come out. You should let the painting talk back to you. With wood engraving you have to have a more precise approach, particularly when dealing with letterforms, architecture and portraiture. Engravings that are primarily autographic allow more freedom to explore on the block, but the scale and the relief process puts a limit on the image. Although it is slow the actual technique is so mesmeric that it makes you go on.'

George Tute's enormous airy studio is filled with his own work, past and current, as well as work by other painters he admires – Keith Vaughan, Ivon Hitchins, Cedric Morris, Alan Reynolds, David Jones. Steeped in the traditions of English Neo-Romanticism, and despite Neo-Romanticism's relegation to the margins of contemporary art fashion, Tute has remained true to its principles. A mixture of carefully observed objects, semi-abstract imaginary designs, and vorticist abstract forms and patterns are woven into the opulent stuff of his creation. Now, after more than fifty years working across a variety of media, he finds that the different processes begin to link up. As he says, 'all these things are part of you, a summary of your life and experience.'

Tute's predilection for art seems to have come out of the blue. He was born in Hull in 1933, into a Yorkshire fishing community. His grandfather died in a fishing accident, and his grandmother had brought up her five children on her own. The family must at one time have been prosperous because her house was full of paintings – mainly Scottish paintings of the 'brown' school. At the start of the war Hull was bombed, and the Tute family was evacuated to Fleetwood in Lancashire. Throughout the war George's father served in the Royal Army Medical Corps, mostly in India, while his uncles were in the Navy.

Opposite page: Militant Forms, c. 1963, 250 × 300 mm

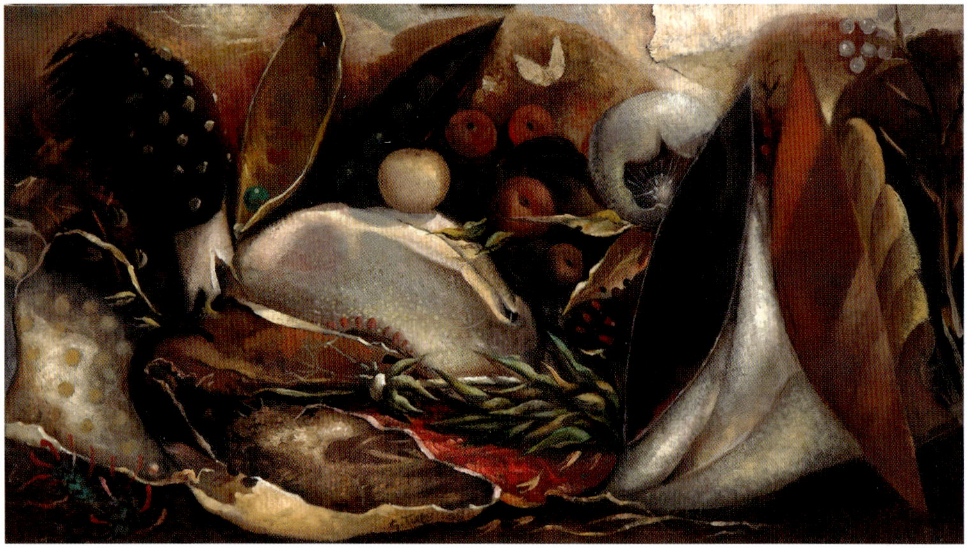

Nature Morte, oil, 2006, 500 × 700 mm

George Tute's interest in art revealed itself when he went to Bainse's Grammar School at Poulton le Fylde. He also spent much out-of-school time drawing and practising watercolours, encouraged by Mr Crosswell, a retired miner and art teacher whom his mother paid to give him weekend lessons. His father, reunited with his family, wanted George to work in the family business rather than take up what seemed a high-risk occupation, but his mother was determined that her son should make the most of his talents. When George left school aged sixteen she took him to Blackpool School of Art for an interview. The Principal, Mr Hayes, evidently approved of his watercolours and enrolled him into the four-year diploma course.

The National Diploma in Design introduced Tute to a wide range of disciplines, including pottery, modelling, lithography and relief printing, but the cornerstone of the teaching was traditional drawing. The tutors at Blackpool were bent on training their students to be teachers in their turn. Tute, however, along with some

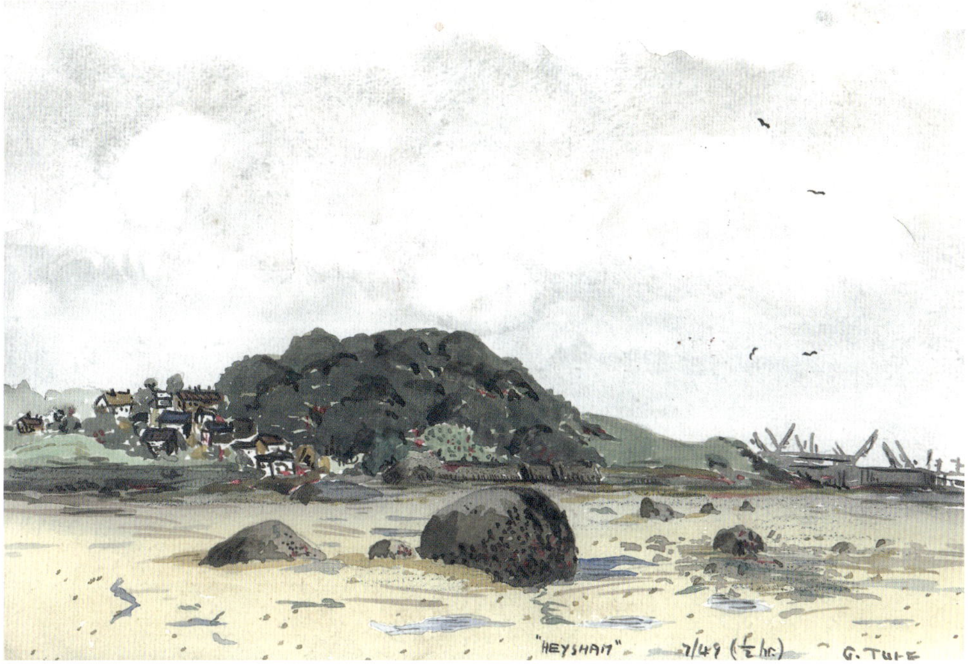

Heysham, watercolour, 1949, 150 × 200 mm

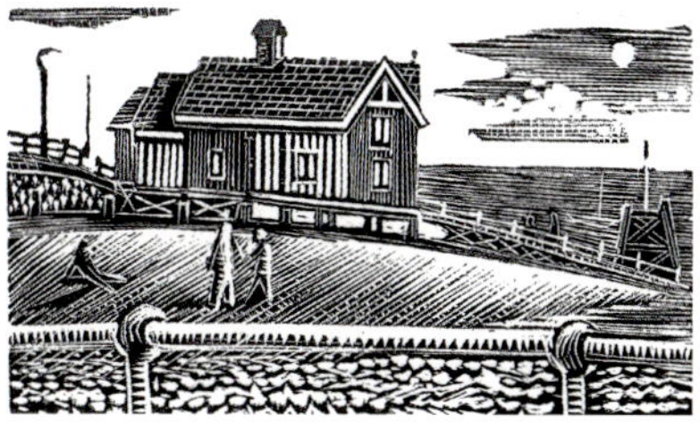

Lifeboat House, Fleetwood, 1950

fellow students, was more interested in becoming a full-time painter. The whole group applied to the Royal Academy Schools and all were accepted. Relishing their first time away from home, the Blackpool students embarked on the five-year course at the Royal Academy, then under the Keepership of Henry Rushbury, and later Peter Greenham. Tute spent his evenings at Regent Street Polytechnic doing a further National Diploma in Design, with Illustration as his main subject. Welcome variation to the student year came when the Royal Academy gave Tute and the Blackpool group permission to live and work in St Paul-de-Vence in the south of France. Although the house they found was primitive, without running water or modern facilities, it was ideal for their purpose. The three winter terms that they spent painting there were magical times. For a long time France was Tute's great love and Cézanne a major influence. Both were later superseded by

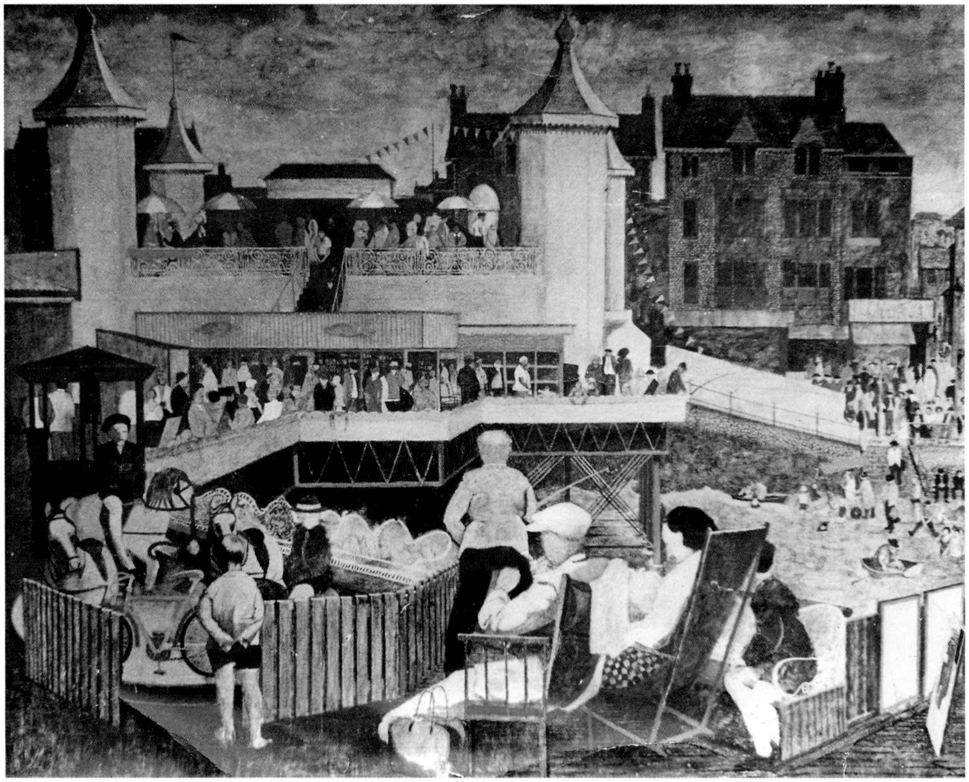

Blackpool Central Pier,
NDD Examination Painting, 1953,
3 ft × 4 ft

love for Germany, where his wife's family live, where he spent a sabbatical year, and where he worked on his first large *Sunflower Field*.

After nine years at art college Tute was called up for national service. He was sent to RAF Bridgenorth, where his activities included 'square bashing' and where he was cajoled into engraving – incising a dog's name on a bronze medallion for his billet corporal. Transferred to RAF Hendon, Tute worked as an Artist/Designer in the Exhibition Display and Design Unit which comprised an architect, technicians, and carpenters as well as artists, their job being to design exhibition stands and other items for recruitment, including the occasional large mural. Tute spent most

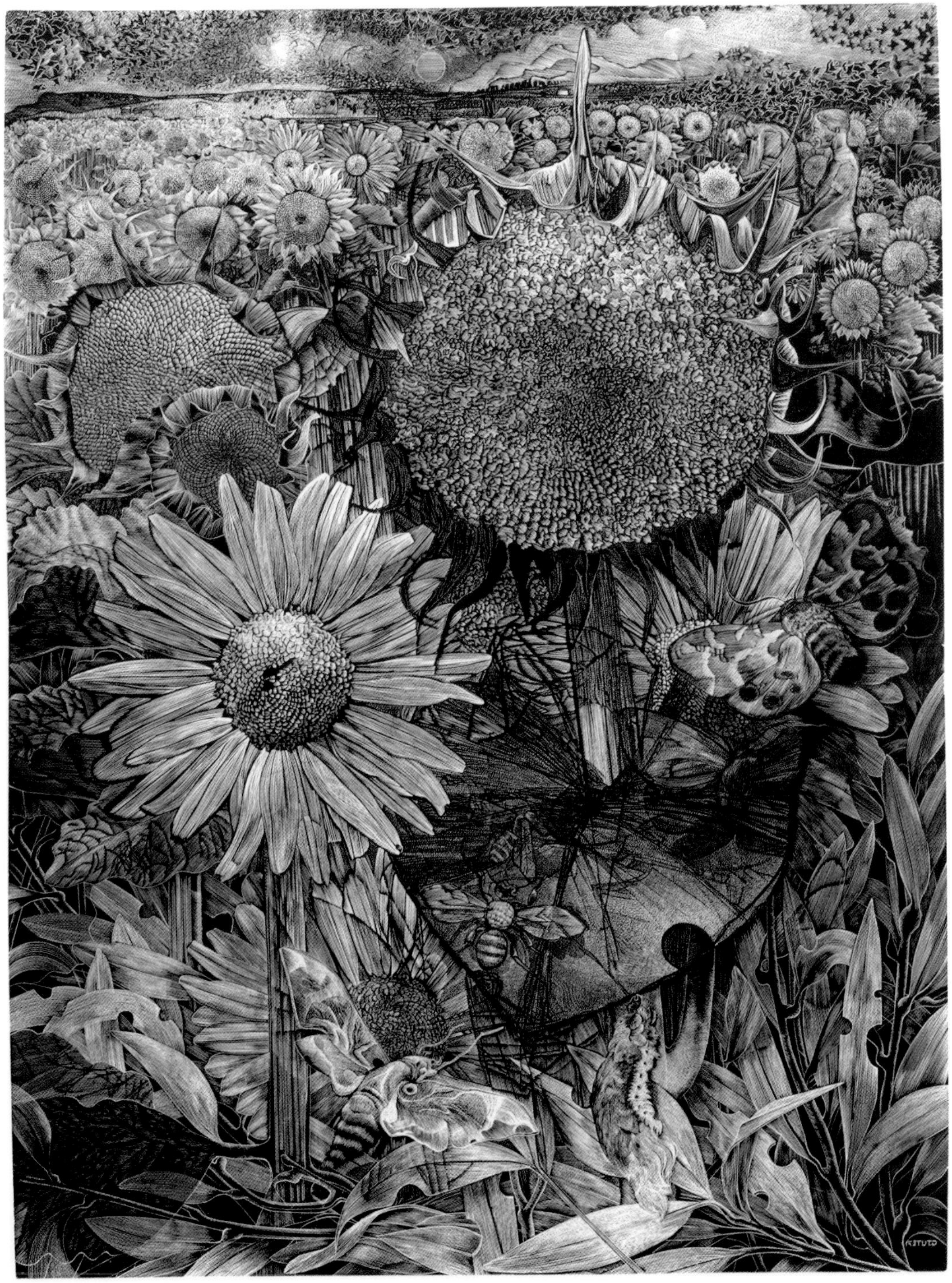

Sunflower Field, c. 1971,
402 × 304 mm

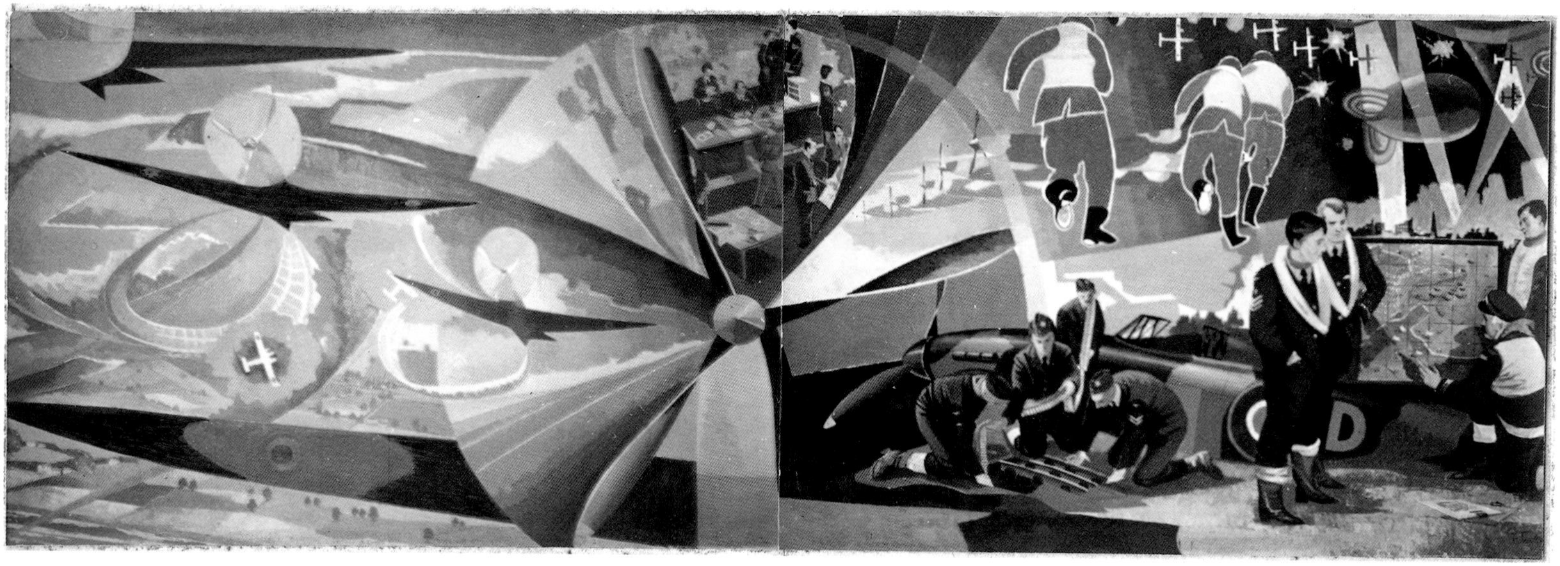

Battle of Britain Mural, RAF, 1959, 6 ft × 20 ft

of his time working at Adastral House in Holborn, which happened to be opposite the Central School of Art. Seizing every opportunity, he took himself to Gertrude Hermes' evening classes in wood engraving at the Central. In Blackpool and at the RA he had already made engravings that had been exhibited with the Society of Wood Engravers and the Royal Society of Painter Printmakers (at that time known as 'Painter-Etchers').

By the end of national service Tute had accumulated a portfolio full of autographic engravings and commissioned illustrations, including *Dandelion Heads* for the magazine *Stocking Monthly*. His early prints show him experimenting to find ways of amalgamating many different observations and experiences within one block. The experiences were building up. While at the Royal Academy a letter from Budapest addressed to William Hogarth had been passed to him for a response. This strange letter, from a student at the Budapest Academy of Arts who was desperate, during the Russian invasion, to obtain heart pills for her father, led to a

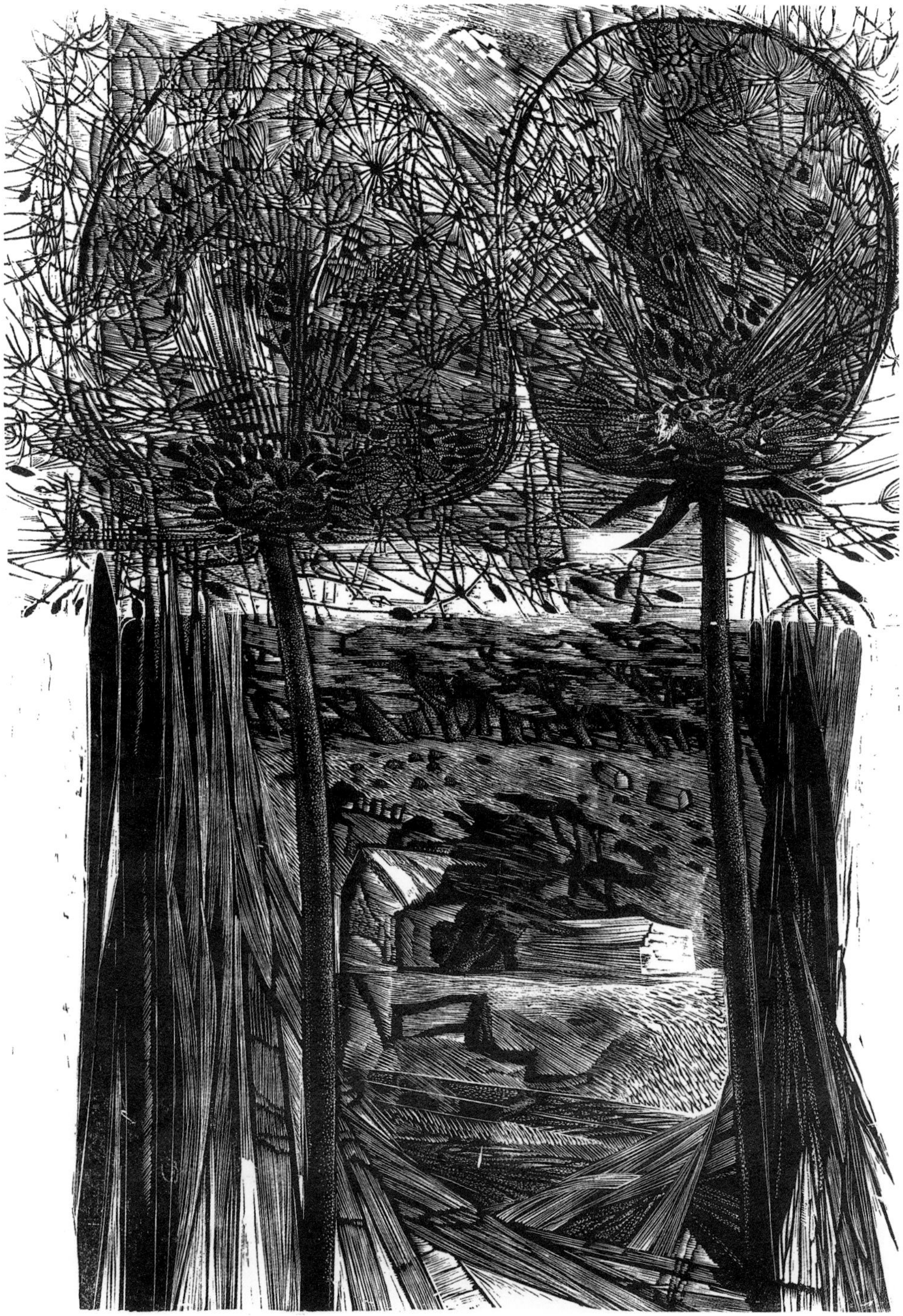

Dandelion Seed Head,
Stocking Monthly, 1959,
200 × 150 mm

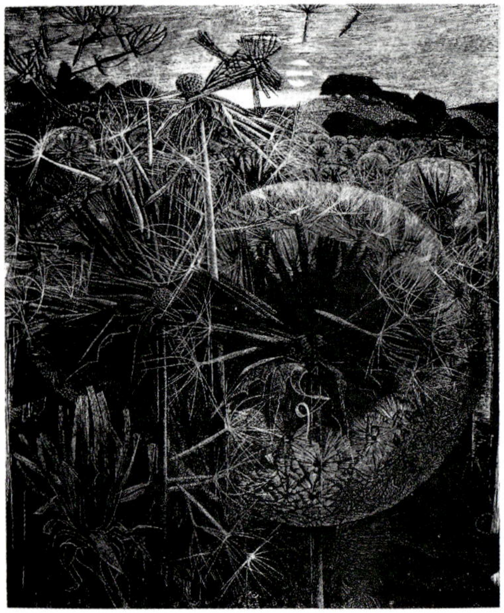

visit and a longstanding connection with Hungary. It was in Hungary that Tute first saw the enormous fields of sunflowers that prompted many later images. Wood engraving seemed the ideal medium for weaving together different motifs, the finished block when printed giving a remarkable sense of completeness and a quality that painting could not emulate. He now asserts that 'after fifty years I have squared the circle between wood engraving and painting – the concerns are the same and both are celebratory.'

Dandelion Field, 1962, 250 × 200 mm

Op Art Painting, oil, 1965, 550 × 750 mm

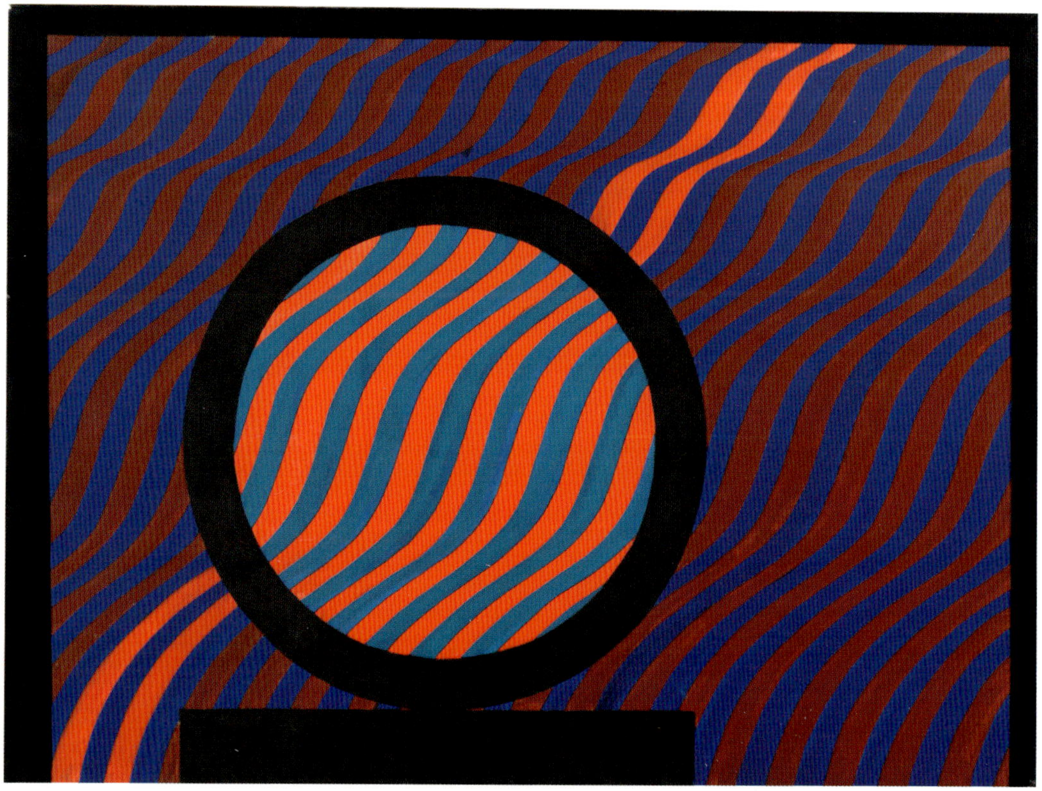

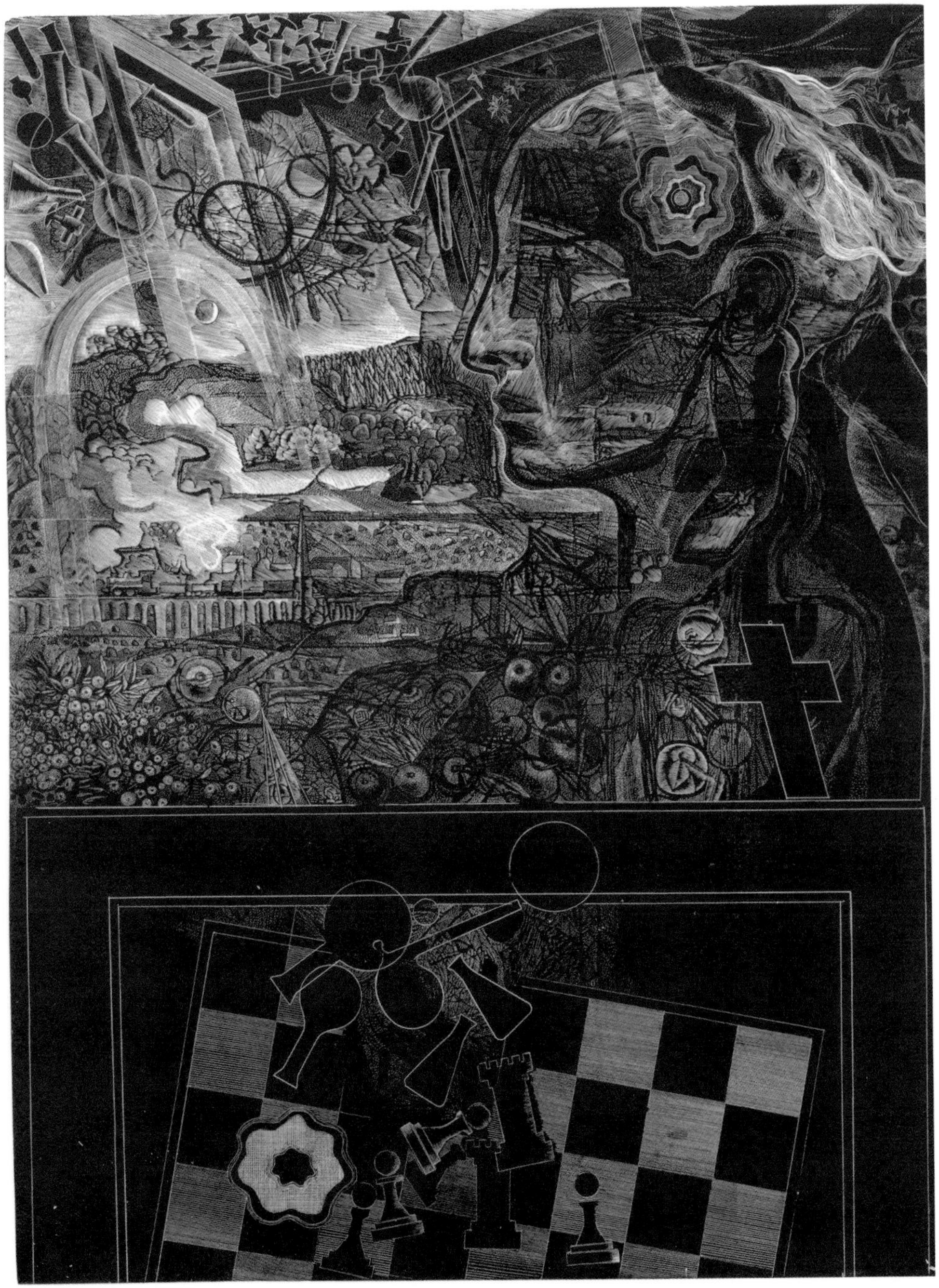

Illustrated Man, c. 1972, 400 × 300 mm

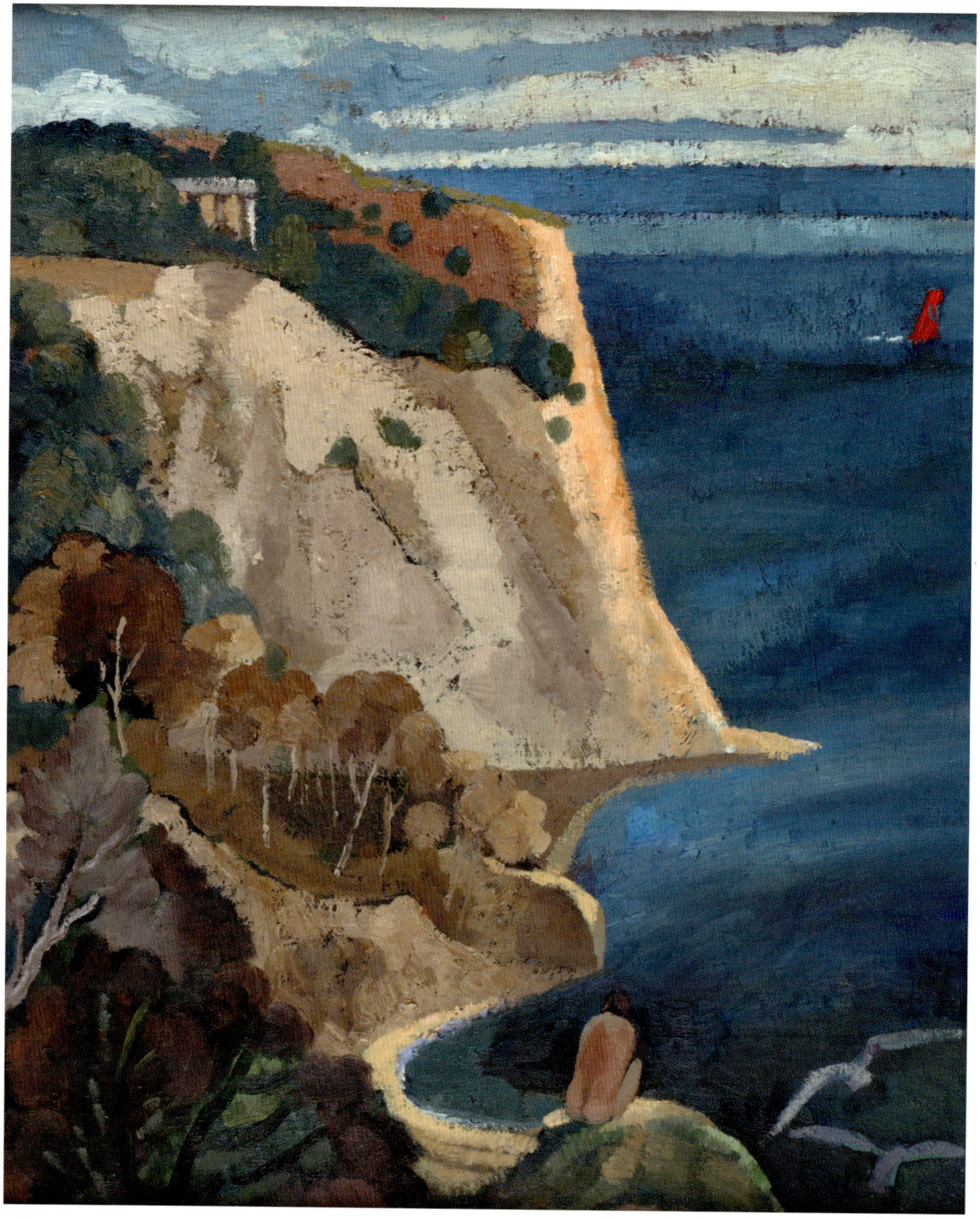

Rugen, oil, c. 1990,
600 × 400 mm

Thirty years of art teaching followed, first at York School of Art (where Tute met his wife, Iris Stoltenberg-Lerche) and then at the West of England College of Art, Bristol. The college was undergoing a period of unrest due to William Coldstream's reforms, and Tute, representing 'new blood', was welcomed into the Graphics Department on the strength of his graphic work. He continued to teach in Bristol through its many changes, eventually becoming Principal Lecturer and Director of Studies in the Department of Graphic Design. He also broadened his horizons with sabbaticals in Germany and Italy and, in 1987, by doing an MA at the Royal College of Art, where he conducted a practical investigative analysis into multiple colour printing and wrote a thesis on approaches to wood engraving that is still available for perusal in the RCA library.

UFO 's Over Fenland, Readers Digest, 1973

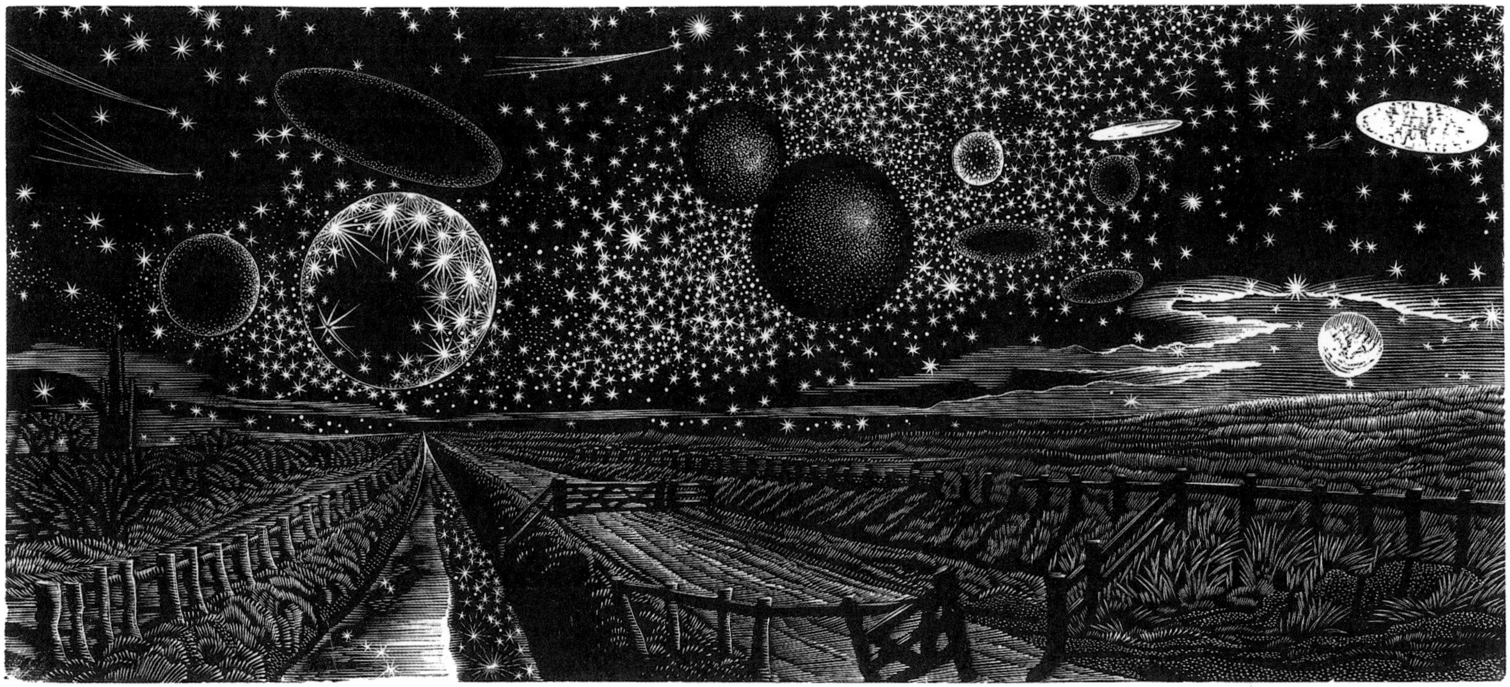

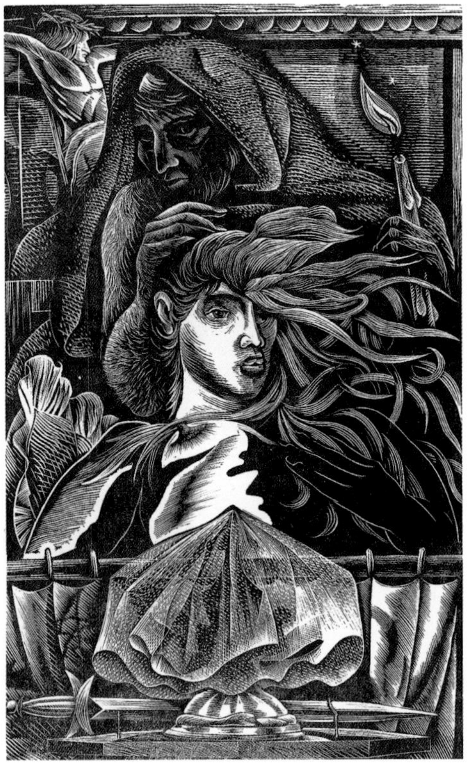

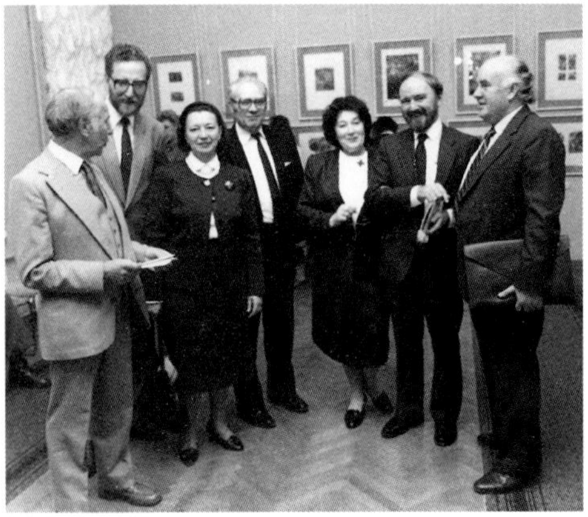

Retirement from teaching in 1987 left Tute free to pursue his own work and also to devote more time to promoting the practice of wood engraving. From the late 1950s he had exhibited work with the Royal Society of Painter Printmakers and with the Society of Wood Engravers, becoming a member of both societies in the early 1960s. He was vitally important to the revival of the SWE in 1984. When he was elected Chairman the rump of the old Society still existed, and a renewal of interest in the medium was created by exhibitions in Hereford, commercial publications such as *Campaign* magazine, various lectures, conferences and workshops in Bristol, and teaching in some art schools. Tute's role was that of a catalyst, bringing together a diverse group of strong-minded individuals whose main aim was to ensure a good re-start for the Society. 'The Civil Service Club was the venue for the first meeting which was chaired by John Newson; subsequently the committee meetings were held in Hilary Paynter's Richmond studio ... My own attitude as Chairman was that the more committee members the merrier, as I did not want to see a repeat of the problems that had led to the demise of the old Society ... The first exhibition of the new Society – being the 47th Exhibition – was held at the Garden Gallery, Kew, in 1984 and was followed by a number of travelling exhibitions in the same year ... I edited and produced the Society's journal which ran for two editions before being transformed into *Multiples* ... One of the main events of my chairmanship was the visit to Russia in October 1986, at the beginning of *Glasnost*. William Butler, Secretary of the Bookplate Society, had floated the idea after the second Hereford exhibition, and through his contacts in Russia we had the opportunity to visit Moscow, Bukhara and Samarkand, lecturing on wood engraving and staging an exhibition of our work in Moscow and then donating it to the All-Union Society of Book Lovers.'

George Tute's energy and experience as a practising artist helped to raise the profile of the Society and of wood engraving in general. His own work was to be seen in many exhibitions at the Royal Academy, the Royal West of England Academy, and

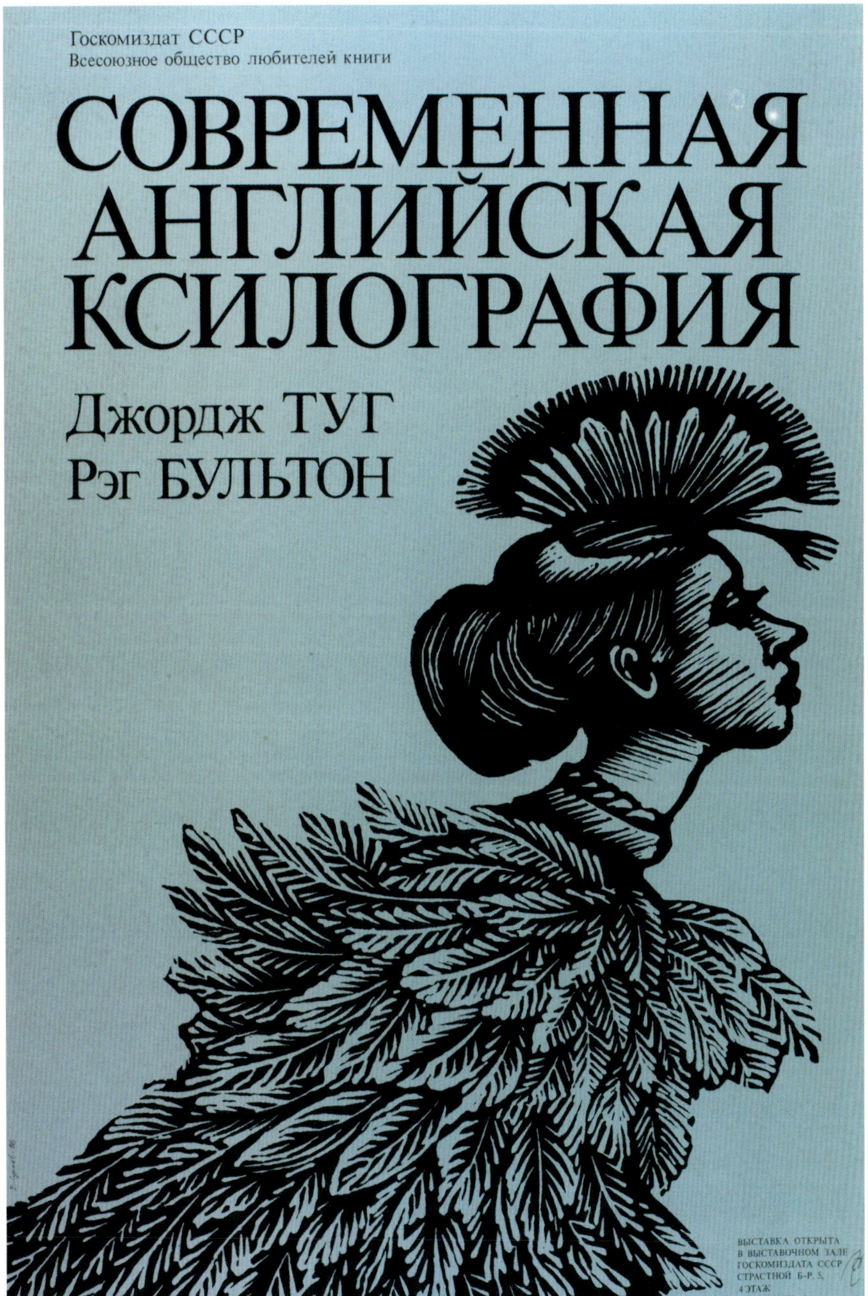

Opposite page, top: For The Monk, Folio Society, 1984, 164 × 102 mm

Opposite page, below: Private view Moscow, A. Kalashnikov (right), R. Boulton (left) and G. Tute (second right), 1986

This page: Poster for Moscow Exhibition, 1986

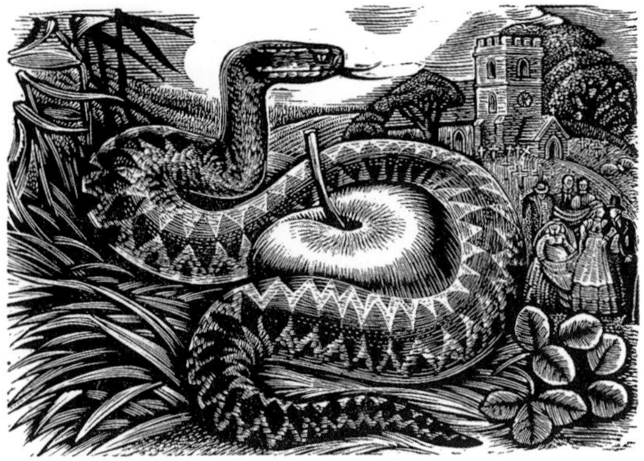

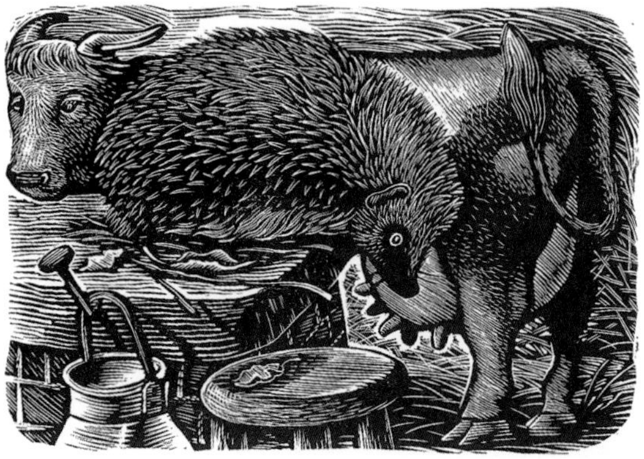

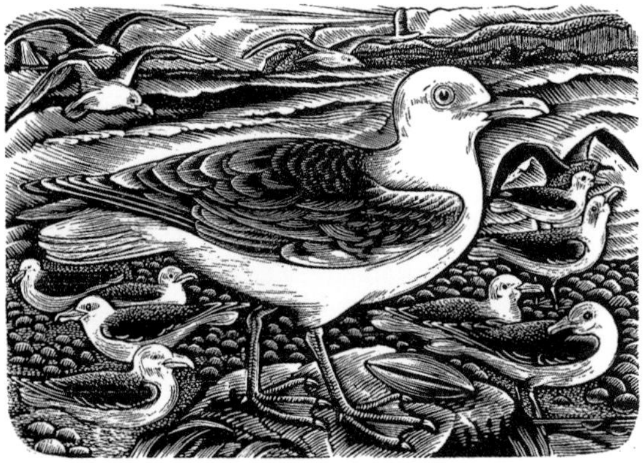

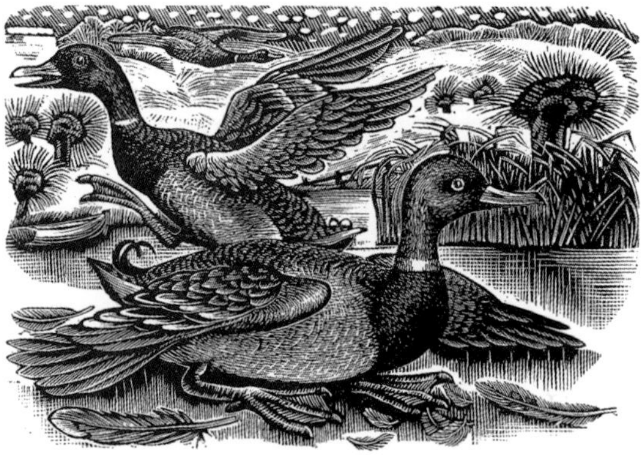

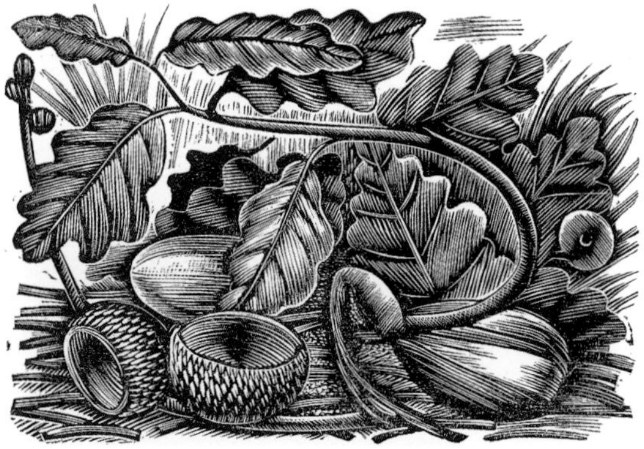

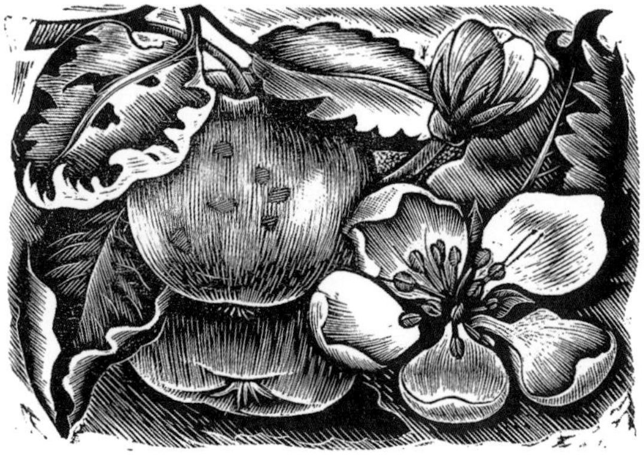

Both pages: For Under the Hawthorn,
Sybil Marshall, Dent, 1981

in private galleries. He undertook commercial work for the whisky distillers, Glenmorangie, fulfilled a major commission for wood-engraved-based murals for The Galleria shopping mall in Bristol, and illustrated many of the Folio Society's books. Musing in the Society's newsletter, he wrote: 'Wood Engravers are a peculiar lot, but lack of tenacity is not one of their failings. Isolated in their ways, with an inside-out, back-to-front, monochrome vision of the world in miniature, they use a technique which requires time and patience as well as optimisim to keep going through those tedious hours of scorpering, chiselling and spitsticking, before the final print dashes their hopes or revives their faith.'

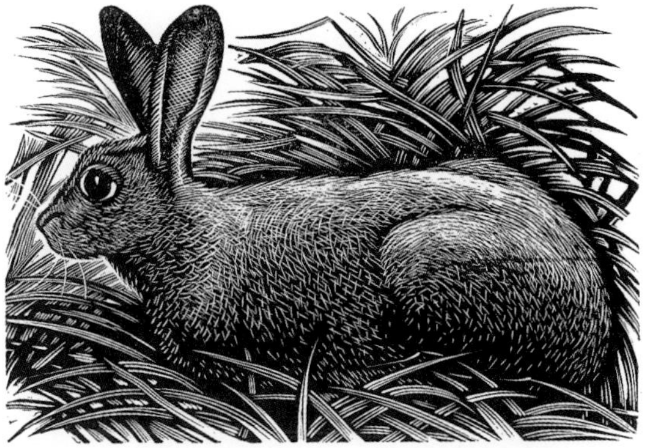

Intricate mark-making, non-natural lighting, and surreal assemblages of real and imaginary forms are the hallmarks of George Tute's art. The rich coloration of his painting is echoed in the subtle range of darks and silvery greys that he achieves in his engraving. Despite their delicate, feathery cuts, his dandelions and sunflowers have a grandeur that belies their size. The exquisite mark-making in engravings such as *Silbury Man* and *Transition* gives to the exploration of his inner world the peculiar intensity that is unique to the medium.

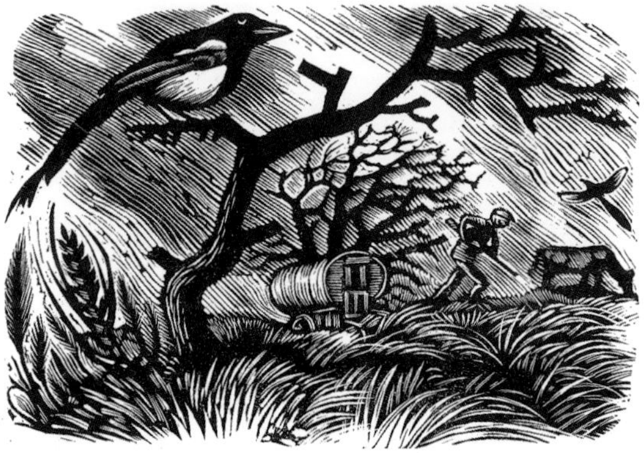

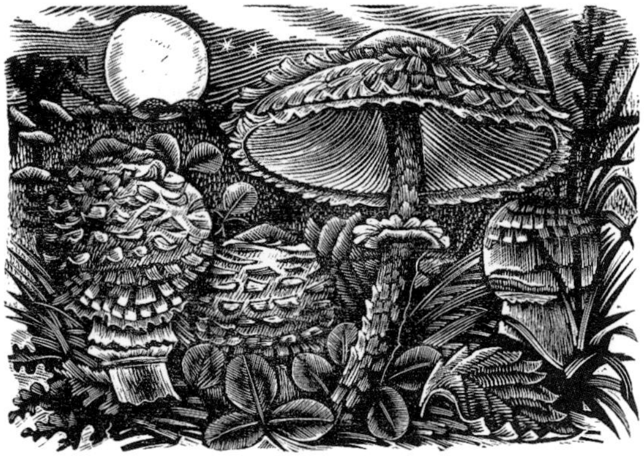

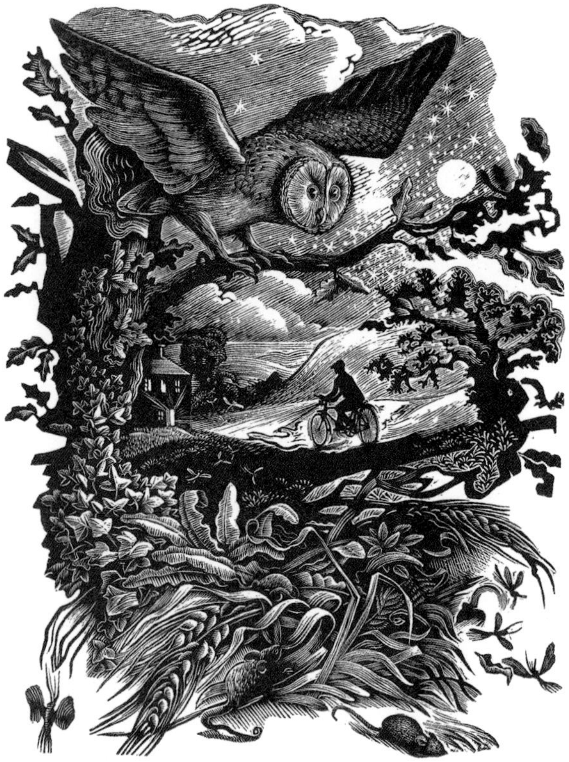

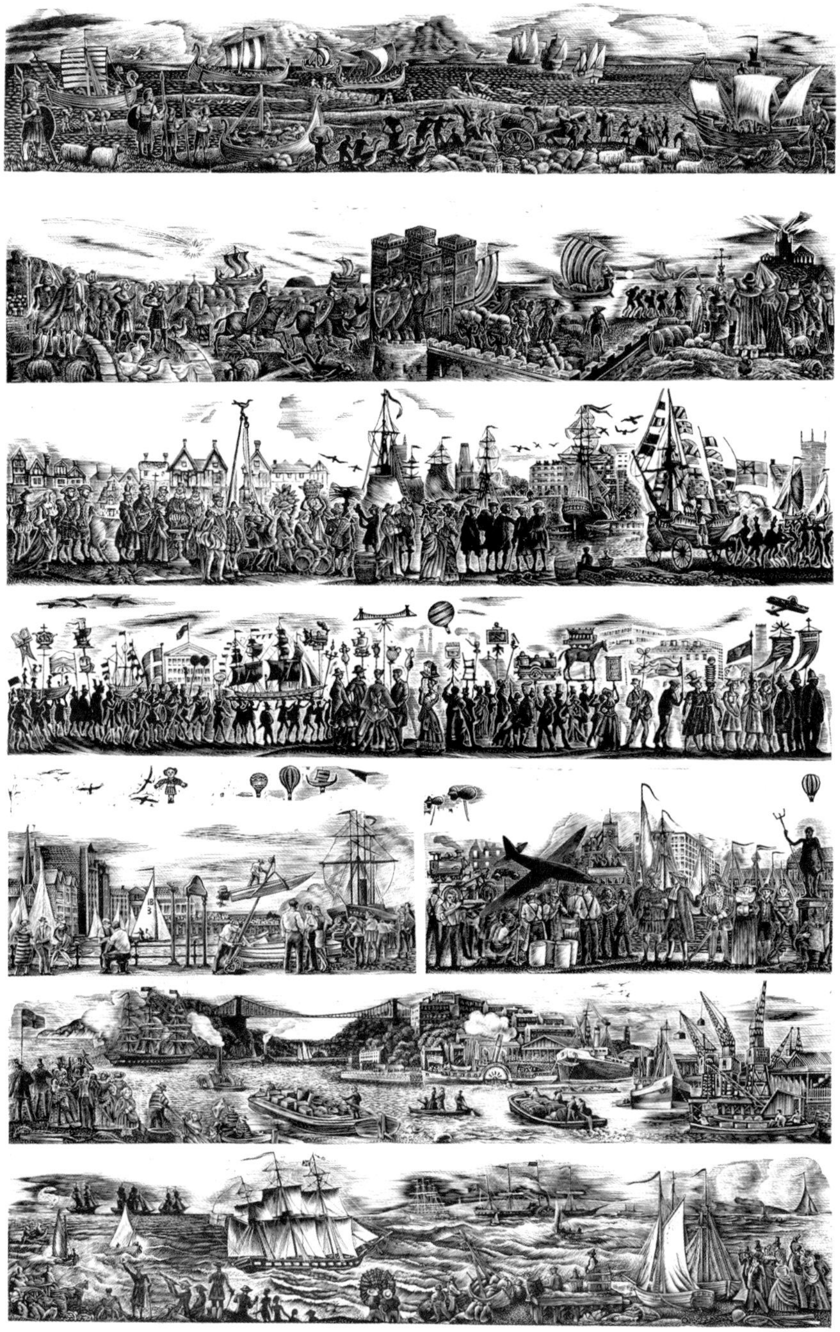

Cycling to the Distillery Tain, Glenmorangie advertising campaign, 1984, 198 × 150 mm

Engravings for Murals at the Galleria, Bristol, c. 1994, 500 × 300 mm

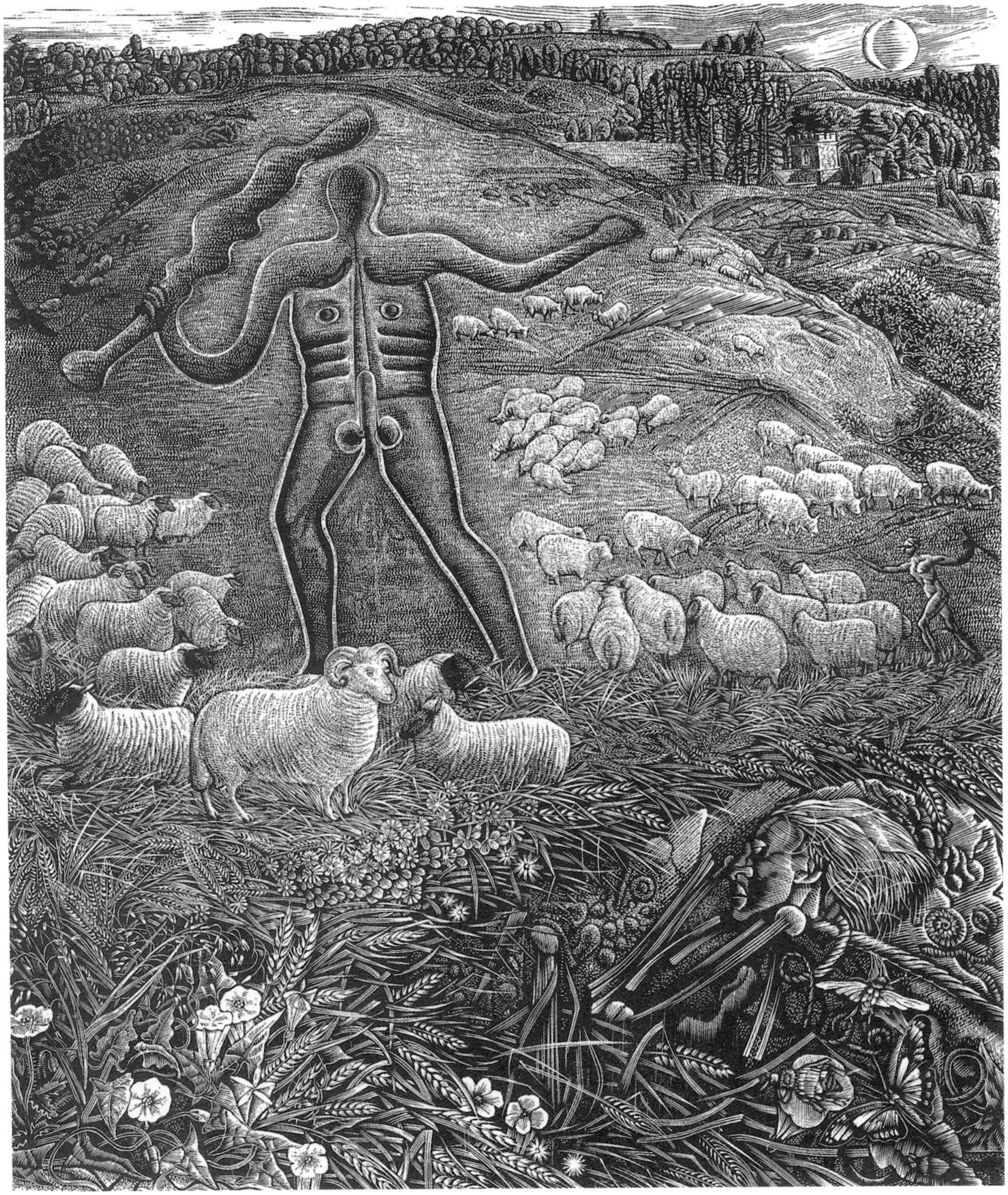

Cerne Abbas Giant, for proposed private press edition of Bone Dreams by Seamus Heaney, c. 1978, 223 × 194 mm

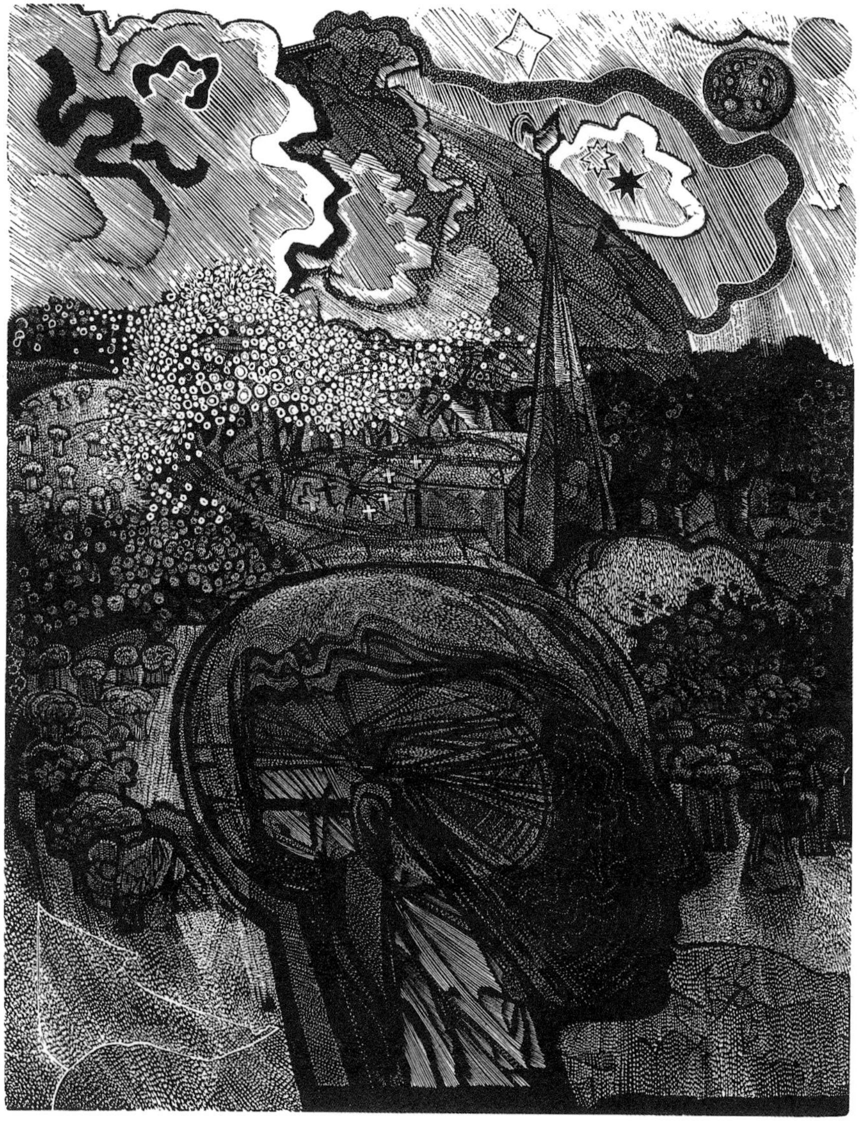

Silbury Man, 1969

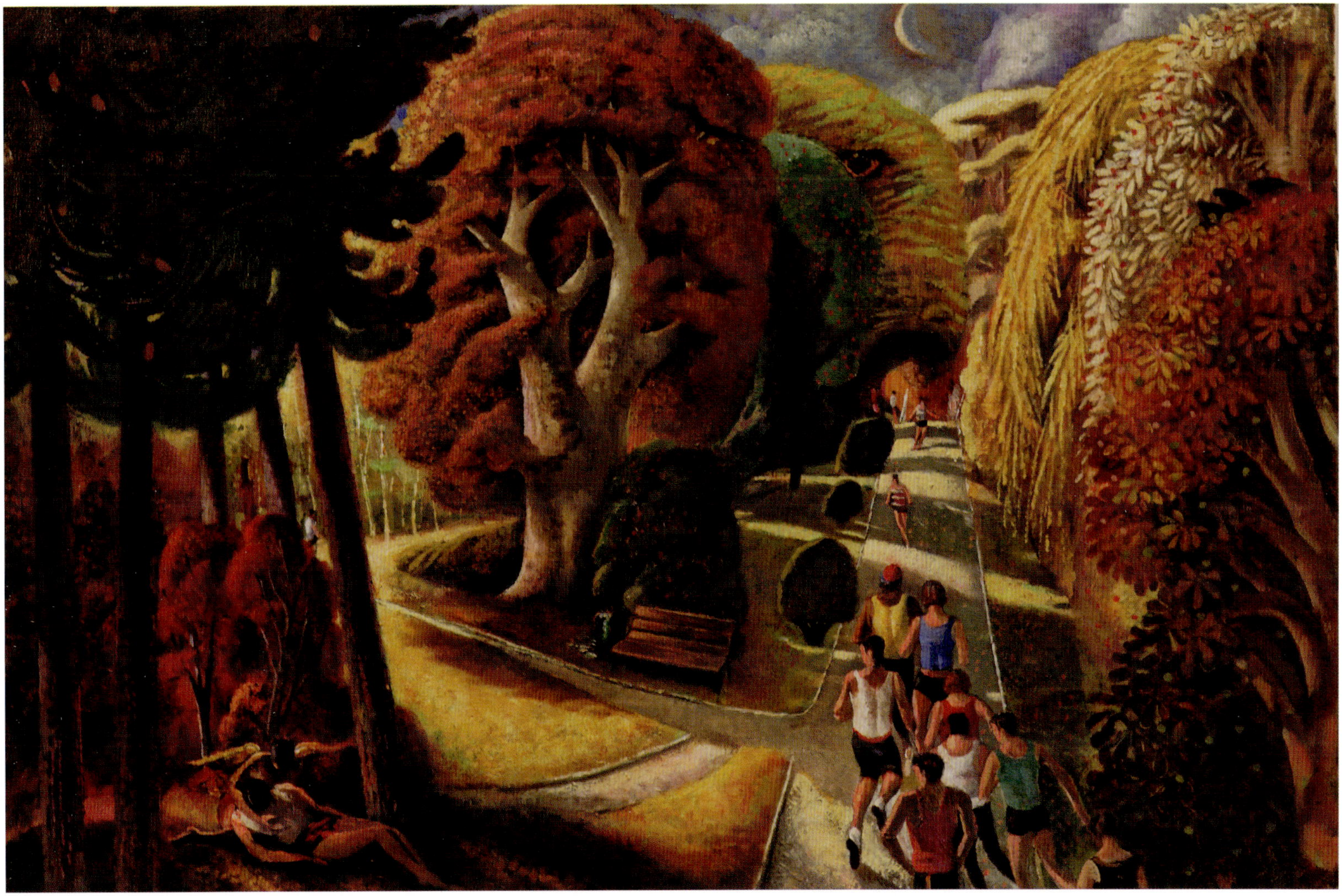

Joggers on the Downs, oil, 2006, 500 × 800 mm

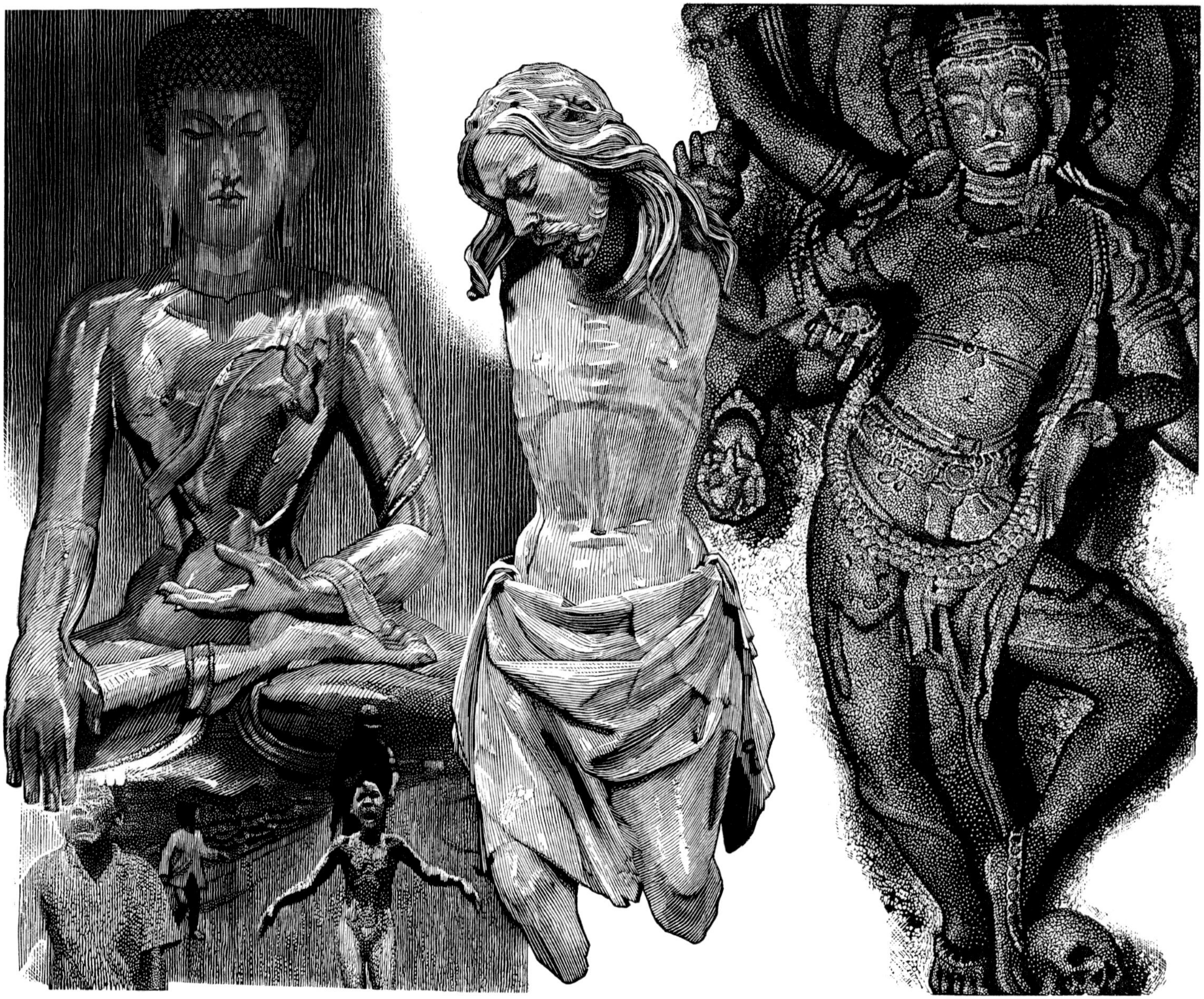

SIMON BRETT: *Three Torsos, 2000, 200 × 250 mm*

3. In Pursuit of the Soul

Simon Brett

Chairman of the Society of Wood Engravers 1986–1992

'To tell the truth and to save my soul; or at least bring it into being.' When questioned about his artistic aspirations, Simon Brett delves deep. He sees his art as a vocation, a way of being in touch with the fundamentals of human existence as well as a means of bringing understanding to others. His work is concerned with the human condition – the strengths and weaknesses of people in the real world and in the imaginary worlds of others. Brett is formidably well-read and possesses a strong sense of history. He combines erudition with acute visual perceptiveness, and the images he creates are complex *mille-feuilles* of ideas and sensory experiences.

Simon Brett was born in Windsor in the middle of World War II. When his father returned from the North African and Italian campaigns after the war, he found a job as Steward of Saint Bartholomew's Hospital in London. For Antony Brett, son of the actress and famous Edwardian beauty Zena Dare and adored grandson of Viscount Esher, post-war life compared poorly with the easy affluence of the pre-war years, and the flat in Bart's which became his home was something of a come-down. Only the Brett family lived full-time in the hospital, reaching their second-floor flat by way of the grand staircase decorated by murals painted by William Hogarth in 1735. As a boy Simon Brett passed these every day, and they were among the first paintings to make an impression on him. Within his family art was thought of as light entertainment, represented mainly by theatre and cinema. Real life was the hospital, where Simon saw patients lying in the wards or being wheeled outside in their beds to take the air in the hospital square. The high window of his attic bedroom was blocked by the Portland stone balustrade that edged the walkway round the hospital's roof. Where the stone was protected from the weather a deep encrustation of soot formed, and from a very young age he was fascinated by these layers of velvety black.

Because, in the bombed-out City of London, deserted at night, there were no other children to play with, Simon Brett was sent away early to boarding school. The bleak north Yorkshire moors and the monastic austerity of Gilling and Ampleforth became the environment in which he grew up. Gilling Castle was the preparatory school for Ampleforth College, and the Catholic education offered by both schools was crucial to the development of his mind and his imagery. Although the surroundings were visually arid, the Great Chamber at Gilling, used as the school's refectory, contained wonderful dark Elizabethan panelling with delicate linear inlay and splendid stained glass windows with heraldic designs in black and orange. These made a vivid impression on Simon, who had already shown a keen interest in art. When he moved from Gilling to Ampleforth, his arrival coincided with that of the stone carver John Bunting, who taught rigorous pencil drawing. Simon spent all his spare time in the art room, where Bunting introduced him to the work of David Jones and Eric Gill. It was the example of John Bunting and his wife Romola that first made Simon aware of the possibility of a cultured way of life combining art and faith.

Towards the end of his school years Simon Brett had to make a choice between studying Art or English. Both parents and teachers felt that art school, rather than university, was where he should go. Because John Bunting had trained at St Martin's, the nearest art school to his home at Bart's, Simon applied for a place there and started at the age of seventeen. Although he eventually specialised in painting, in his second year he encountered wood engraving, taught by Clifford Webb. Simon chose this as his once-a-week option because he liked the look of it and because he recognised it from books.

The one member of the family who took art seriously was his great-aunt Dorothy Brett, then living in New Mexico. She had been at the Slade with Mark Gertler and

Dora Carrington, at Garsington with Lady Ottoline Morrell, and had travelled with D. H. Lawrence and his wife to New Mexico. When the Lawrences moved on she stayed, remaining in New Mexico for the rest of her life. She had started a correspondence with her great-nephew during his schooldays, and when Simon left art school she suggested that he join her in New Mexico so that she could 'make a proper artist' of him. Adopting a semi-naïve style, Dorothy Brett painted the native Pueblo indians and their customs. The best of her work displays a strong sense of design, her richly decorative paintings capturing something of the inner life of the people and their complicated ceremonials.

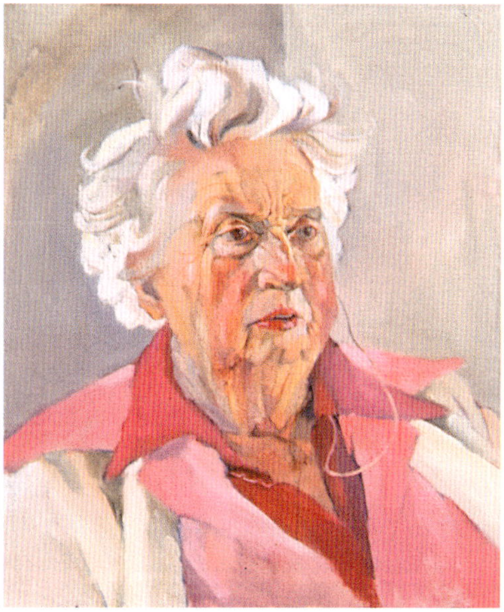

Dorothy Brett, small version 1966
approx 51 × 38 cm (20 × 15 in?)

For two years Brett lived near his aunt, partly funded by one of her wealthy friends and partly by selling his drawings and paintings. He painted many landscapes, but his major work there was an ambitious twelve-foot long triptych of the *Raising of the Cross*. He had thought: 'I am the same age as Delacroix was when he painted his

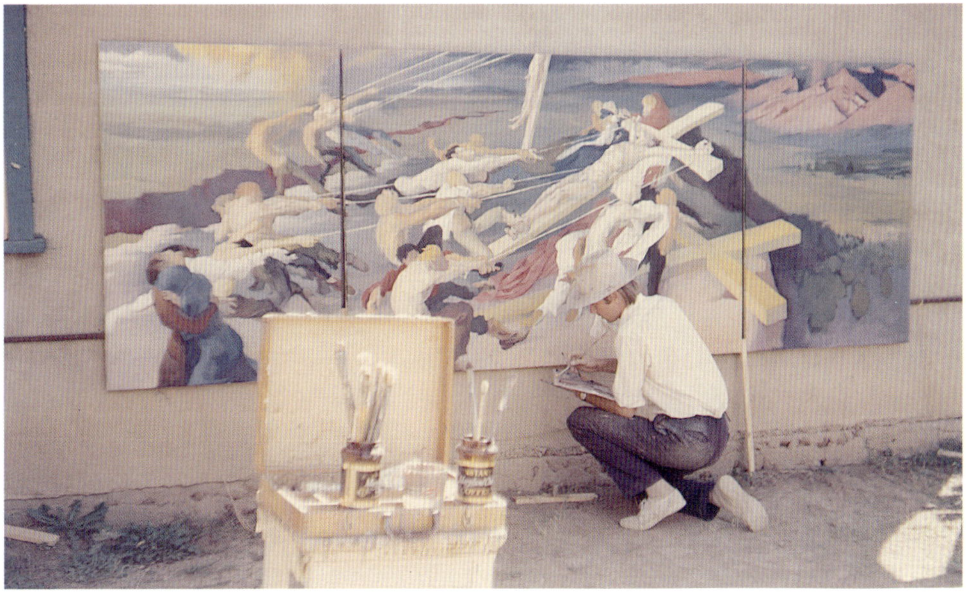

The Sangre de Cristo triptych.
Simon Brett at work on the painting,
New Mexico, 1966

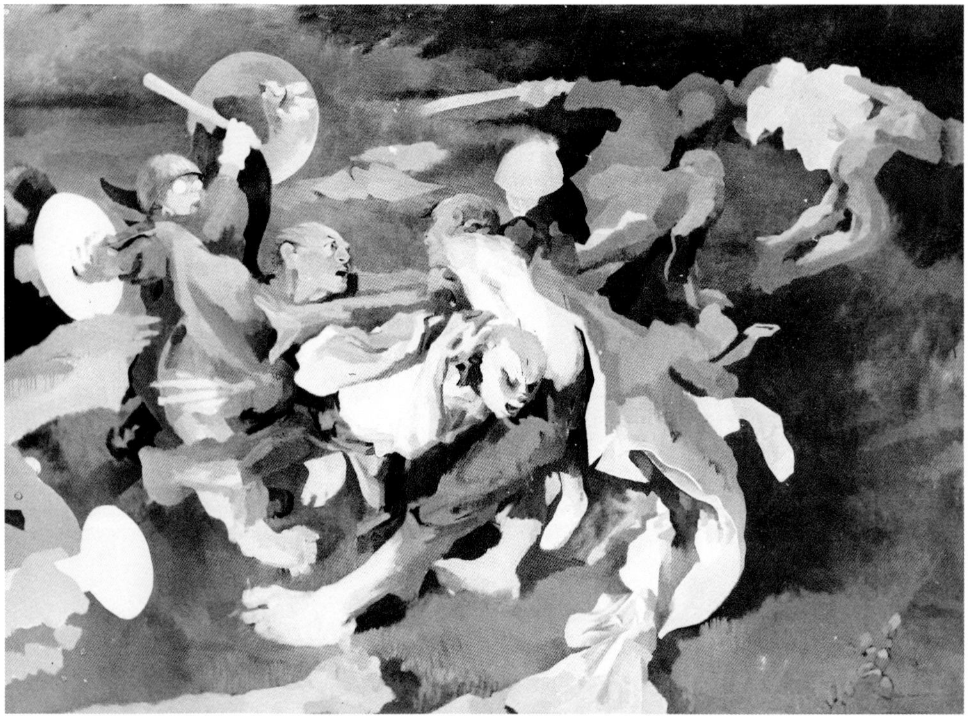

The London triptych, 1968. The centre panel, Malchus's Ear, depicting the arrest of Christ. Oil on canvas, 122 × 183 cm (4 × 6 ft)

Dante and Virgil, so I must try something on the same scale.' Brett's triptych is a study of human figures in extremis, with the Sangre de Cristo mountains in the background. Although the religious impetus behind the picture is strong, it contains perhaps more motion than emotion.

Although the young artist was building a useful reputation in New Mexico, the culture seemed too remote from the European art that had nurtured him, and he returned to London to continue to make his way as a painter. In 1968 he painted a London triptych of the *Arrest of Christ* (by riot police). Various odd jobs supplemented his income until he found a position as a companion to a retired clergyman in the south of France. During the two years he spent in Les Arcs, near

Draguinan, he painted steadily, making a third large triptych portraying the *Conversion of Saint Paul*. In his paintings he synthesised a Cézannesque treatment of the landscape with a more mannerist handling of the figures. However, he had no success in exhibiting these large pictures and his efforts to make a life as a painter ran out of steam.

In 1971 Brett took a teaching job at Marlborough College, in Wiltshire, and for the next twenty years worked there three days a week, lecturing on art and helping to formulate the highly successful methods of teaching instigated by the Head of Department, Robin Child. Although teaching fed his understanding of art, it left Brett with little time for painting. However, he had begun to receive commissions for wood engravings, mainly bookplates, initially through his mother who was then working in a Bond Street stationers' shop, and also through colleagues at the college. A collaborative project to publish an illustrated book on Saint Gregory came

The Conversion of Saint Paul, 1970, oil on three canvases, the left panel depicting Christ's lament over Jerusalem. Approx. 122 × 370 cm (4 × 12 ft)

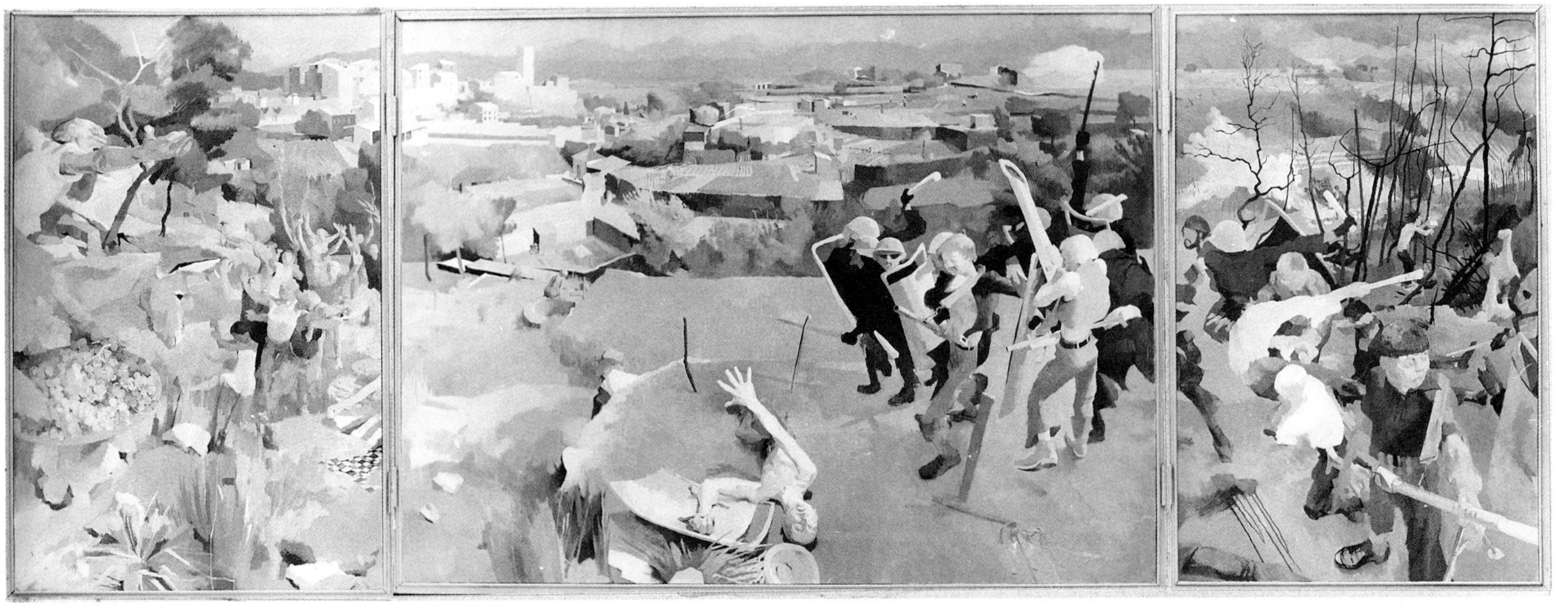

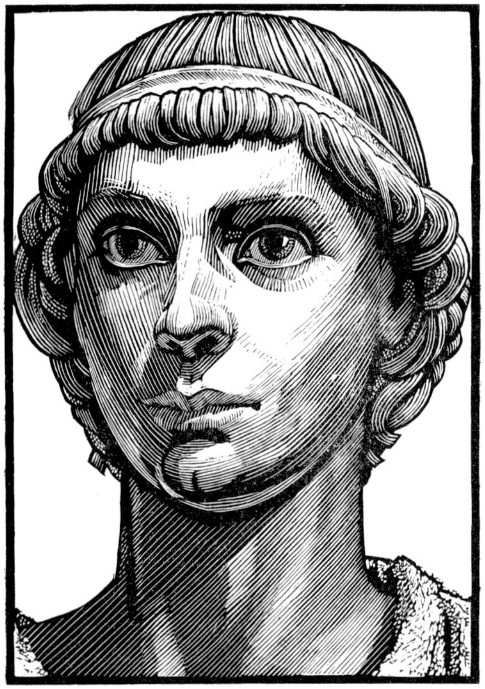

Above: Pericles 1, 2005, 103 × 73 mm

Right: Saint Gregory, for The Animals of Saint Gregory, 1981, 185 × 127 mm

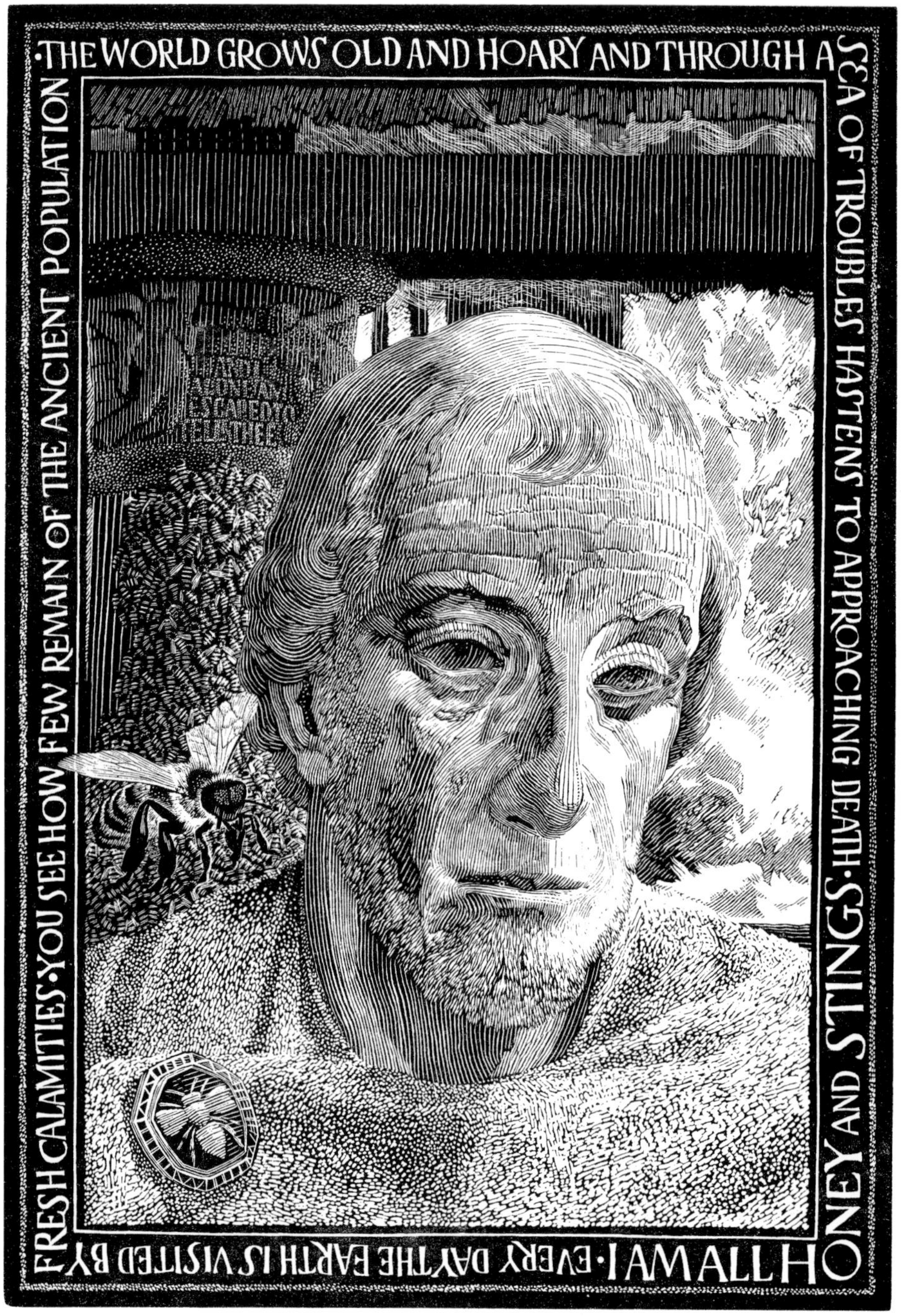

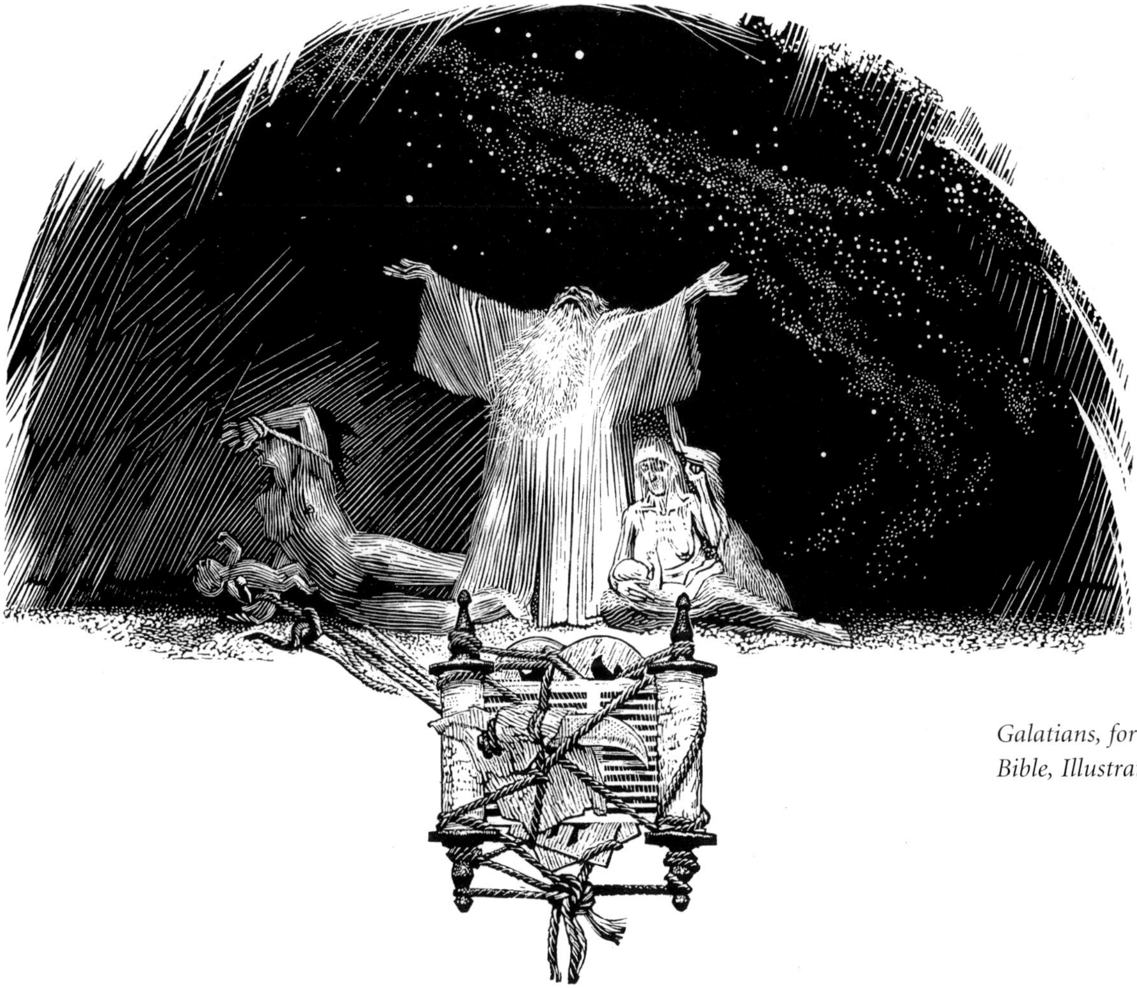

Galatians, for The Reader's Digest Bible, Illustrated Edition 1990

through an acquaintance at the local church. This book proved a success, winning the Francis Williams Illustration Award sponsored by the National Book League and the Victoria and Albert Museum. Brett found himself with a small publishing business on his hands and a growing reputation as a religious illustrator. His Paulinus Press published a number of limited-edition and commercial books,

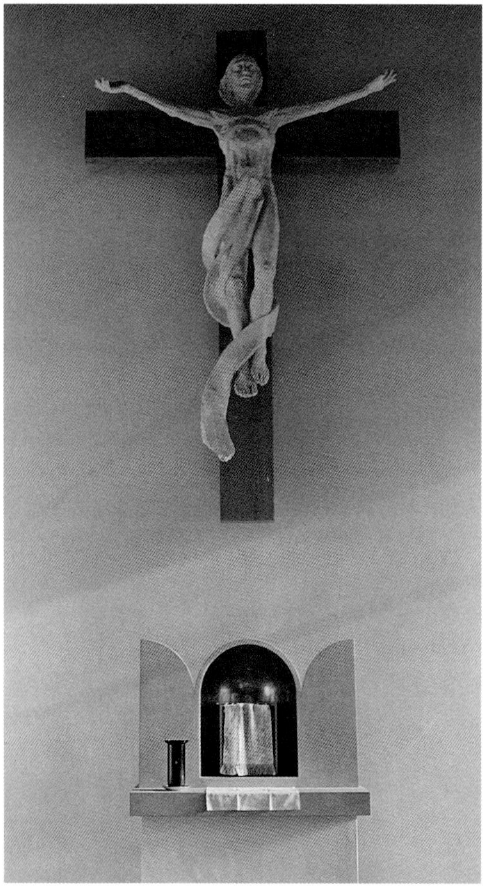

The sculpture of The Risen Christ in St Thomas More Church, Marlborough, photographed before the decoration of the tabernacle housing or its destruction. The decoration may be seen from the ensuing prints.

Opposite page: Axe of God, 1987, 200 × 255 mm

continuing in existence until 1989, when a request came from the *Reader's Digest* to help illustrate their new edition of The Bible. This commission prompted Brett to give up both publishing and teaching and become a full-time wood engraver. To replace his teaching salary he set himself the target of completing one wood engraving a week.

It was in wood engraving that Simon Brett found himself. He loved drawing and, acutely sensitive to qualities of line and varieties of tone, he enjoyed the accretion of engraved marks through which the form emerged. He appreciated the 'less is more' nature of engraving, where a simple vocabulary of marks can create solid forms and wide spaces as well as a vast range of painterly tones. The forms could also contain psychological depth, as is evidenced in his heads of *Saint Gregory* and *Pericles*, or the mother and child in *Hannah Jane*.

A couple of years after his arrival at Marlborough Simon Brett had married Juliet Wood, whose former husband had been the previous head of the art department. Simon and Juliet were committed members of the local Catholic church, for which in 1977 Simon had made a life-size figure of the Risen Christ, designed to hang above a tabernacle decorated by Juliet. When this tabernacle was removed from the church without discussion and found chopped up in the car park, they felt they could not worship there any more. To come to terms with his feelings about this event Brett made a large engraving entitled *Axe of God* (1987). When a later period of family difficulties led to some therapeutic gardening, Brett noticed that the redesigned garden echoed the shapes of tabernacle and cross. Eight years later this led to a second engraving in which, in a reversal of the bible story, Adam and Eve are shown fleeing from God's burning house into an ordered garden. These two engravings engendered an on-going series reflecting on religion and war. *Ordnance Survey*, prompted by the Hungerford massacre, is a complex pictorialisation of the closeness of tragedy. *Three Torsos* presents, in statue form, the presiding deities of

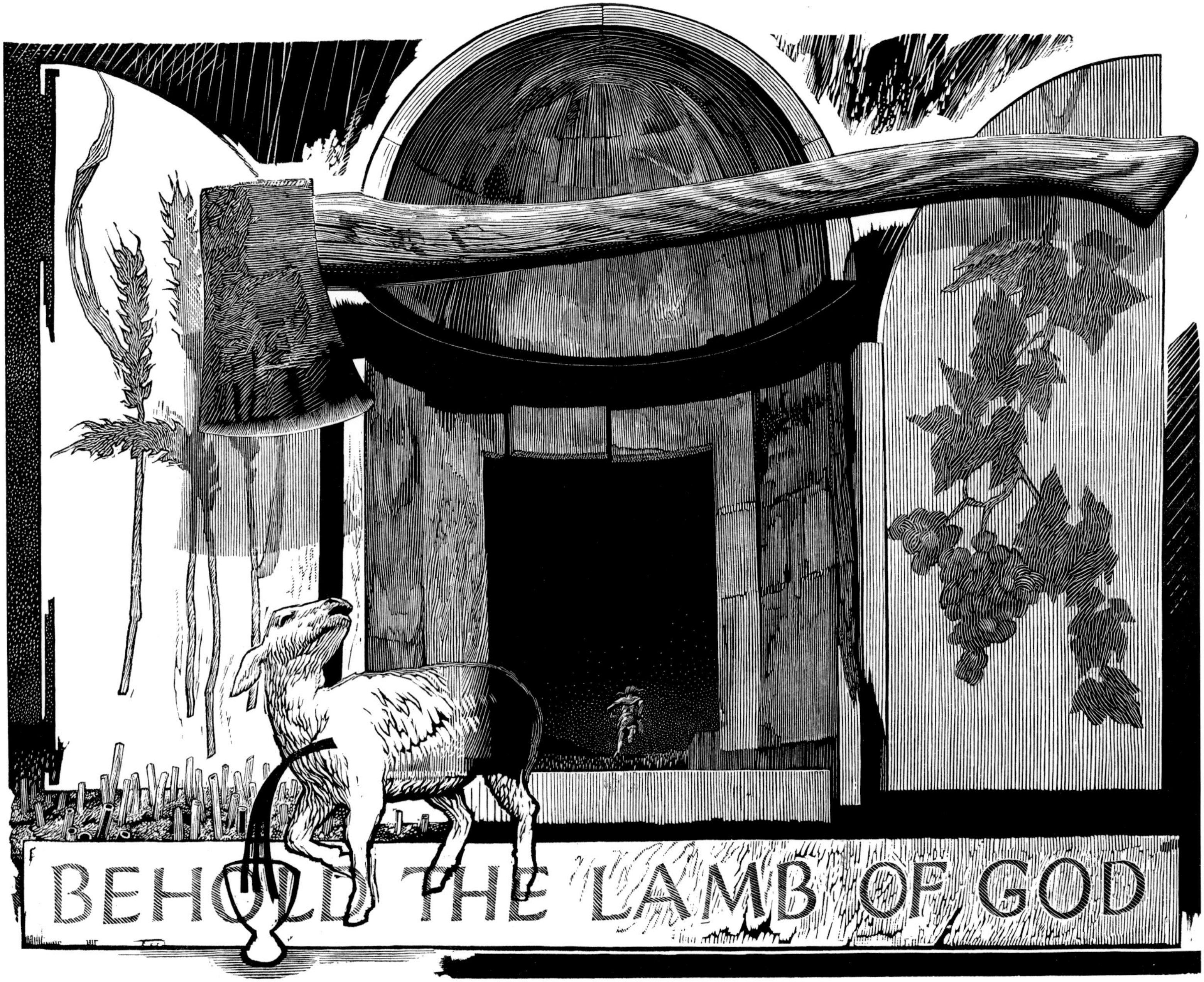
BEHOLD THE LAMB OF GOD

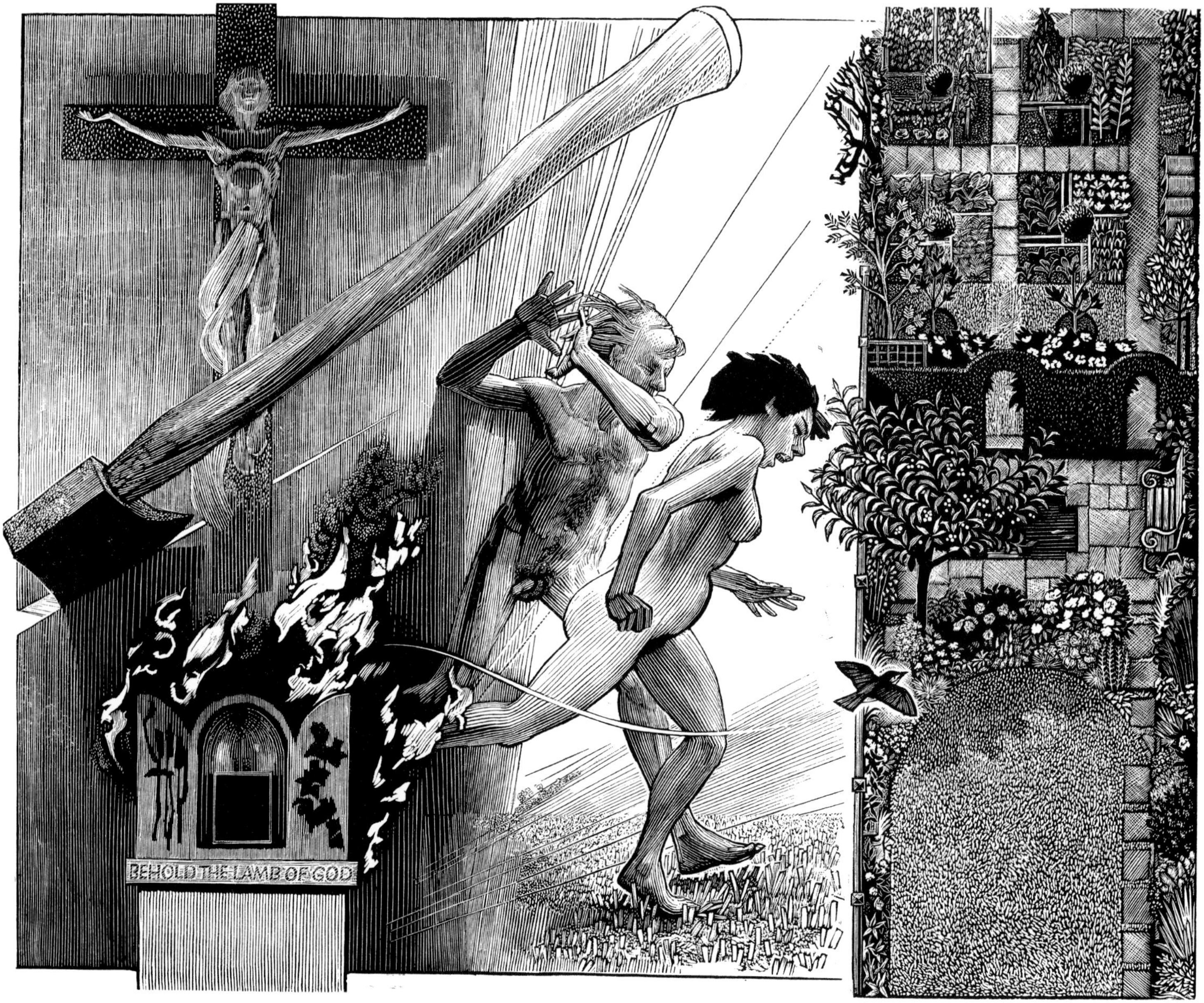

Garden Plan, 1995, 202 × 255 mm

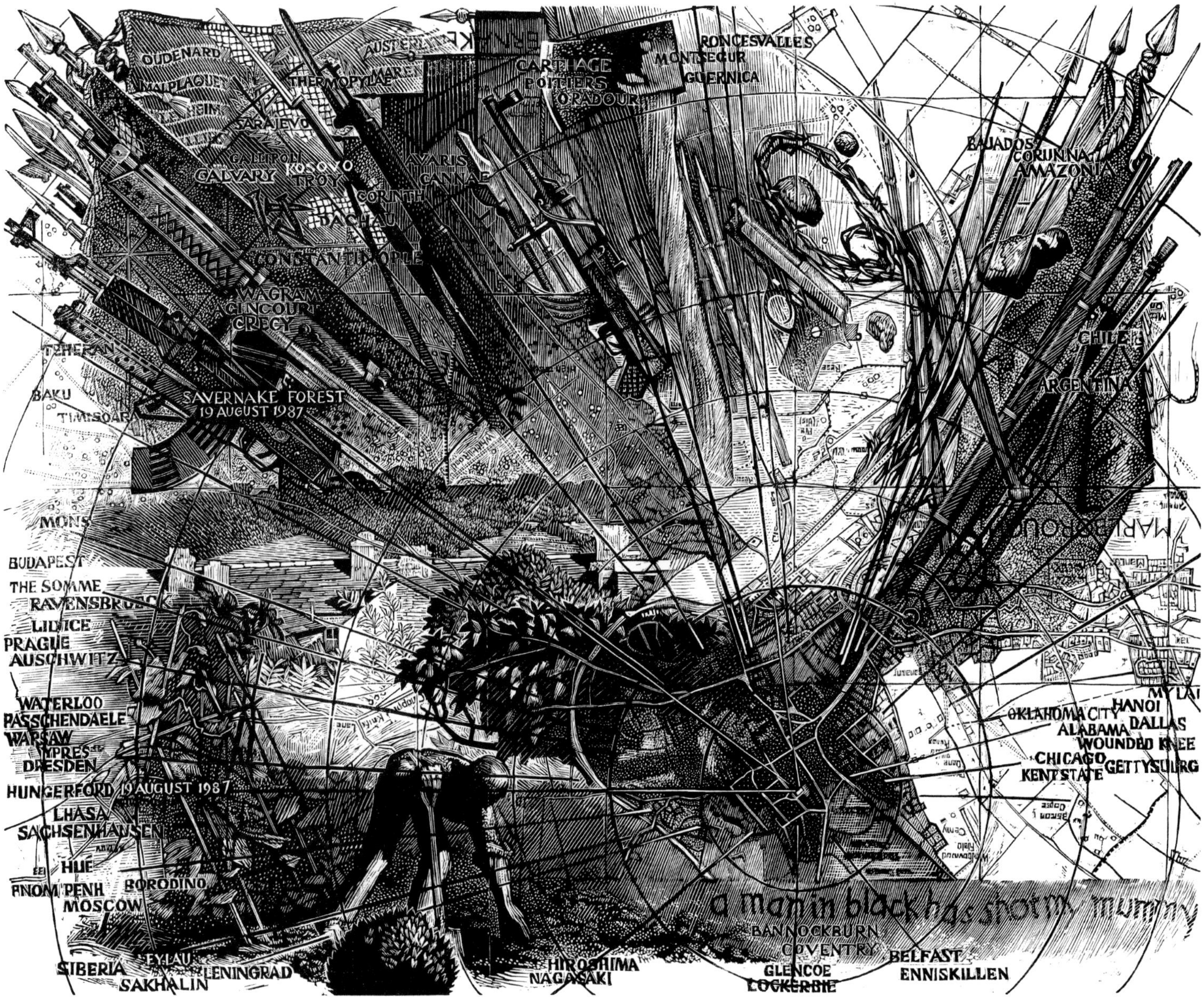

Ordnance Survey, 1995, 200 × 255 mm

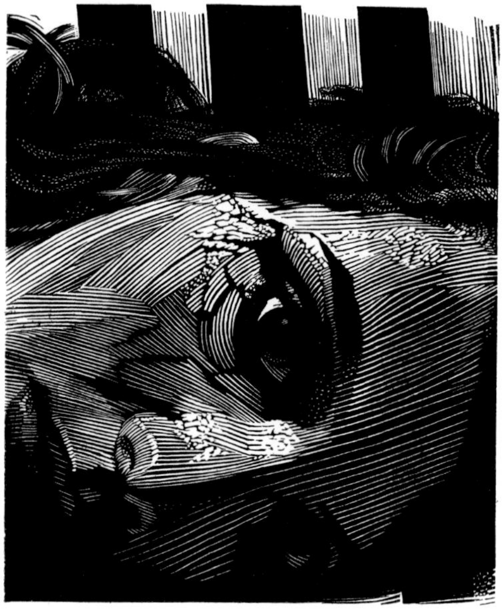

The Dark Lady, for Shakespeare's Sonnets, Folio, 1989, 90 × 75 mm

three major religions, suspended above the reach of real human misery. The layering of visual and literary allusions within these autonomous engravings shows Brett at his inventive best, with his faith as a prime motivation. As he says, 'my thought is so structured by my Catholic background that I have not rejected it.'

Simon Brett combines his working practice with promoting the cause of wood engraving, writing extensively on its processes and practitioners. He organised the 50th exhibition of the Society of Wood Engravers, *Engraving Then and Now* (1987), which showed work by every traceable member, past and present. He organised the 75th anniversary show, *Wood Engraving Here and Now* (1995), and as well as writing the catalogues for these exhibitions he has compiled a series of handbooks culminating in the worldwide survey *An Engravers Globe* (2002). As Jim Horton of the American Wood Engravers Network wrote, 'Any student of wood engraving would have to become aware of Simon Brett. Not only for the stunning virtuosity of engraving skill and vision, but also for his eloquent writing. He is an inspiration and a working textbook. The added bonus is that he has proved to be an accessible and encouraging person.'

The demanding commissions that have come Simon Brett's way have increased his range of subject matter and liberated his imagination, requiring as much delving into the self as into the minds of others. This fusion of ideas and engraving skills has made Brett one of Britain's most eminent illustrators. He is perhaps at his best in his engravings of people – the heroines and villains of classic literature, the heroes and thinkers of classical times. The timeless solemnity of his heads of Marcus Aurelius, the concentrated force of his Arthurian knights, and the lovely liquefaction of *Shakespeare's Dark Lady*, show the breadth of his vision, while its expression in his chosen medium combines the visual and the literary in ways that are now effectively taboo in modern painting.

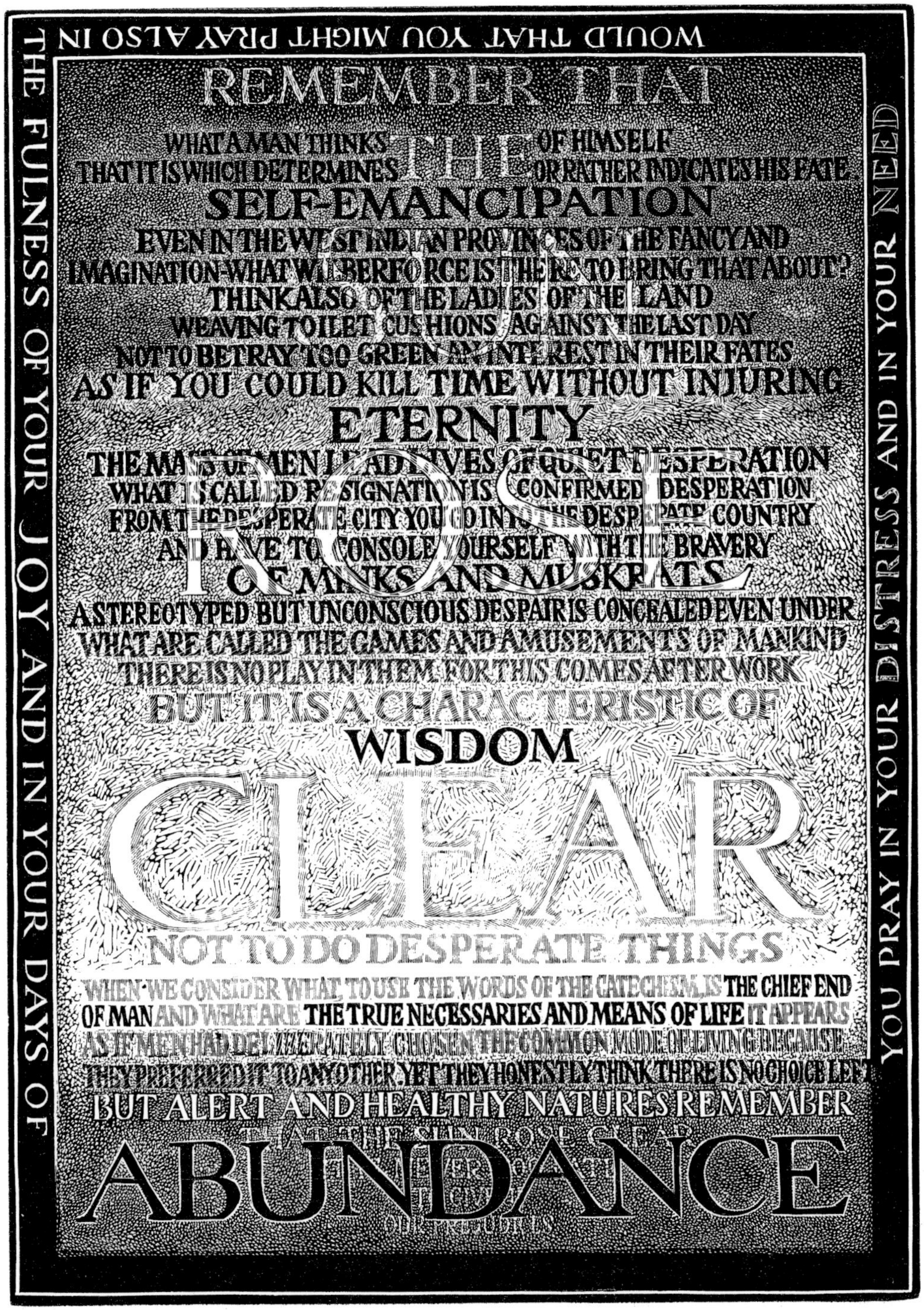

Text, 1983–84
Commissioned by Michael Taylor Rare Books for a collection of Contemporary British Lettering, this sets a passage from Thoreau's Walden, repeating over itself, with words from The Prophet by Kahil Gibran running round the border and joining in with Thoreau's at the end.

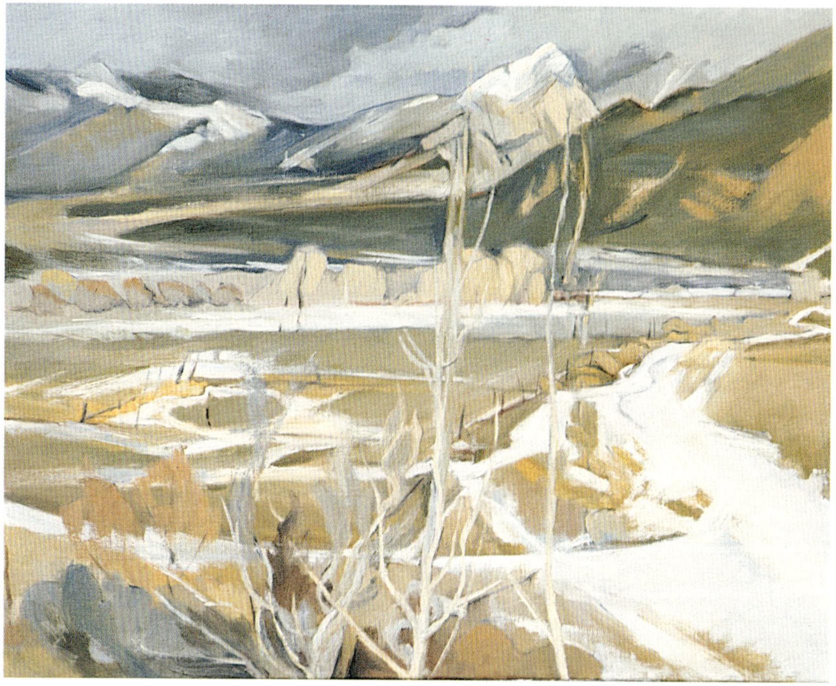

Above: Winter in Taos, 1966, approx 61 × 76 cm (24 × 30 in)

Below: Trees in New Mexico, 1965–56, approx 61 × 76 cm (24 × 30 in)

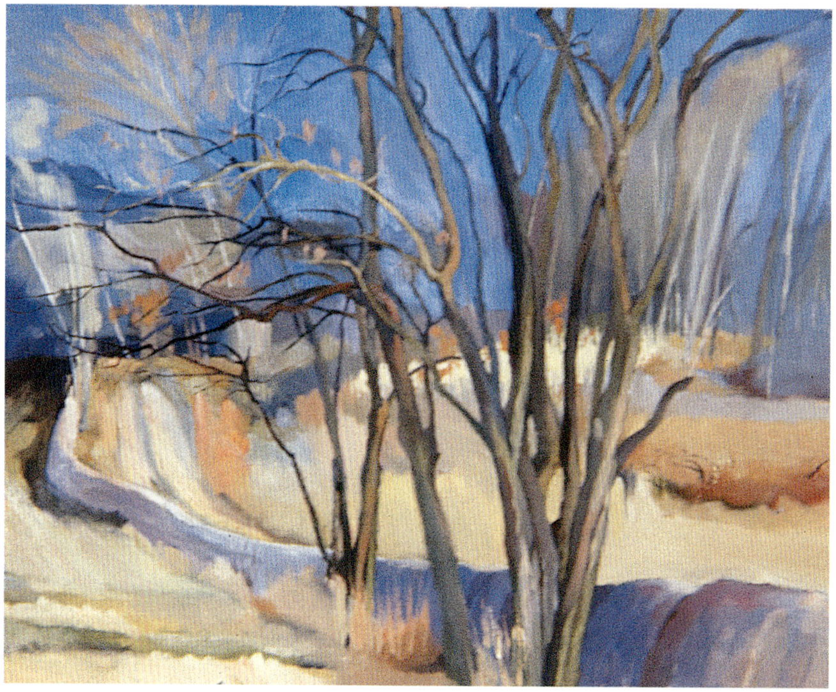

Opposite top: Brucefield Mains, 2001, 124 × 314 mm

Opposite bottom: The Manor, Priors Marston, 2005, 130 × 360 mm

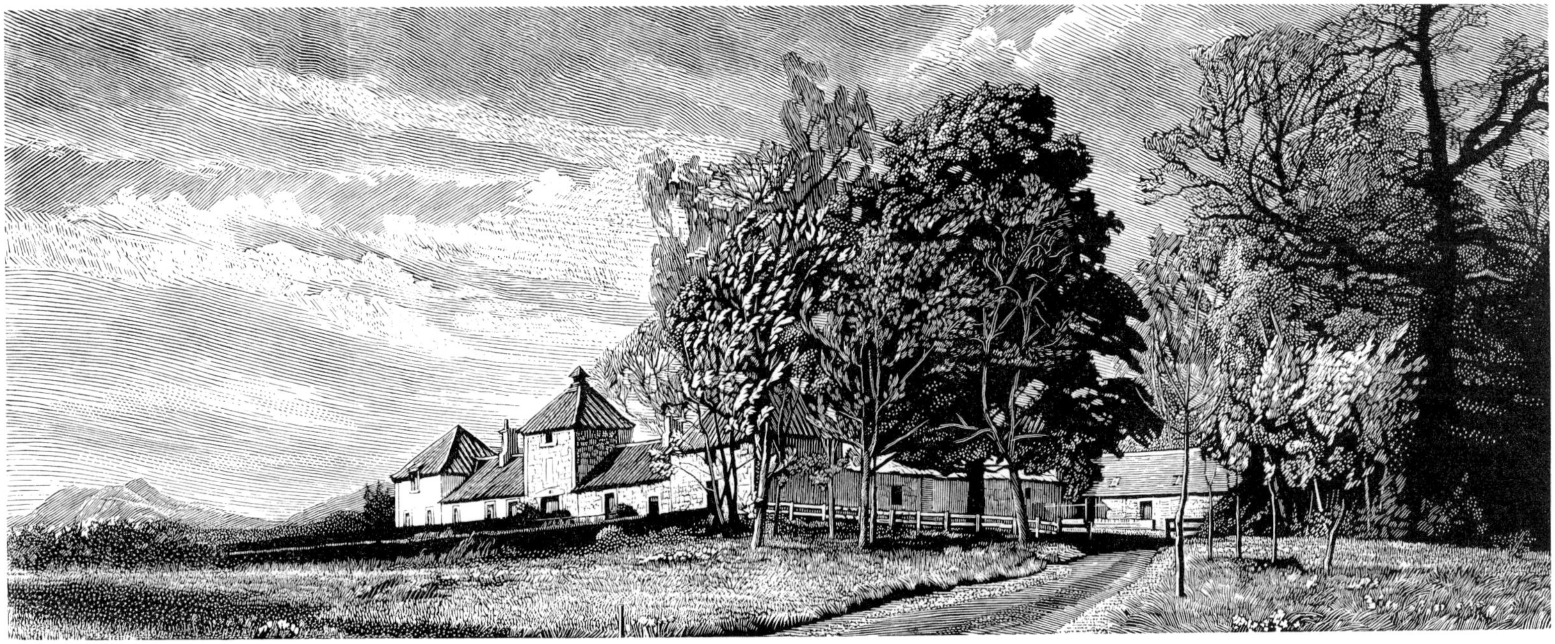

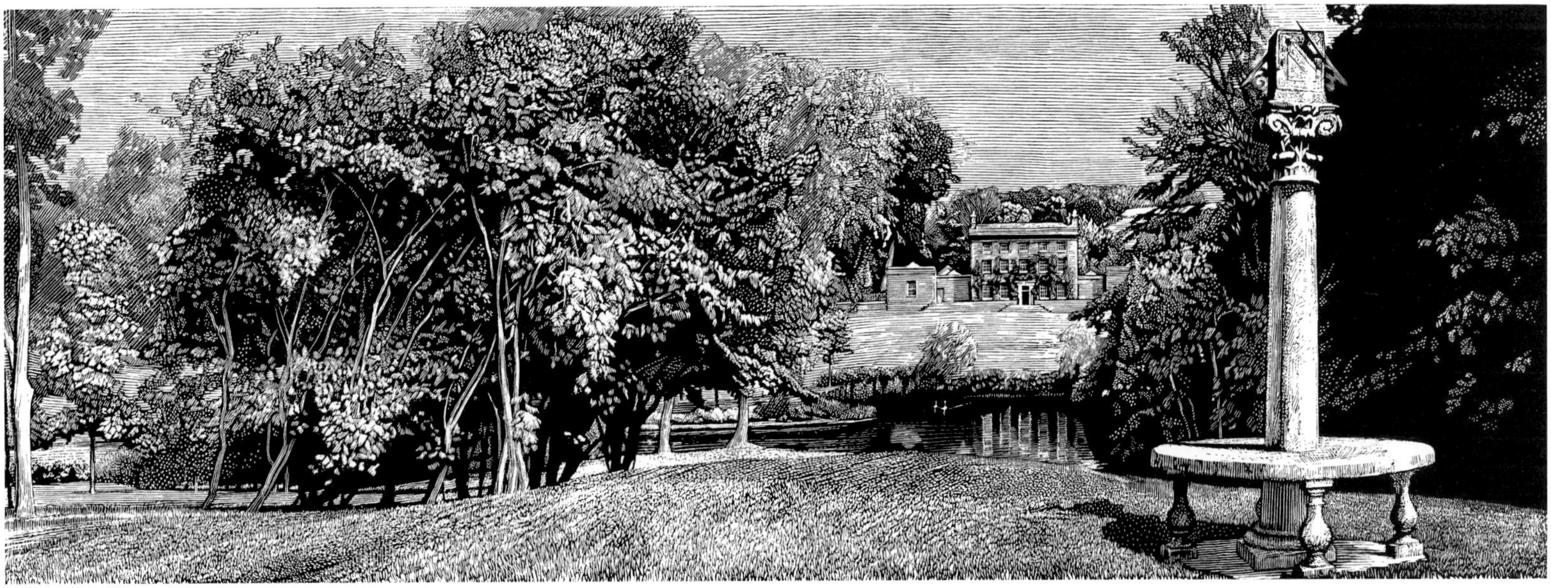

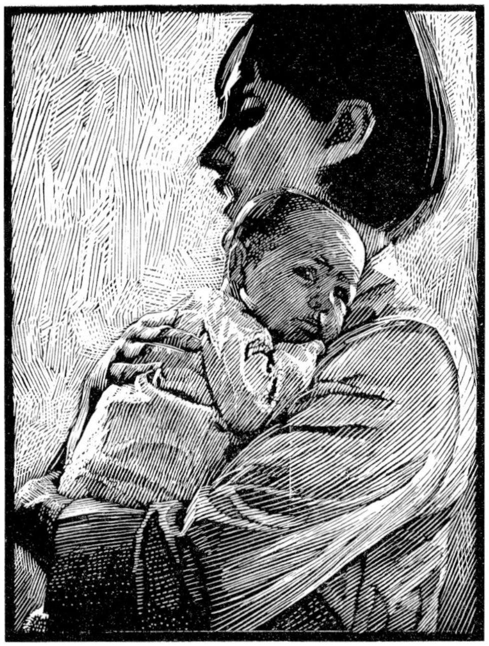

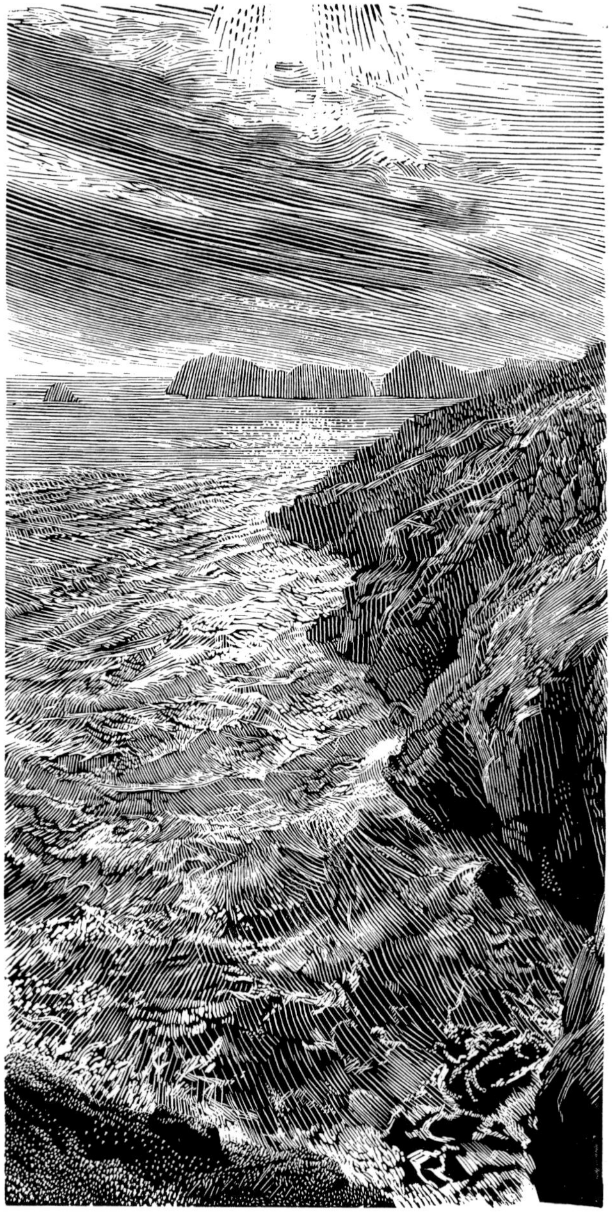

Above: Marie and Hannah Jane, 2005

Right: Ramsey Island, 1985

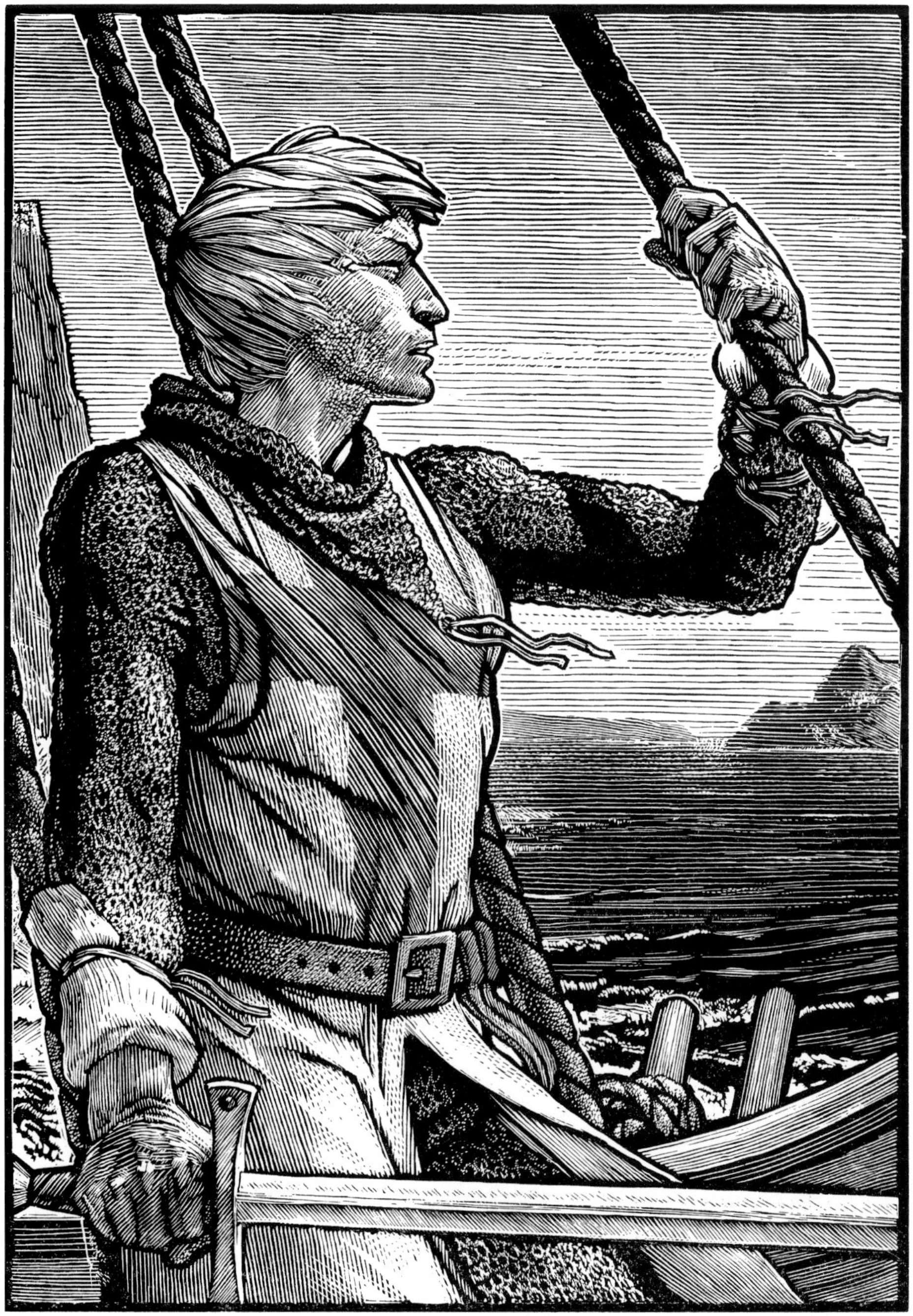

Perceval on the Ship for Legends of the Grail,
Folio 2007, 200 × 140 mm

Right and opposite page: Perceval and Lancelot,
for Legends of the Grail, Folio 2007,
two blocks each 200 × 140 mm

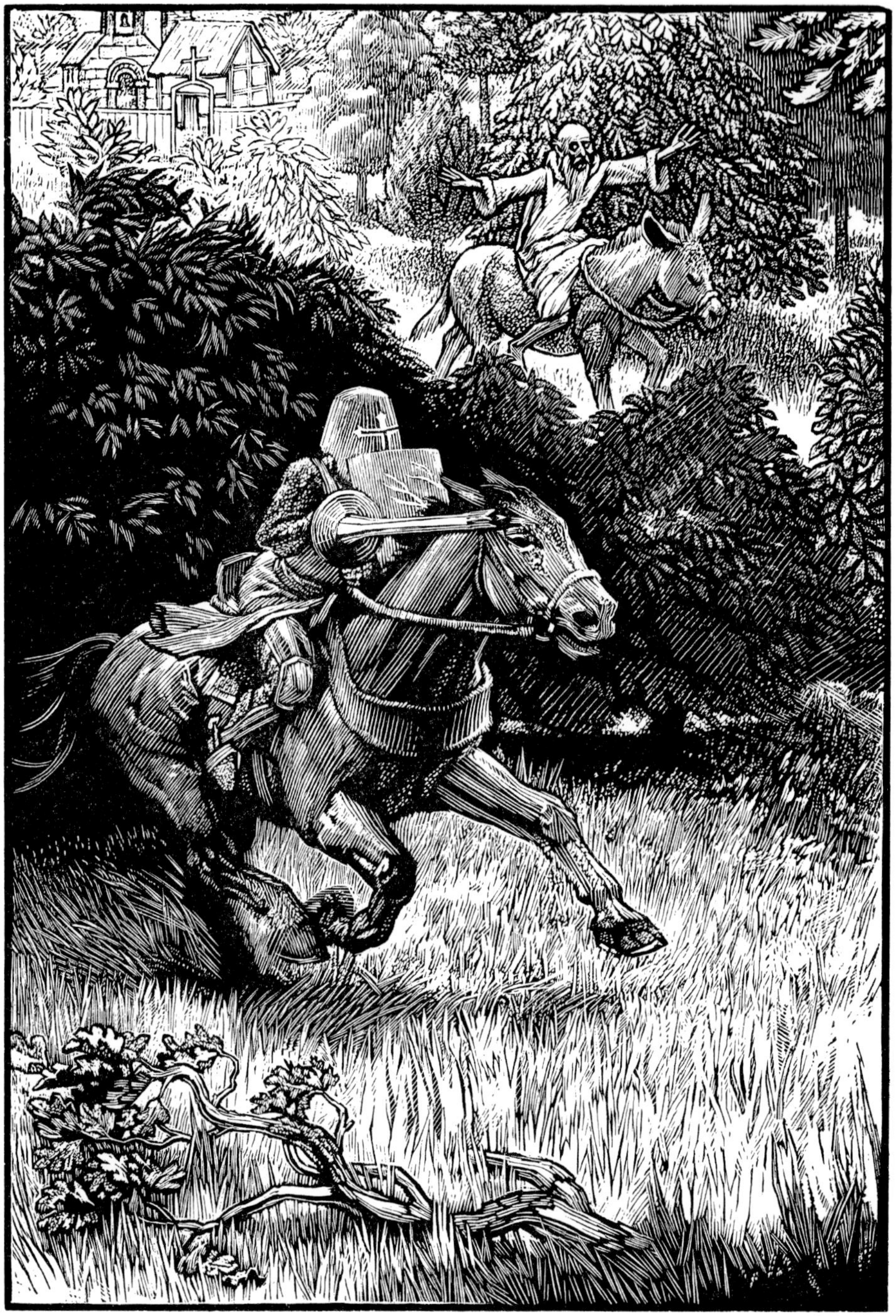

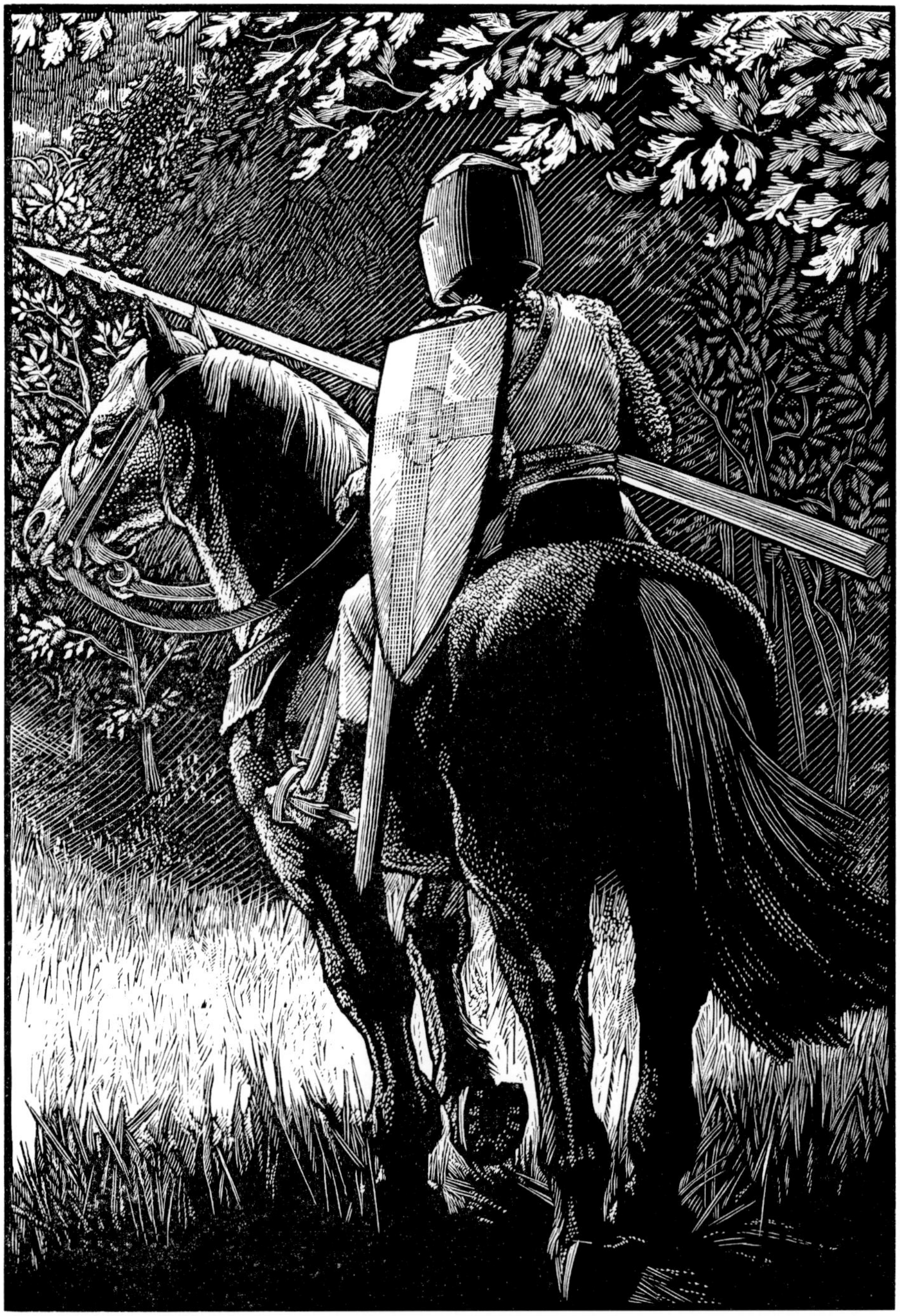

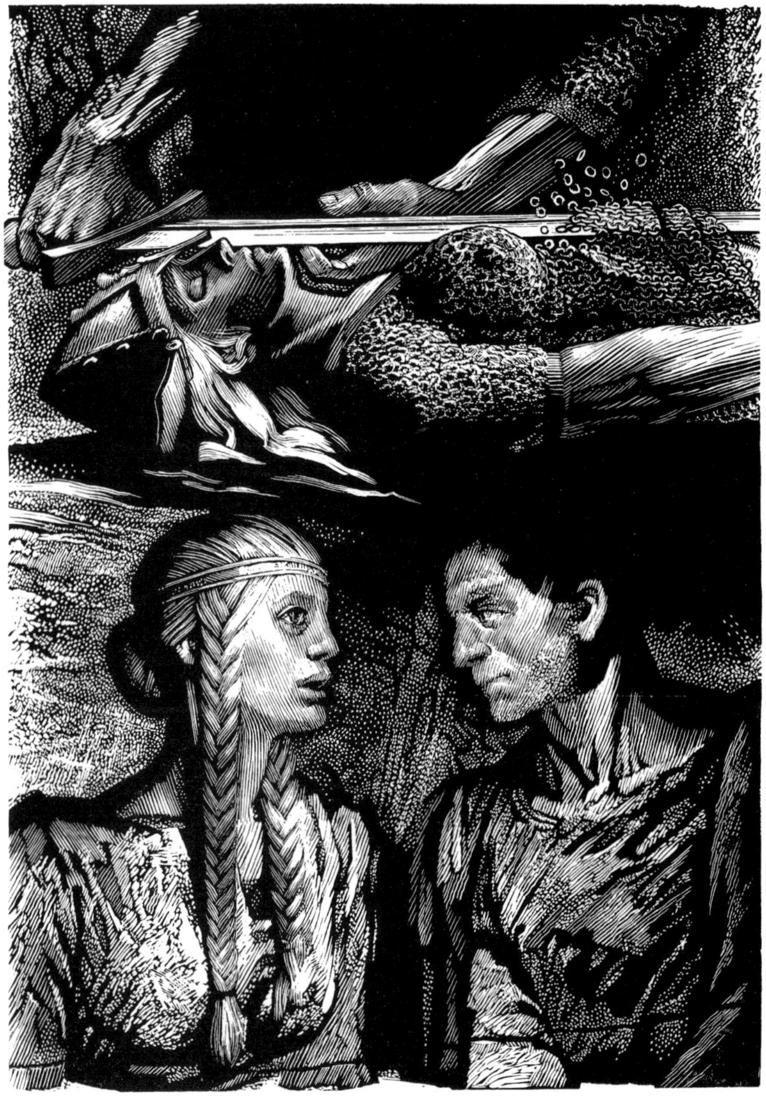

Wisdom Songs, for Legends of the Ring,
Folio 2004, 200 × 140 mm

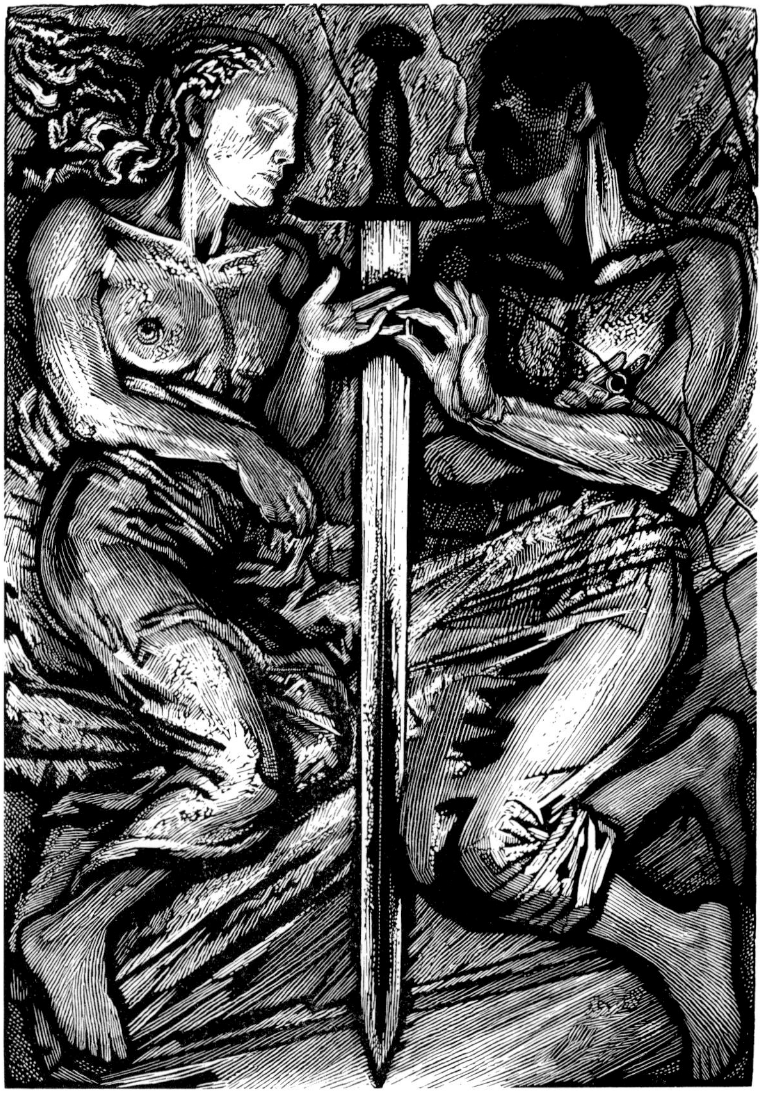

The Sword Between, for Legends of the Ring,
Folio 2004, 200 × 140 mm

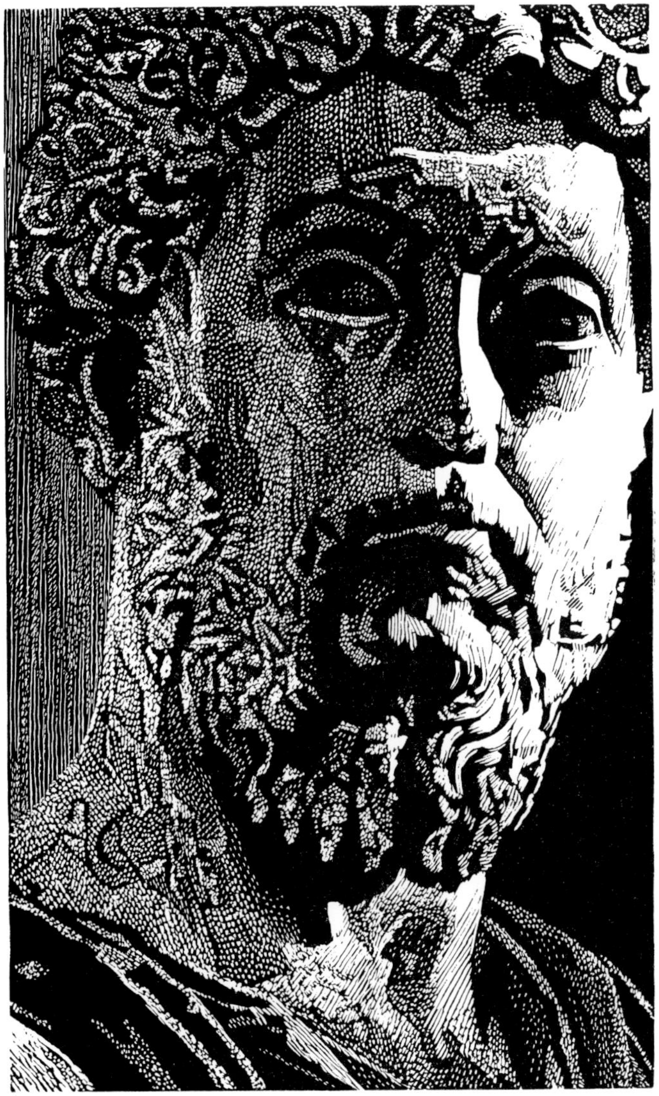

Marcus Aurelius VIII, for Meditations,
Folio 2002, 150 × 90 mm

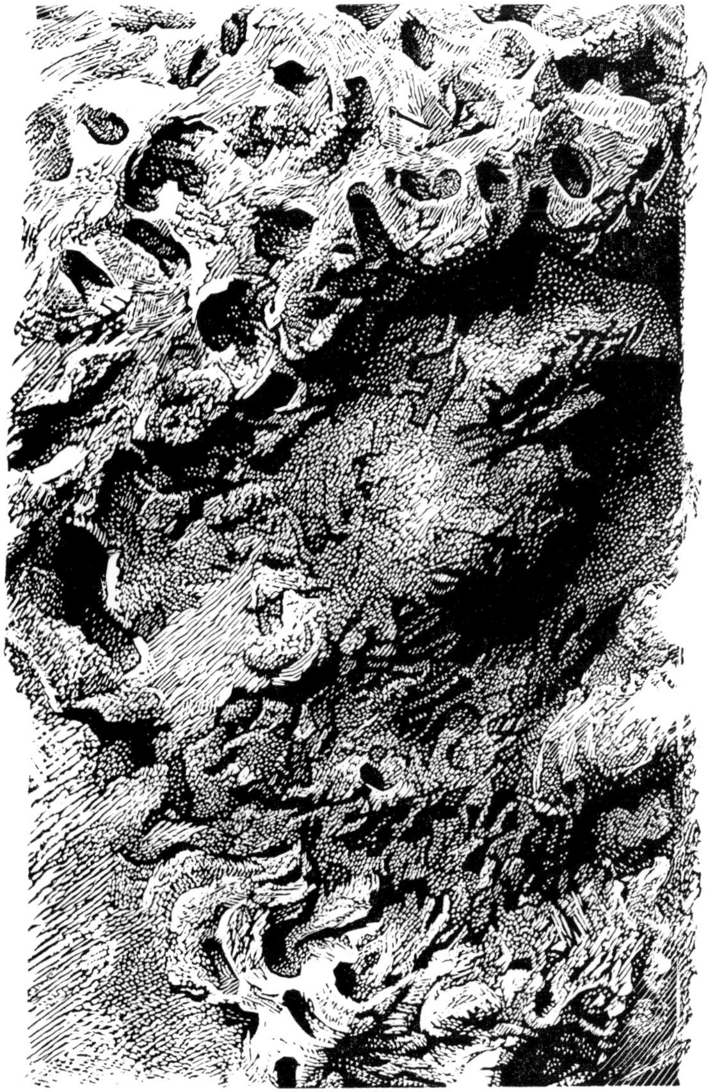

Marcus Aurelius XII, for Meditations,
Folio 2002, 150 × 90 mm

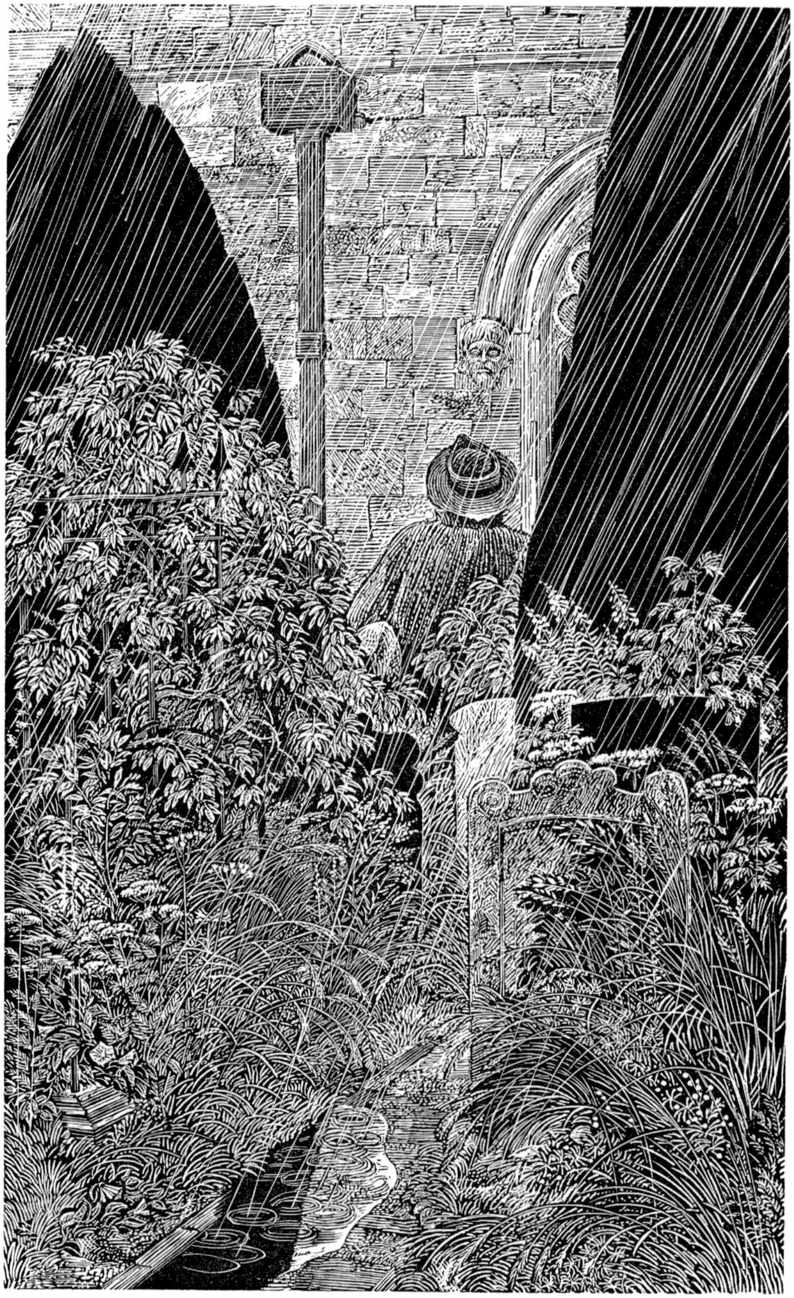

IAN STEPHENS: *Rain, 1998, from A Month in the Country by J. L. Carr, Folio Society, 1999*

4. Quiet Corners

Ian Stephens

Chairman of the Society of Wood Engravers 1992–1995

Landscape is the central motif in Ian Stephens' imagery, but he is less concerned with the grand sweeps of moor or mountain than with quiet, unnoticed corners of country that he knows well. He is deeply interested in the land, in the way it has been used and altered by the people and creatures that inhabit it, in the effects caused by weather and changing seasons, and in the contrast between its past and present appearance. Although now a town dweller, at heart he is a countryman like his hero Thomas Bewick. As he says, 'I have a strong feeling for Mr Bewick. He got it right. Bewick was a radical in his day and though his work may look cosy now, when it was done it was fresh and honest, describing things as they were. It was his direct observation, his birds, and the little vignettes that intersperse pages in his books – that's where he really comes good. There was nothing approaching his birds and animals at the time, nothing.'

It was perhaps Bewick's example – his ability to condense whole worlds into tiny spaces, his truth to nature, and his utter lack of bombast – that enticed Ian Stephens into choosing wood engraving as his primary means of expression. That important model, combined with his innate skill at working with wood and his love of the material itself, proved an irresistible combination. His father, a farm worker, possessed a natural sense of design, and Ian recalls him drawing a perfect apple in soft pencil for his two small sons. Ian used to haunt him as he worked out of doors, hedging and ditching, and he remembers wandering off aged three or four to find his way to the farm where his father worked. 'I loved being outside. If I am having a duff day now, all I have to do is walk across a field. I love the country and have a fair knowledge of it. I was steeped in it. Dad would be cutting a hedge somewhere and I would be there helping him. It has formulated the way I think.' *The Hedgecutter*, one of the first engravings Stephens made, many years later, is

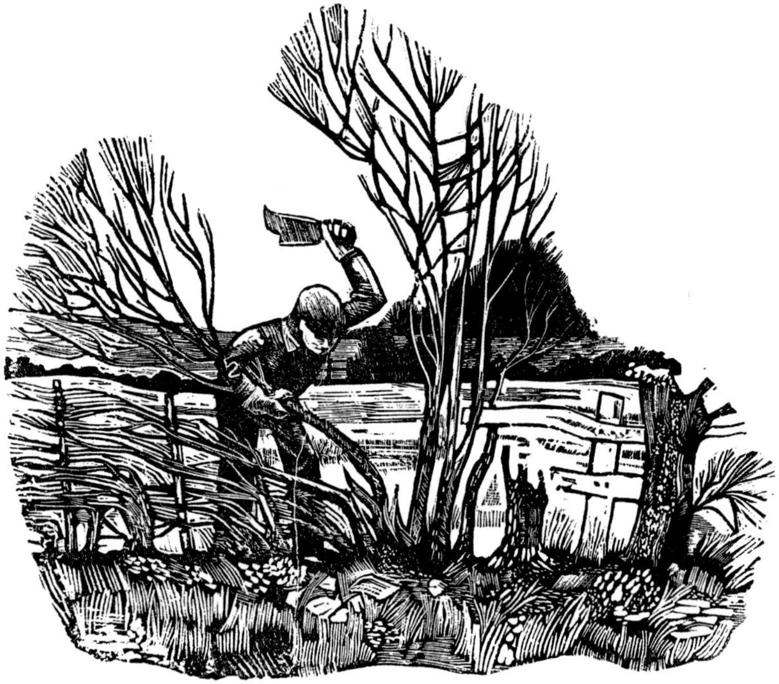

The Hedgecutter, 1973

based on memories of his father laying a hedge. In it he made the novice's mistake of failing to reverse the image; his father was right-handed, not left-handed.

Ian Stephens' parents were Welsh. In the 1930s they moved with their families from Wales to the Newport Pagnell area. His mother's family were fine singers, and in the extended family there were great-aunts and great-uncles with magnificent voices. Ian was the first in his family to make anything of the visual arts. He drew from an early age, and was always encouraged to make his own Christmas cards. He bought rough notebooks and filled them with drawings. When he was sixteen, he was asked by one of his schoolteachers if he had ever thought of going to art school, because his compulsion to draw might come to something. Stephens found a place at Northampton School of Art and for four years commuted there by train while continuing to live at home.

Northampton School of Art was then tiny, with between two and three dozen students. Frank Cryer taught painting, lettering and illumination; Peter Cubitt taught Life Drawing and most of the other disciplines that students were expected to incorporate into the final diploma; Tom Hughes and Henry Bird completed the team. Cubitt was an excellent draughtsman and an important influence on the young Stephens. 'He was a very fine man. I have never seen anybody able to control the line as he did. And he had a way of looking at you if you were getting a bit pretentious, a little gentle smile that would put you right.' Stephens chose Illustration as his main subject, with Lettering and Illumination as secondaries. Then destined only for use in books, Illustration was done mainly in black and white pen and wash. This suited Stephens well because he had discovered he was colour blind. He has always regarded his colour blindness as an advantage, because it honed his sensitivity to variations in tone when an ability to depict tone and texture was of primary importance. English literature also formed a central part of the course, as it was necessary to read and interpret the books and to stick to the text when illustrating them. In the art school a counsel of perfection prevailed. Cryer would say 'Never take short cuts, never fudge. Make sure you have achieved what you set out to do. Never exhibit anything that you're not sure is as good as it could be.'

During his last weeks at art school Stephens happened to see one of Lawrence's catalogues with engraving tools in it. He had previously been given the King Penguin book of Bewick's engravings and had loved the look of them. But he had thought of engraving as a dead art and was astonished to find that blocks and tools were still obtainable. He bought a few blocks and four tools from old Mr Lawrence and for his own private enjoyment began teaching himself how to engrave. The art school had steered its students towards teaching as the steadiest way of earning a living, and Stephens duly took up his first post as an art teacher, continuing, after a short interlude in an advertising agency, where the speed of work required was a surprise to him, to teach at a boys' secondary modern school in a rough part of Northampton. After twelve years there a bout of glandular fever forced him to quit, and he got a job in a printer's studio preparing artwork for print. 'That was good experience for me because it got me up to date with techniques and there was a huge variety of work, all urgent. You prepared a piece of artwork, passed it on to the plate maker, and saw the finished job going out of the door the same afternoon.' A job with a fishing magazine followed, and then an appointment as a graphic designer with Odhams Leisure Group, a large mail order publisher best known for cookery and knitting books.

Throughout these years Stephens kept his own private work going, experimenting with etching and linocutting at the art school in the evenings, and engraving at home. In the 1970s a friend discovered a dismembered press waiting for the scrap merchant outside the door of a backstreet printer. He collected and assembled what turned out to be a fine Columbian Press, made in 1818, and gave it to Stephens on permanent loan. This press enabled Stephens to print his own blocks and encouraged him to branch out into other forms of relief printing.

For Ian Stephens wood engraving was a case of love at first sight. He found he had a natural facility for it, enjoying the control necessary for cutting the boxwood blocks. He appreciated the fact that there was no room for empty gesture and that the precision required for cutting the blocks prevented any tendency to slickness. Although he made many experimental engravings he found he could never allow himself to go completely abstract, but always returned to something that was readable as a landscape. His subjects were mostly local scenes re-imagined from drawings done in odds and ends of sketchbooks. From a neighbouring shop he

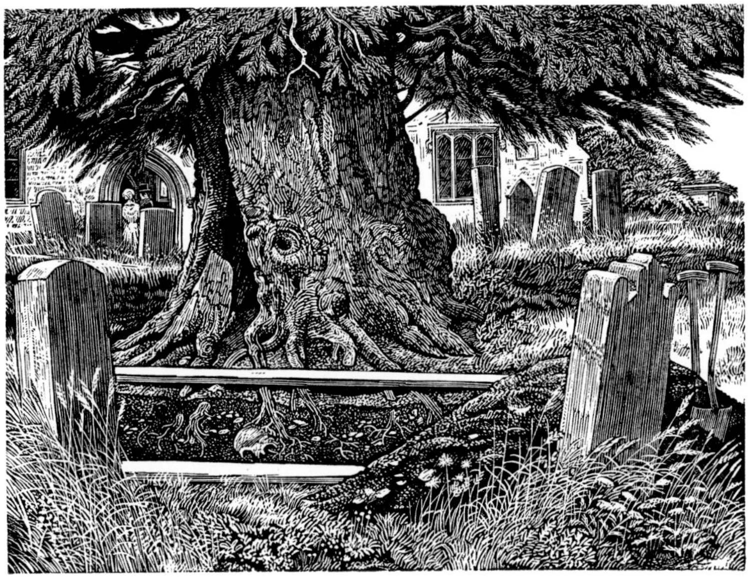

Tennyson as landscape: Old Yew, 2005 for the Folio Society Tennyson, 2006

obtained his first commission – a local landscape to be used as a Christmas card. A steady trickle of commissions followed and in the early 1990s the trickle turned into a flood when the Folio Society approached him. Tennyson was by far the most time-consuming of the books he illustrated for the company. 'Tennyson's poems are beautiful but often very long (*In Memoriam*, for example, is eighty pages) and so full of images that choosing a passage to illustrate was difficult. On the plus side, though, the vast majority allowed me to indulge my predilection for landscape subjects.'

In 1984 Ian Stephens was invited by Hilary Paynter to be in at the start of the revival of the Society of Wood Engravers, and he has been assiduous in promoting its cause. As he says, when he became Chairman the Society was up and running. 'All I had to do was jump aboard the wagon and keep the momentum going for my three-year stint. A topic that occupied our attention … was the lack of tuition or

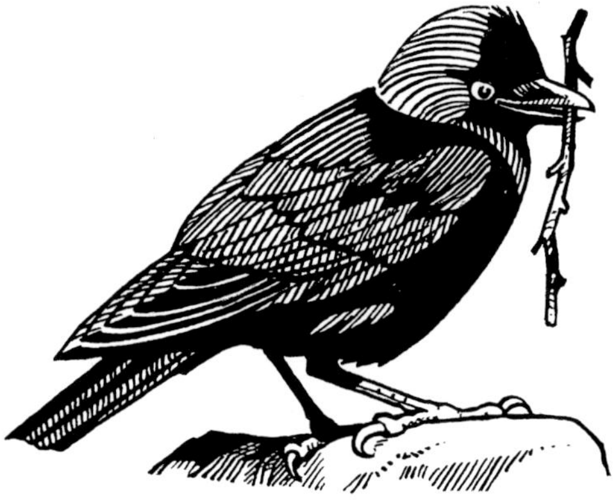

Jackdaw drawing c. 2006

courses in wood engraving at British art schools and colleges. Since my tenure it has become all too clear that art schools that teach any skill-based subject at all are as rare as hen's teeth.'

As Chairman Stephens helped to organise the important touring exhibition *Wood Engraving – Here and Now* which started at the Ashmolean in Oxford and showcased the work of fifteen of the best living wood engravers. Although the necessary selection proved a somewhat poisoned chalice, the exhibition adhered to its brief of showing wood engraving as Fine Art, and as a primary means of artistic expression for 'exploring visual ideas or the human condition'. It brought together an eclectic mixture of subjects and techniques and demonstrated the range and stature of contemporary work in the medium. Stephens has continued to be a consistent contributor to the Society's annual exhibitions and has exhibited widely elsewhere. He was elected Fellow of the Royal Society of Painter Printmakers in 1984. He also keeps in touch with events in the wider art world through his connection with the iconoclastic newsletter *The Jackdaw*, which features his eponymous illustrations. A natural modesty and dislike of ostentation belies Stephens' distinction as an artist. As he says, 'I think of myself as an illustrator who sometimes manages to strike a chord in a piece of work and art finds its way in.'

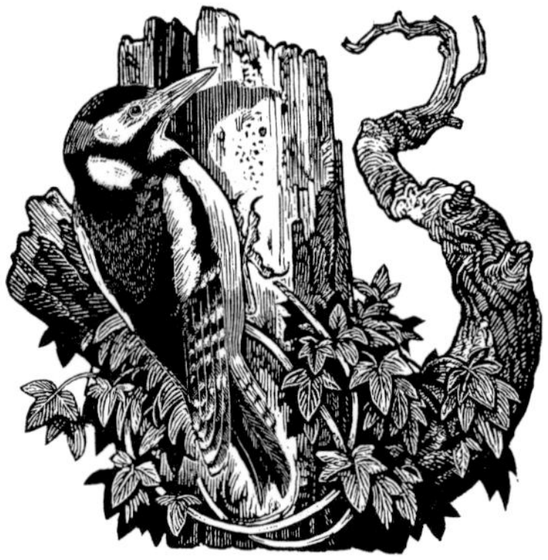

Greater Spotted Woodpecker, 1993

Ian Stephens, true to the Royal Society of Painter-Printmakers' motto – *Never a Day without a Line* – has something on the go all the time. As he works only on boxwood, his prints tend to be small, but their small size increases the intensity of the images. Responding freshly to the forms and textures that he sees in the countryside, he explores the secret life of plants and the creatures that live in and around them, bringing half-seen corners of the countryside vividly to life. His *Devil's Coach Horse* and *Greater Spotted Woodpecker* have a contained sparkle that springs from careful observation without a trace of anthropomorphism. His accurate eye notes what is really there, and pen and ink sketches show him

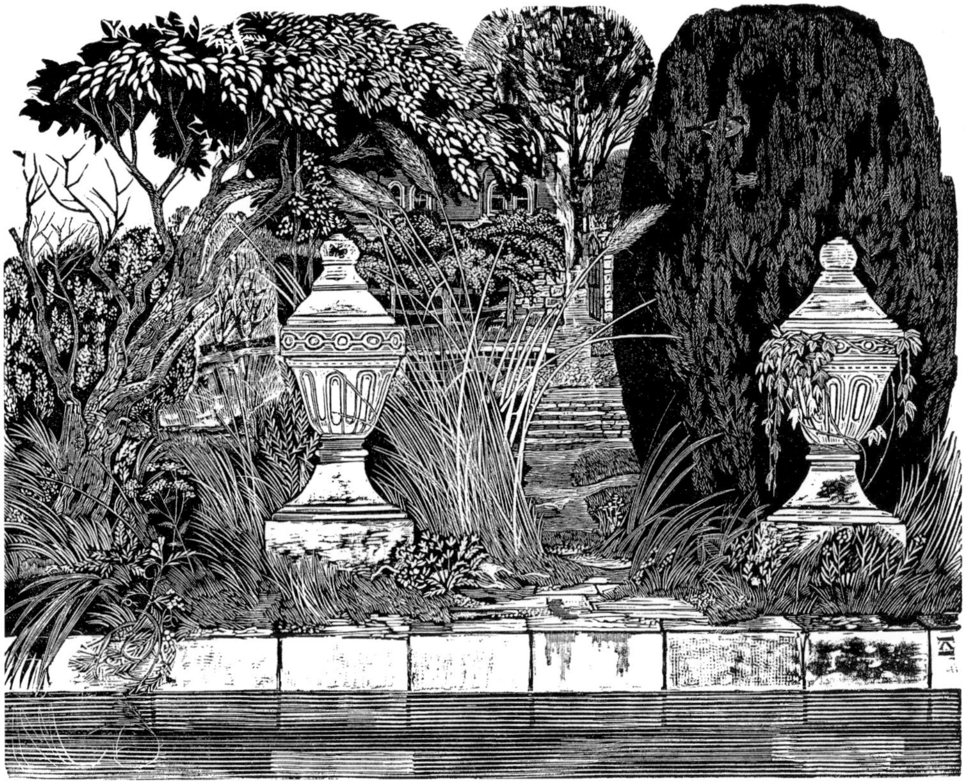

Deserted Garden, 1980

investigating various tangles in nature, later to be explored in images such as *Deserted Garden*, *Rain* or *The Wrong Snow*. Vignettes such as *A Sudden Shower*, *Packhorse Bridge*, or the small pieces made for Milton Keynes Development Corporation, demonstrate not only his interest in the visual effects of weather but also his love of odd combinations (palms and prams, kingfishers and windsurfers) and his choice of off-centre compositions that suggest fleeting observations or chance events. *Midsummer* shows him ranging over the countryside, from his feet to the horizon. *Saling* gives a bravura depiction of plants glowing in intense light.

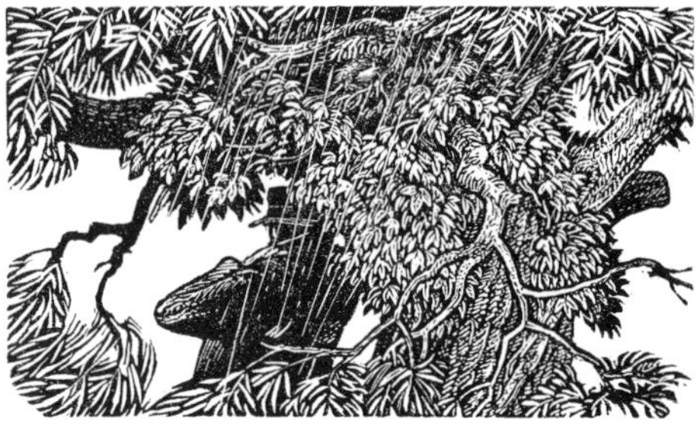

Above: A Sudden Shower, 1997, illustrating John Clare for The Folio Golden Treasury

Right: Saling, 1997

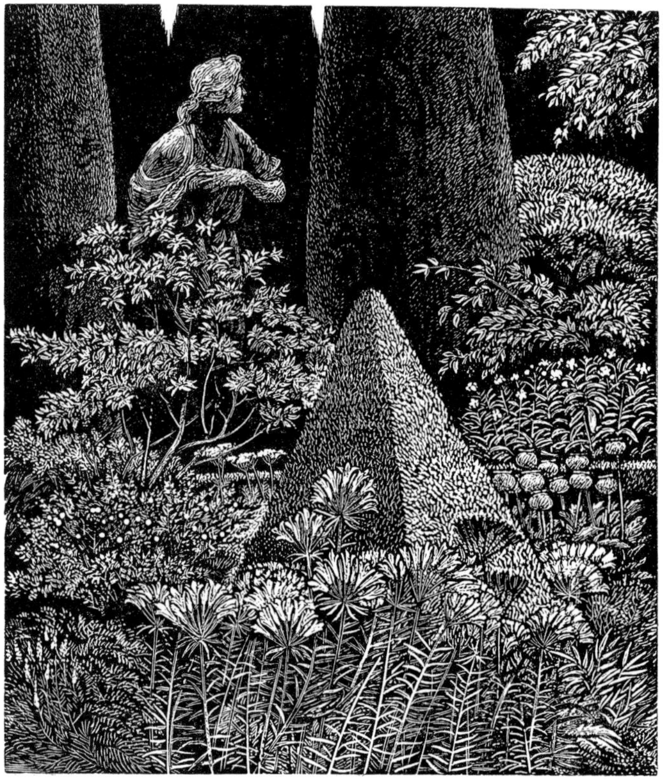

Stephens' attention to detail is immense, and his mastery of detail is matched to his mastery of engraving, which has become the medium in which he relives his experience of the country around him. Like Bewick, he is at his very best when peering under hedgerows or into trees, making visible the hidden life of the natural world.

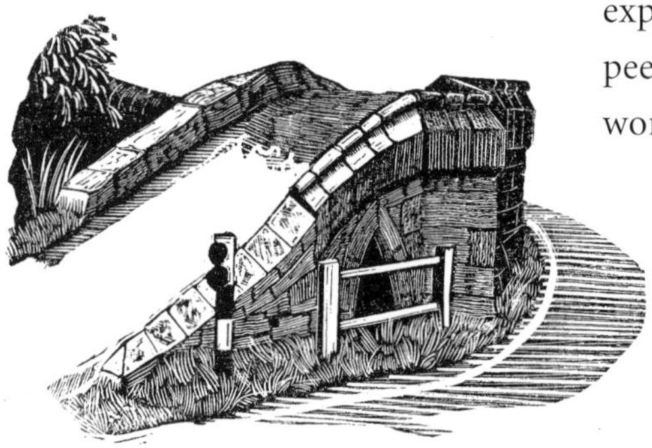

Packhorse Bridge, 1976

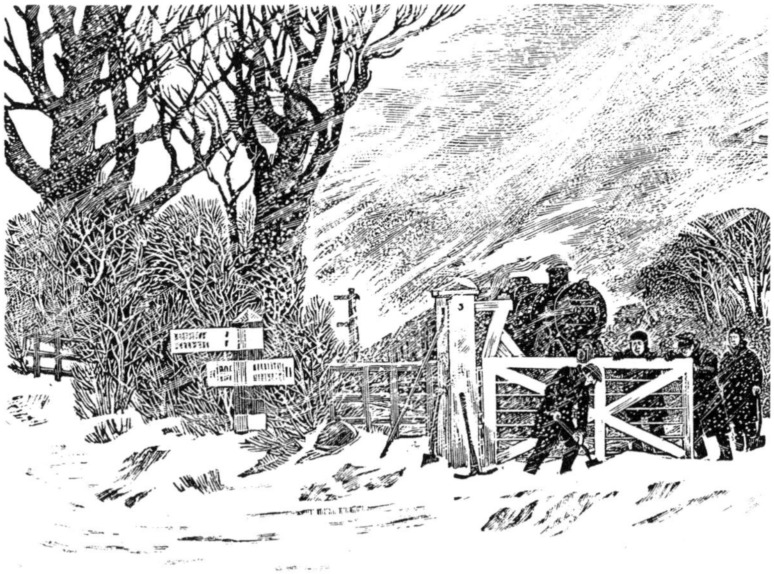

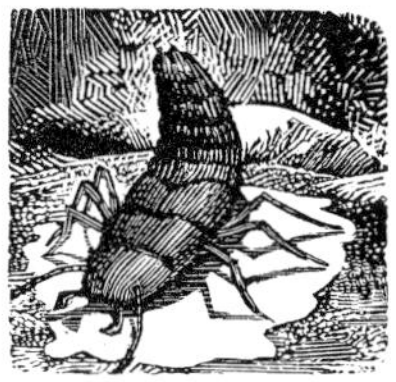

Above: Devil's Coach Horse, 1997, illustrating John Clare for The Folio Golden Treasury

Left: The Wrong Snow, 2003

Below left: Sketchbook drawing, c. 1958/9, later used for The Wrong Snow

Below right: Devil's Coach Horse, pen sketches

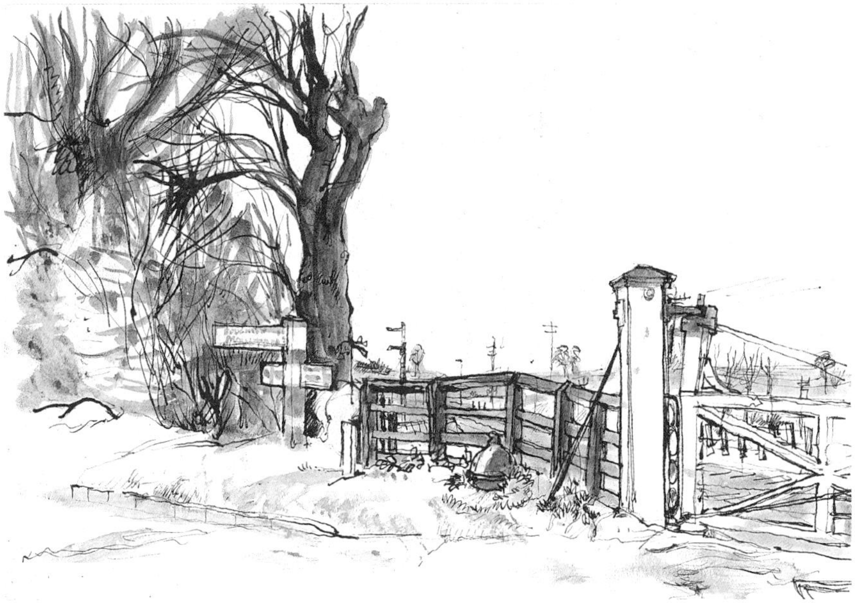

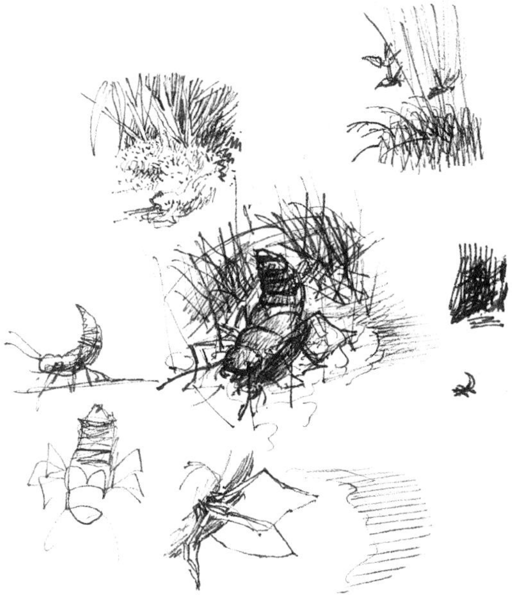

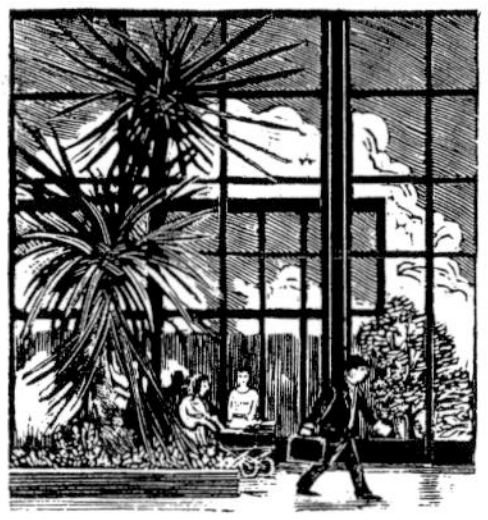

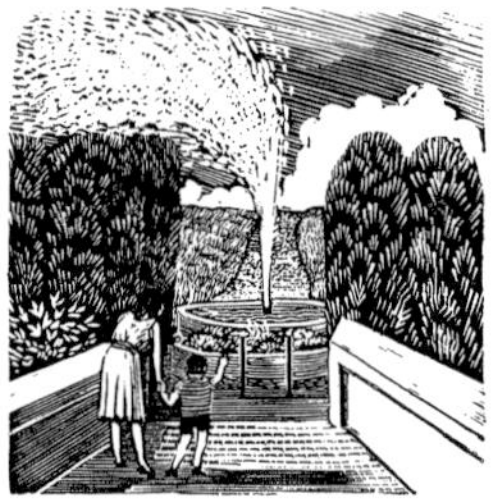

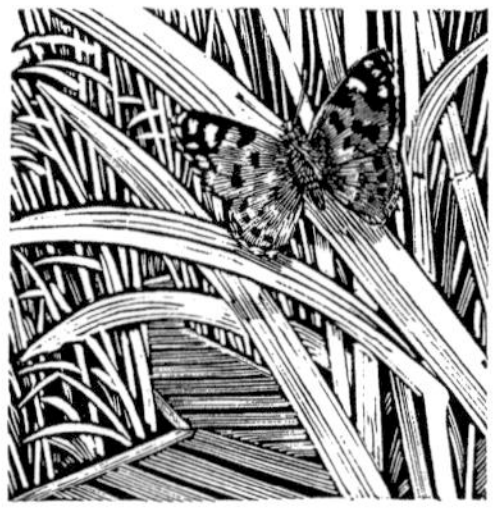

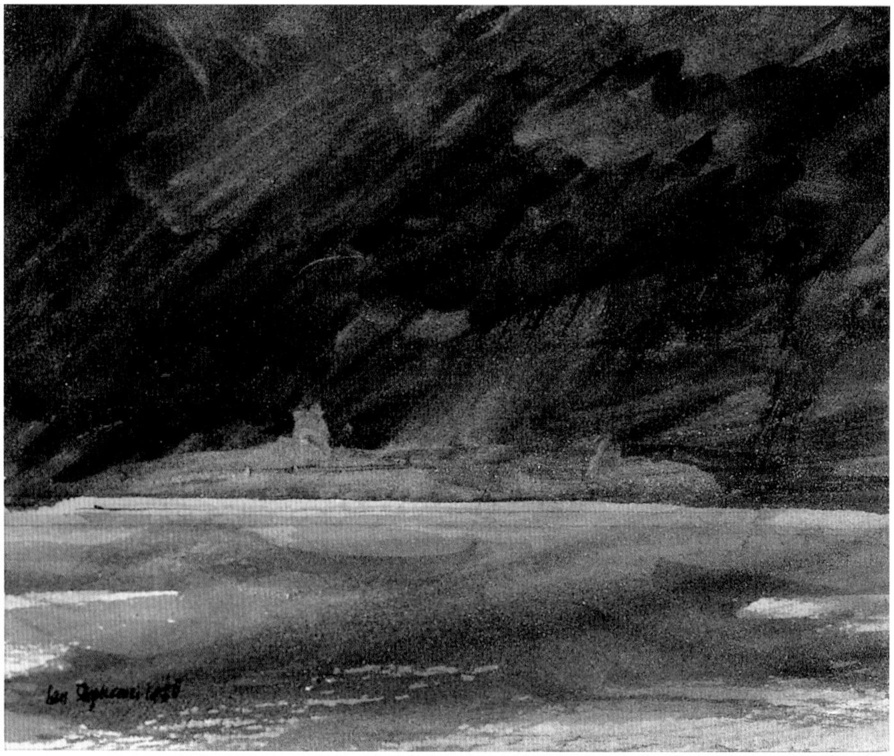

Above: *Farne Islands, watercolour sketch, 1986*

Left and below: *Aspects of Milton Keynes, c. 1986*

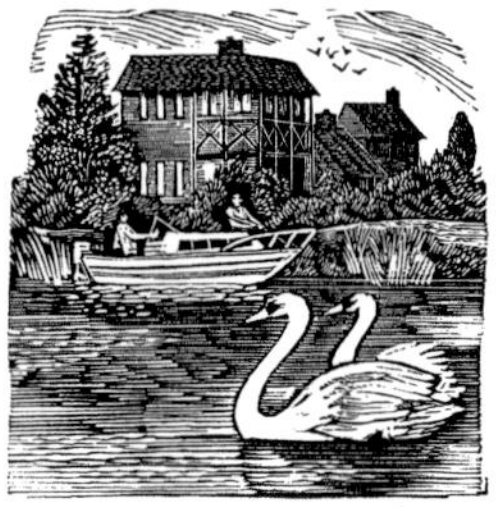

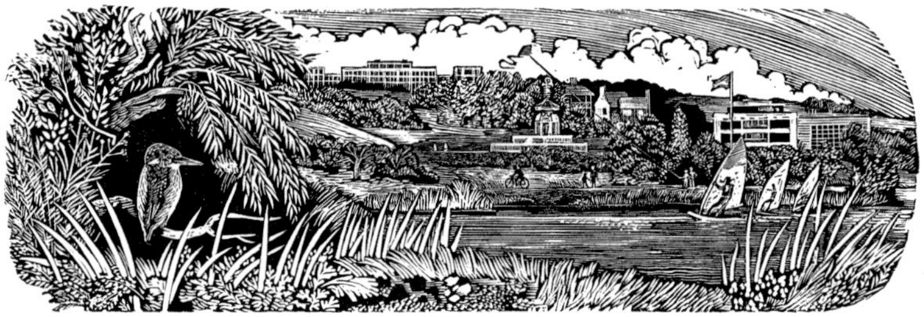

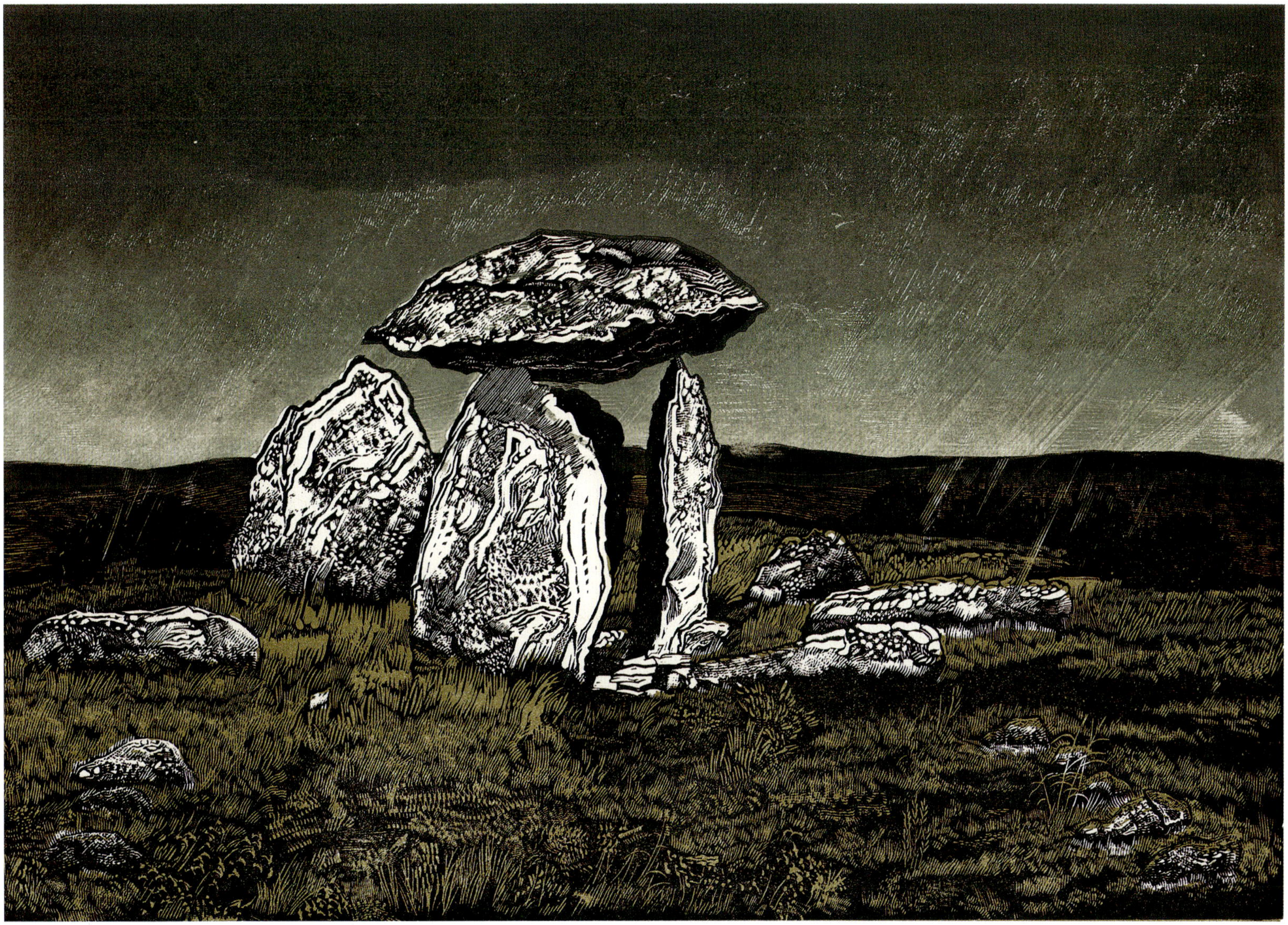

Cromlech: Pentre Ifan, multi-colour linocut, 1976, 212 × 304 mm

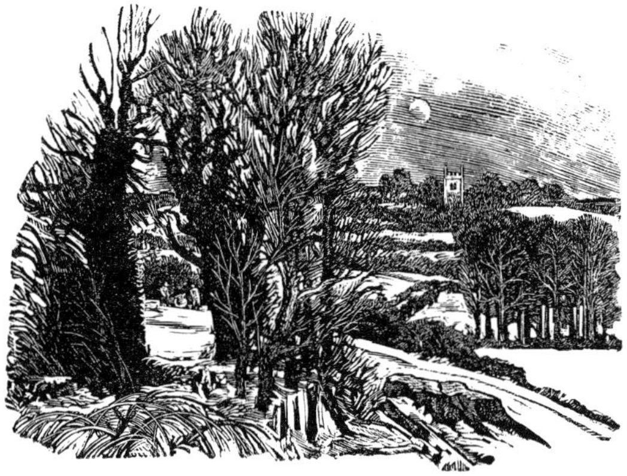

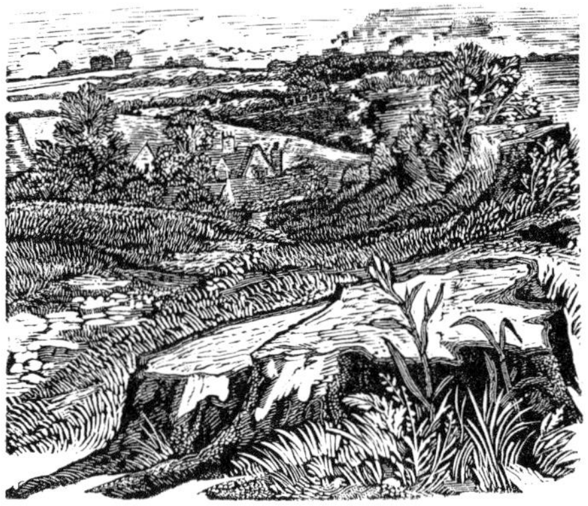

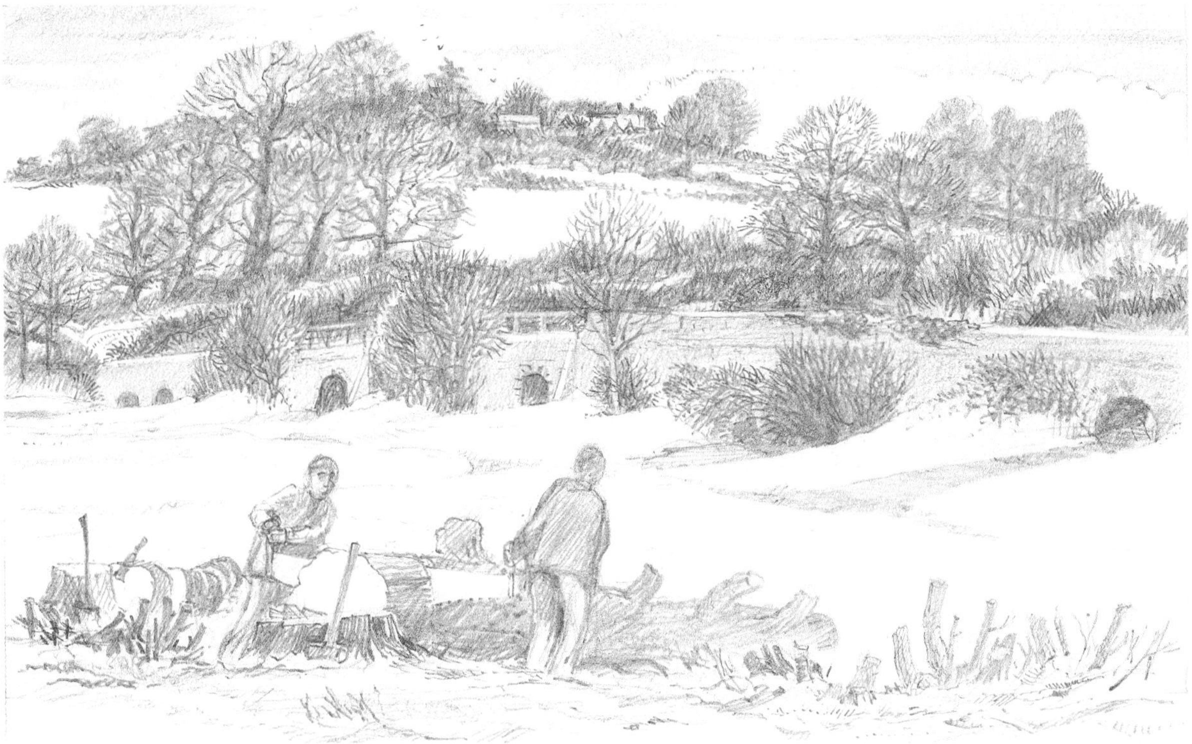

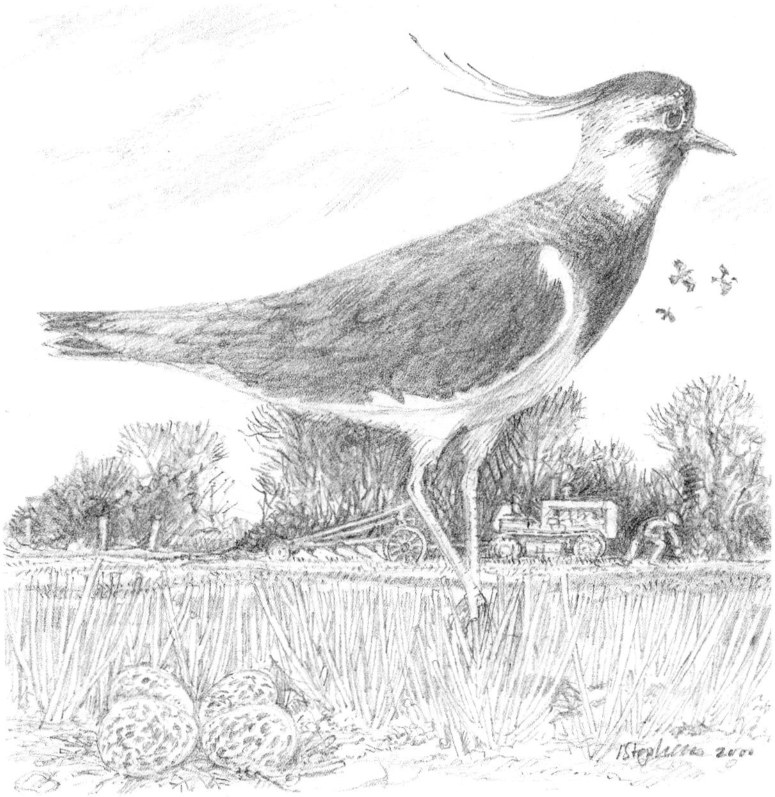

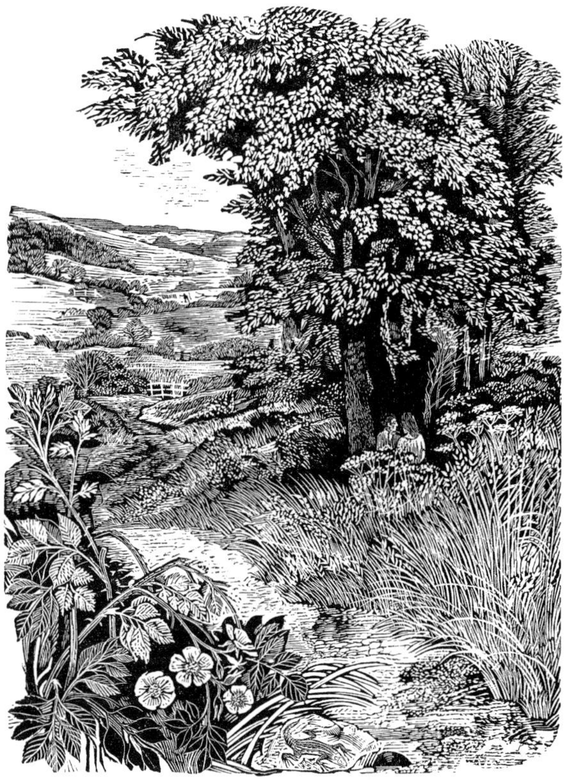

Opposite page

Top left: Thicket c. 1989?

Top right: Abthorpe Elms, 1989

Bottom: Brampton Crossing, pencil sketch for proposed engraving, c. 1995

This page

Left: Study for Millennium Ark project, pencil, 2000

Right: Midsummer, 2007

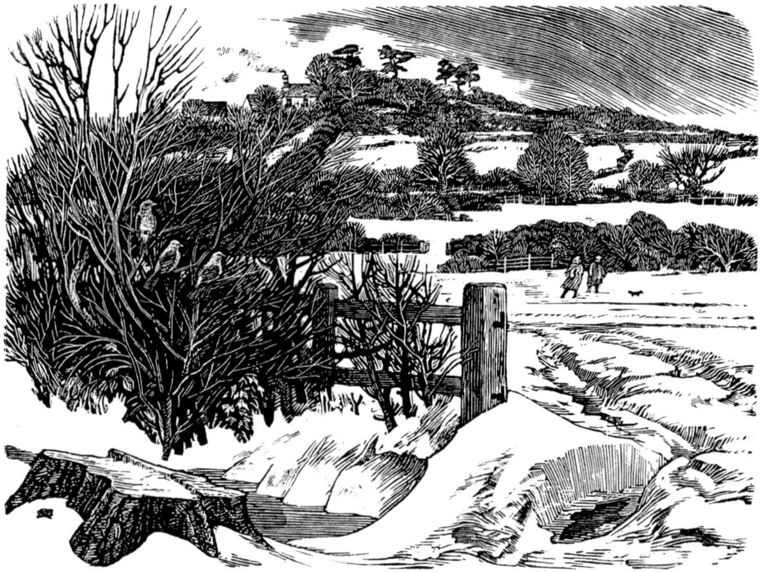

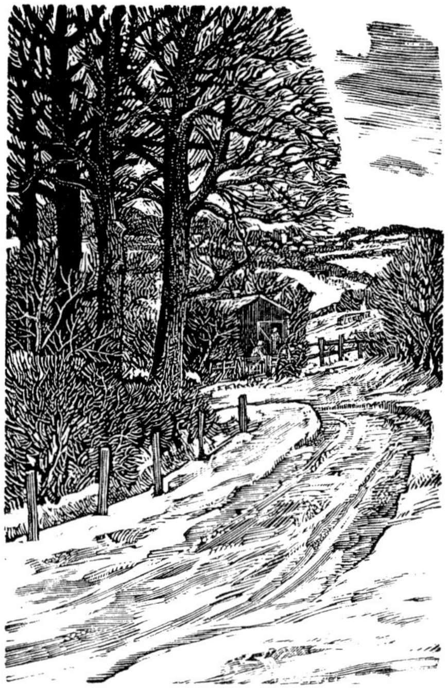

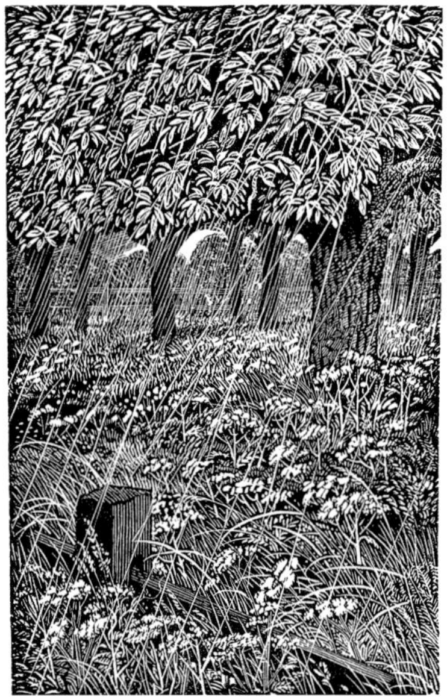

Above left: Winter Fields, c. 1985?

Above right: Shepherd's Hovel, 1996

Left: It Rained, 2007

Opposite: Red Kite, 2008

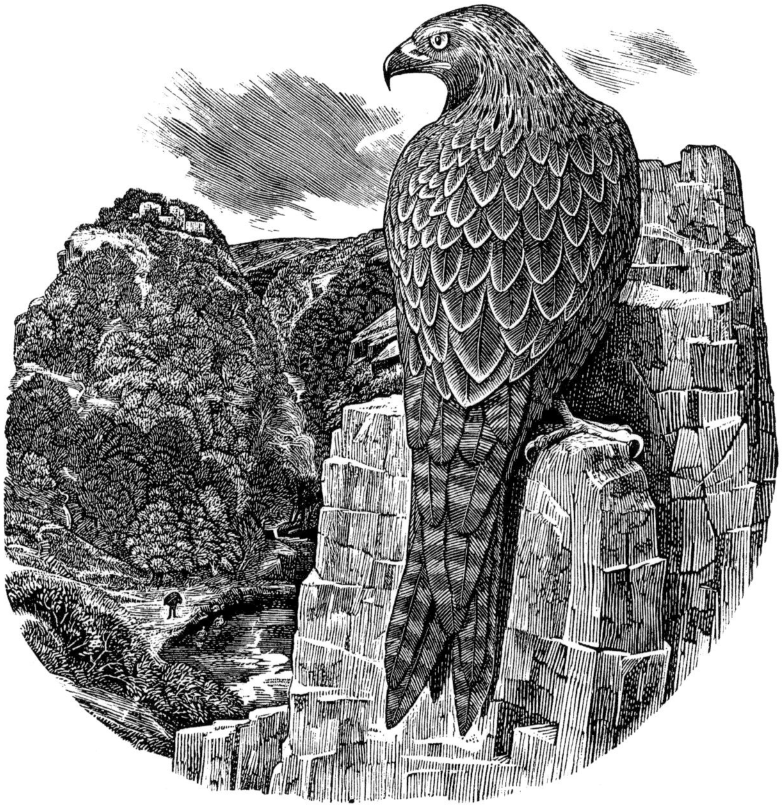

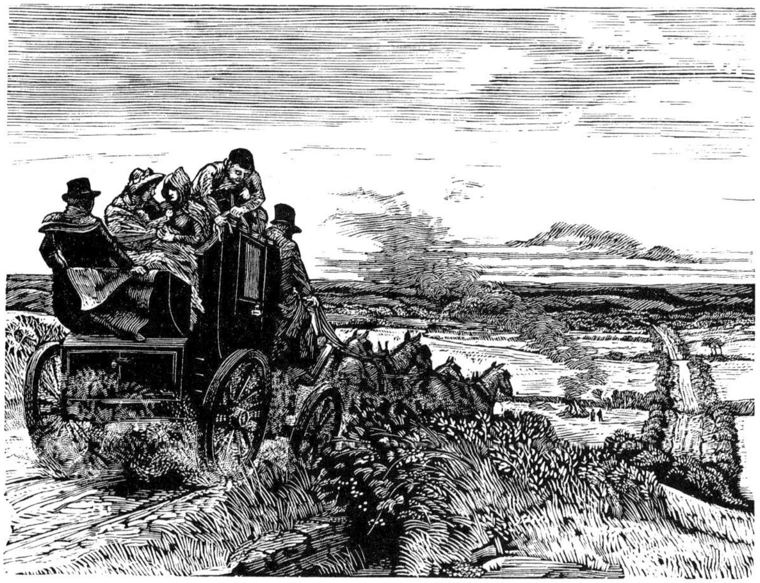

On the Road, from The Tenant of Wildfell Hall, Folio Society, 1991

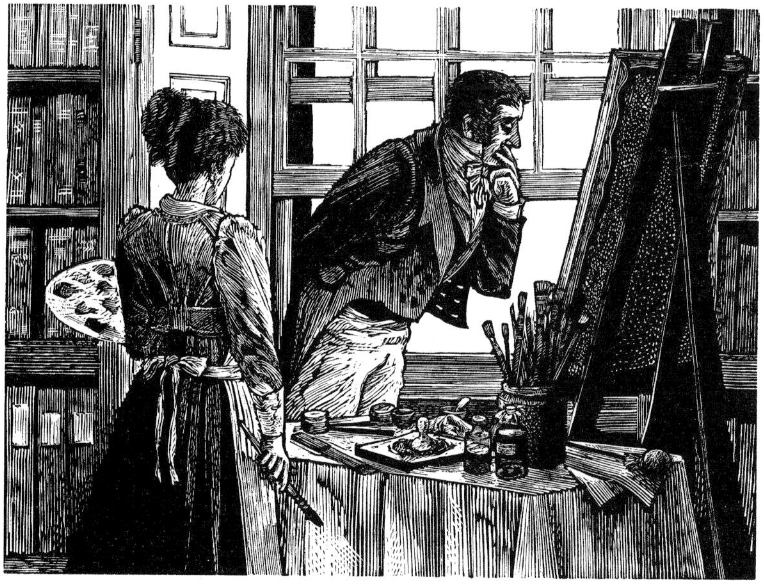

The Expert, from The Tenant of Wildfell Hall, Folio Society, 1991

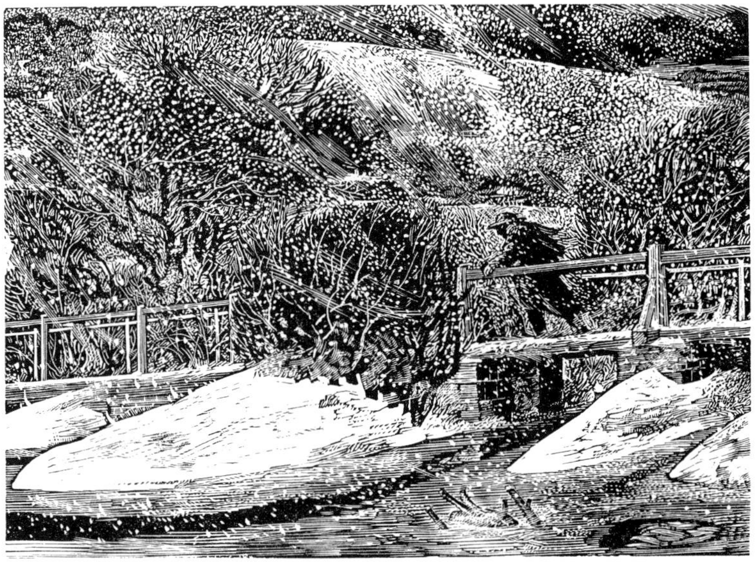

The Causeway Chill, from The Folio Golden Treasury, 1997

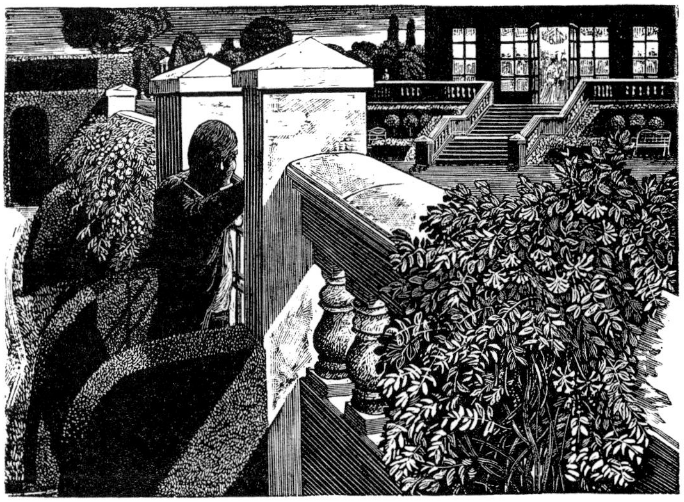

Maud, from the Folio Society Tennyson, 2006

SARAH VAN NIEKERK: *Hirundings of Selborne, 1993*

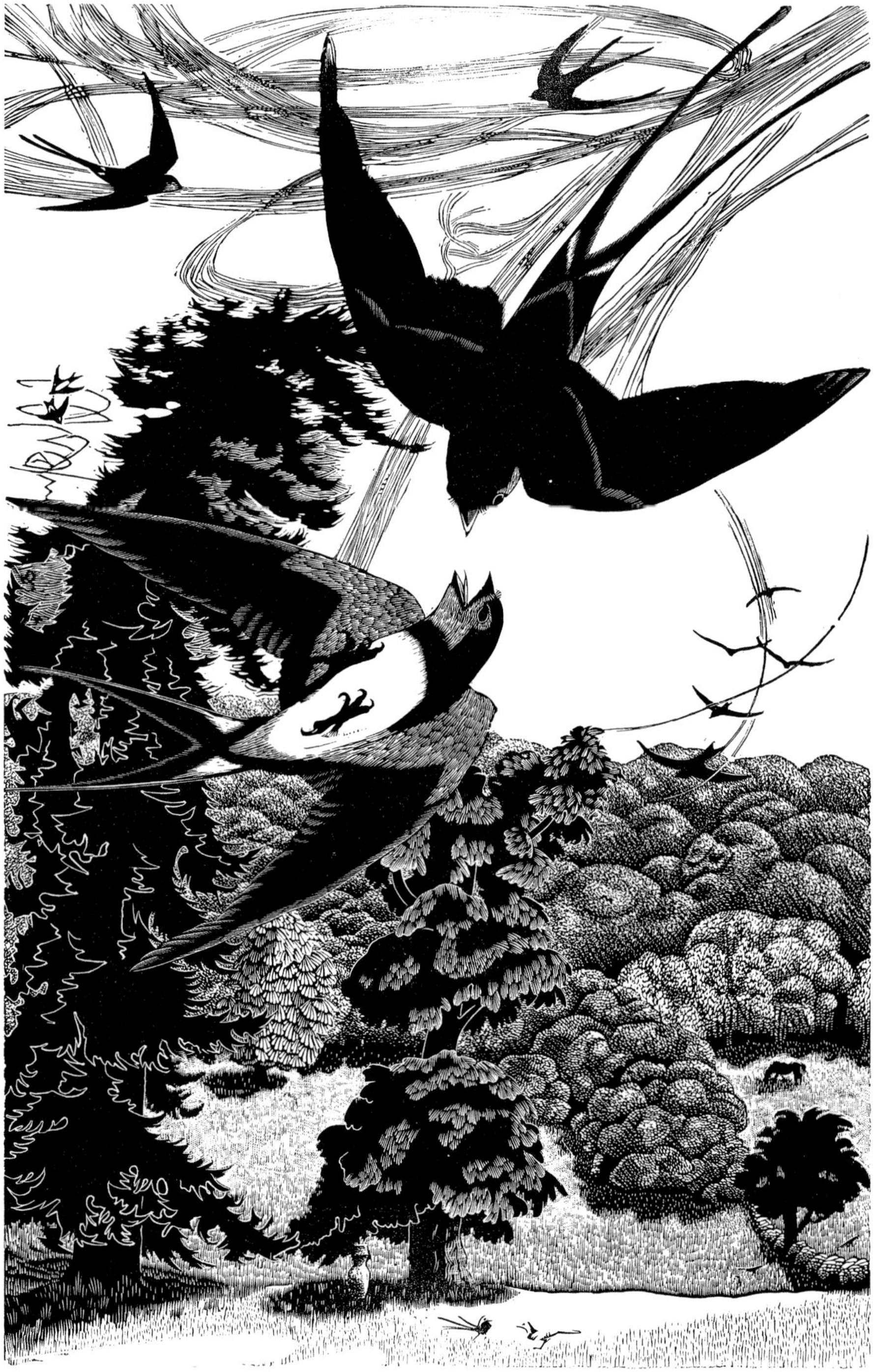

5. The Swirl and Sweep of Nature

Sarah van Niekerk

Chairman of the Society of Wood Engravers 1995–1998

The fluid lines and sweeping curves that are hallmarks of Sarah van Niekerk's images are drawn from acute observation of the world around her, but they incorporate more than simple responses of the eye. They also summarise her vivid response to sound and movement – the crack of the wind, the roar of roiling water, the high-pitched call of flying birds, the deep grunts of animals settling into their bedding. The state of the weather, the noises of the countryside, the touch and taste and smell of things – her art activates all the senses. *Olive Grove* engenders an extraordinary sense of heat. *Mr Henson's Young Tamworths* bristle noisily in their slumber. The *Elvers* feel slippery. The countryside and its creatures, wild or tame, form the cornerstone of her work, and she is expert at bringing out the inner life of the animals, birds, and plants that she depicts.

The sensory accuracy of van Niekerk's imagery, and her ability to find dramatic designs within natural forms, owes much to her beloved teacher at the Central School of Art. Gertrude Hermes' artistic sensibility, both as sculptor and wood engraver, was formed in pre-war Modernism, and the plunging perspectives and abstract patterning in her wood engravings have elements of Cubism and Vorticism. Her influence on her pupil is clearest in van Niekerk's imaginative studies. *Genesis*, with its freely floating lines and circular rhythms, is strongly reminiscent of Hermes' superb *Undercurrents*.

But although she looks for pattern in her subjects, van Niekerk's work is more naturalistic and her mark-making more descriptive of textures found in nature. Her own distinct voice is clearest in designs based on careful observation, where

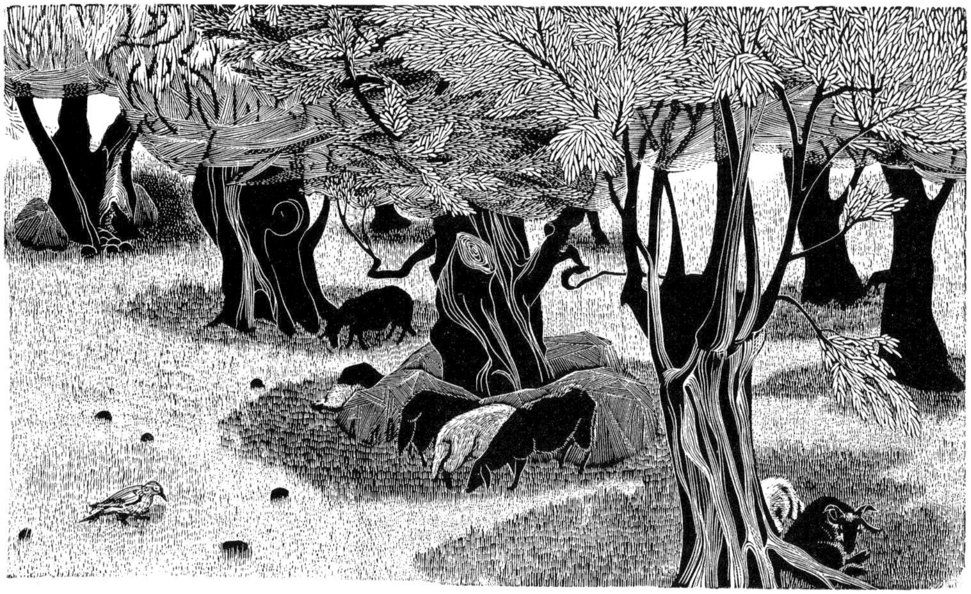

Olive Grove near Molyvos, 1985

steep perspectives and powerful contrasts of black and white are subservient to the reality of the scene. The element of humour is entirely her own. She sees the theatrically funny side of the people and creatures she observes, and engravings such as *The Flautist*, *The Power Machine Show*, *Saturnia* and *Signora Fernando* are both perceptive and entertaining, as is her engraving, for the *Reader's Digest Illustrated Bible*, of Jonah scooting along in the complacent belly of the whale. Much of her work contains an element of gentle caricature.

Although as a child she was always drawing, art seemed very much a subsidiary activity to Sarah van Niekerk, and she had to be forcibly weaned from her determination to be a farmer. Her mother was a painter and drawing and painting therefore seemed a natural part of life, although Sarah saw that her mother's priority was ministering to her husband. Before the war Sarah's father made his living as a writer, publishing novels based on his adventures in New Mexico and

Romania. During the war he was co-opted into the Ministry of Information and from then on moved from one diplomatic posting to another, often working undercover. When Sarah was born the family lived in Berkshire, in what was then the remote village of Inkpen. Sarah remembers that her father was always around, working in the garden, building a pond for her and her elder brother to swim in, or shut inside his double-doored study, writing. It was a rural idyll where life revolved around the seasons. She recalls the thrilling ice storm just before the war, when rain followed by severe frost coated the trees with ice, causing huge branches to fall to the ground.

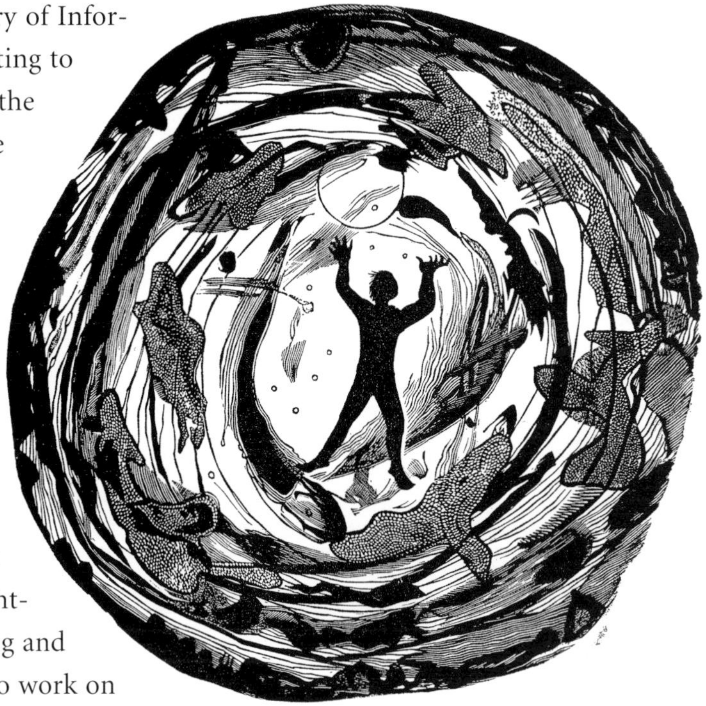

Genesis, 1984

When war threatened Sarah sailed on a refugee ship with her mother and brother to Canada, and then made a nightmarish journey south to the United States, the train dividing and separating her from her mother. Her father followed later to work on secret government missions in America, eventually ending up in Washington, where the family were reunited. Sarah went native, embarrassing her brother with her American accent. All she now remembers about her American school is a day spent drawing leaves.

Back in post-war England the family moved to a farm near Newbury. Sarah loved the farm and was certain that farming was the life for her. At Bedales School her artistic talent was encouraged but she drew only what she loved – the animals on the farm. In order to separate her from her beloved horses her parents packed her off to France to learn French and acquire a bit of culture. In the Jeu de Paume she was struck dumb by her first sight of Impressionist paintings, and she returned many times to look at them. On her return to England, aged seventeen, she was

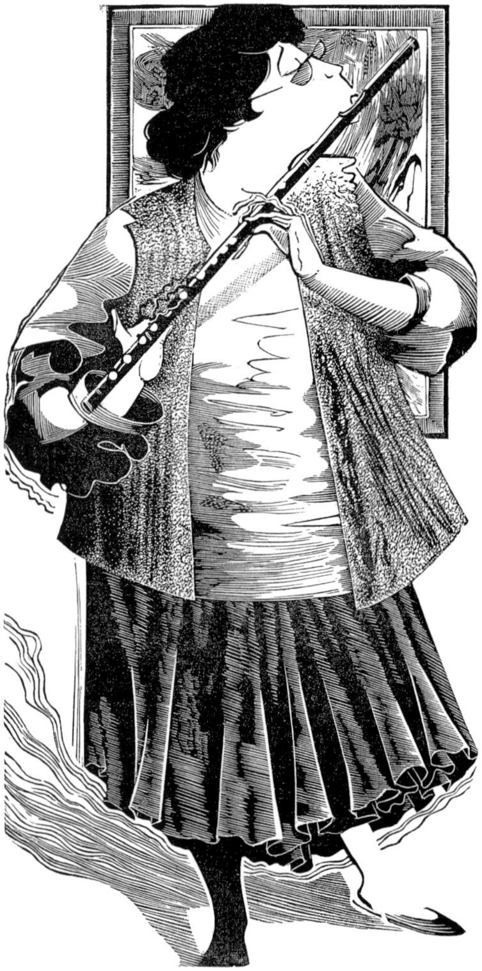

The Flautist, 1991

taken for an interview at the Slade, where her brother was already a student. Professor Coldstream looked at her drawings of farm animals and suggested that the Central School of Art and Design might suit her better. There interviewed by Maurice Kestleman and Jesse Collins, she was offered a place and advised to specialise in Illustration or Graphic Design. She was also steered into Zoo Drawing, taught by Gertrude Hermes, who in turn introduced her to wood engraving. She took to engraving with alacrity, finding 'a positive sensual pleasure in cutting through the silky surface of the darkened block into the crisp boxwood. I loved the satisfying crunch as the scorper lifted little golden curls on its way through the wood to create light in which the composition was slowly revealed and to this day I still do. I still delight in the rich and varied textures that can be created, the sparkling clarity of the cleared white areas and the deepest blacks of any print medium.'

Gertrude Hermes was an inspirational teacher. She treated her students as her own teacher, Leon Underwood, had treated her – as artists from the start. Although she was specialising in Illustration, Sarah van Niekerk hated drawing with a pen and therefore tried to do all her illustration work by wood engraving. She completed the course by taking the Central's brand new Diploma in Wood Engraving. By the time she had finished three and a half years there, a brief, dismal job in an advertising agency and a postgraduate year at the Slade, she had already exhibited widely – with the Young Contemporaries, the Welsh Arts Council, the Society of Wood Engravers and several other organisations. A large colour linocut of *Lorna*, a rhinoceros at Regents Park Zoo, was bought by the Victoria and Albert Museum as well as by several education committees.

In 1956 Sarah married Chris van Niekerk, a fellow graphics student from the Central who had then started work in advertising with J. Walter Thompson. While three small children kept Sarah at home, her own work was confined to conté book

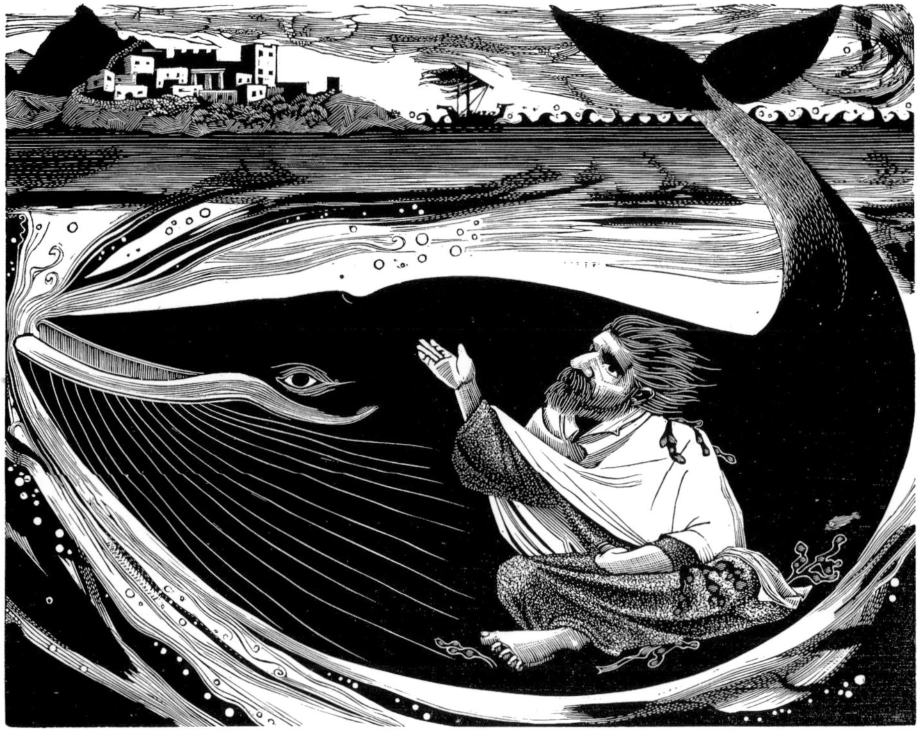

Jonah, for The Reader's Digest Bible, 1990

illustration and engraving Christmas cards. A first commission for a company presentation, to engrave the company's building in Queen Anne's Gate, came through friends of her parents. As she had done no serious engraving for a decade, to get her hand in she worked from her zoo sketches on *Ring-tailed Lemurs*. The Queen Anne's Gate engraving led to other commissions and she began to engrave seriously again. She needed her own press, and consulted Mr Lawrence, to whom Hermes had introduced her when a student. Mr Lawrence's establishment in Bleeding Heart Yard was the mecca for all wood engravers, but the great man would only deign to meet those whom he considered real artists. He obviously took van Niekerk seriously for he directed her to an etcher in Ditchling who owned a

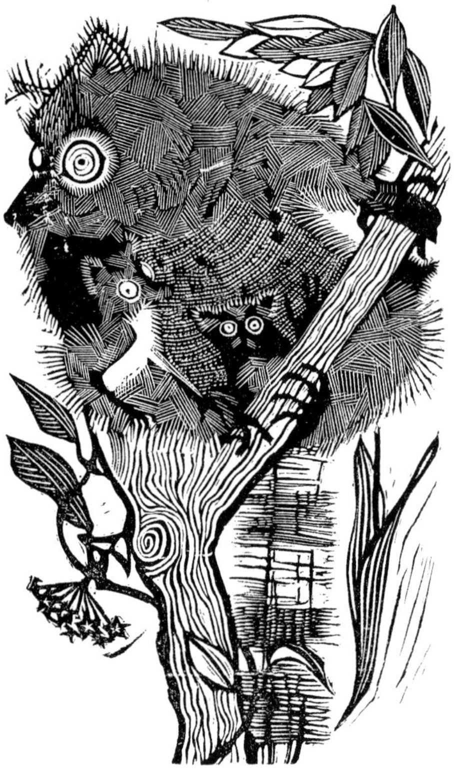

Ring-tailed Lemurs, 1968

collection of presses, and from him she bought the Hopkinson and Cope Albion Press that she still uses. She had always enjoyed printing, and the newly-acquired press started her working again, and on a much larger scale. A series of large colour linocuts of animals followed. Sarah had kept up her zoo drawing because it was something she could do with young children, and two visits to her husband's family in South Africa expanded her repertoire with lions, warthogs, wild dogs and antelopes. A huge mural commissioned by Kew Gardens in 1976 also stretched her design and printing skills.

Many early engravings were influenced by the Welsh landscape, where the van Niekerks spent holidays with the children. When they moved to Oxfordshire the family kept a small flock of Jacob sheep, and sheep began to figure in her work. When *Ring-tailed Lemurs* was accepted by the Royal Academy for their 1975 Summer Exhibition Sarah felt that her career was truly launched. For the following twenty-one years she exhibited at the RA every year, selling in large editions. She was also exhibiting widely elsewhere, and in order to keep up the flow of new images she set herself a target of doing one engraving a month. Although some of these were commissioned engravings, the majority were autonomous prints, inspired by the countryside and the creatures around her.

Over the years Sarah van Niekerk has built up an impressive body of work, autographic engravings as well as commissioned illustration for the *Readers Digest*, the Gregynog Press and the Folio society. Never short of ideas, she prefers working to her own dictates, although she acknowledges that commissions have expanded her horizons and enlarged her vocabulary, especially encouraging her to draw people. Alongside her own demanding working schedule van Niekerk has been an assiduous teacher, running classes at the City Literary Institute, the City and Guilds of London Art School, West Dean College, and, after Gertrude Hermes retired, at the Royal Academy schools. She teaches as she was taught, showing her students the

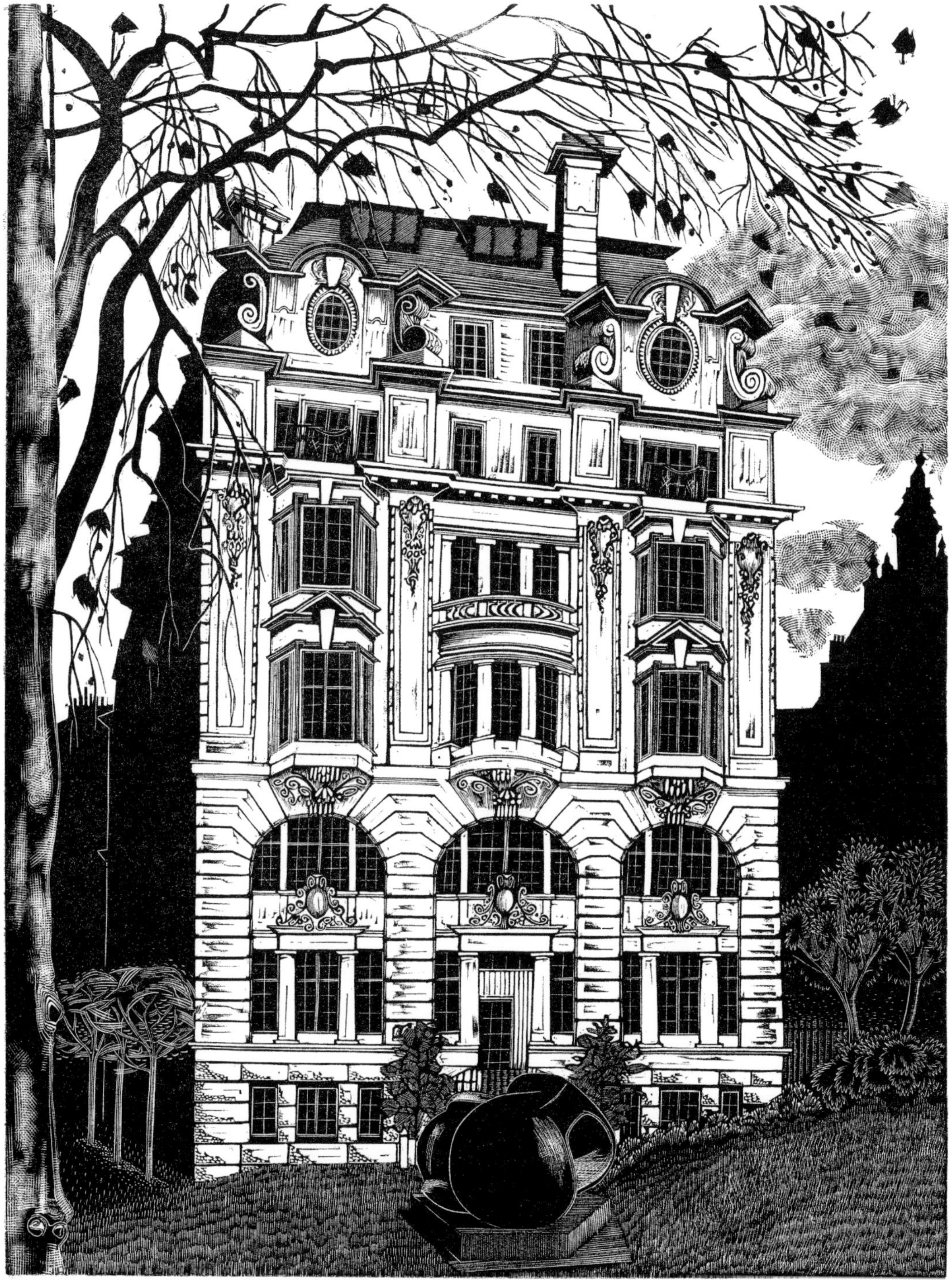

Queen Anne's Gate, 1968,
205 × 153 mm

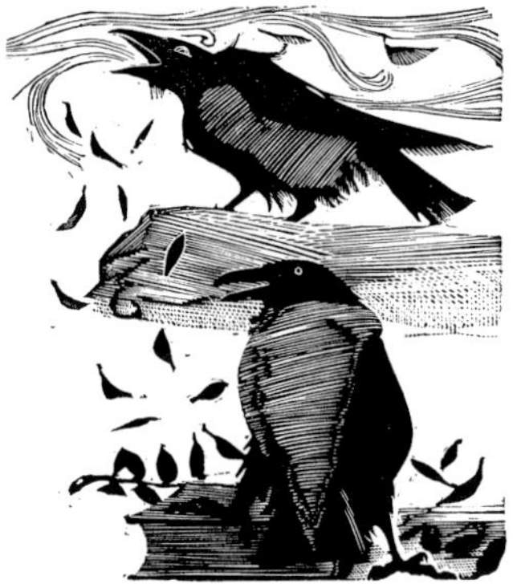

Ravens, 1990

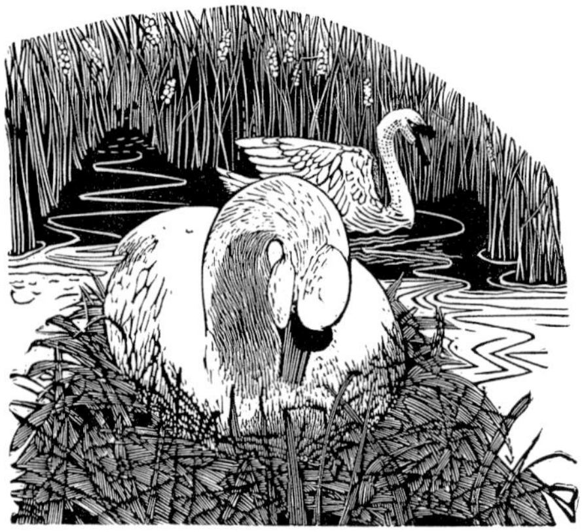

Swan's nest, 2008

Opposite: Nant Pasgan Bach, 1997, 225 × 152 mm

basic essentials while wafting around the studios encouraging them as fellow artists. Membership of the Society of Wood Engravers has kept her in touch with developments in the medium, and membership of other societies – the Royal Society of Painter Printmakers and the Royal West of England Academy – has widened her range as well as confirming her status as a contemporary artist engraver. Wood engraving is the medium in which her unique synthesis of flat patterning, boldly juxtaposed blacks and whites, decorative line, graphic depiction of form, and caricaturist's shorthand can flourish freely. Her work is instantly recognisable in any exhibition.

Van Niekerk works intuitively and spontaneously within the obvious constraints of the medium. She prefers the cut line to the drawn line and enjoys the slow process of letting light into the block. Although she makes preparatory sketches for her engravings, a minimum of drawing on the block leaves her mind clear to 'recapture that first, fine, careless rapture'. As she emphasised in her book in *The Engraver's Cut* series: 'There is a temptation with wood engraving to become too meticulous, too detailed, so that the life of the original impulse is squeezed out. On the other hand, I have never seen a satisfactory engraving by someone who cannot draw. Every part of the block must be considered, no part can be brushed over or scribbled across. The marks are always deliberate, and the tool chosen to bring the appropriate degree of light to that mark. The process of working out the composition on the block, together with the deliberation of the marks, can result in a very static, dead composition, so I make a lot of preliminary drawings and a minimum of drawings on the block so that the imagination is free to invent new marks and textures with the tools in order to let the light in.'

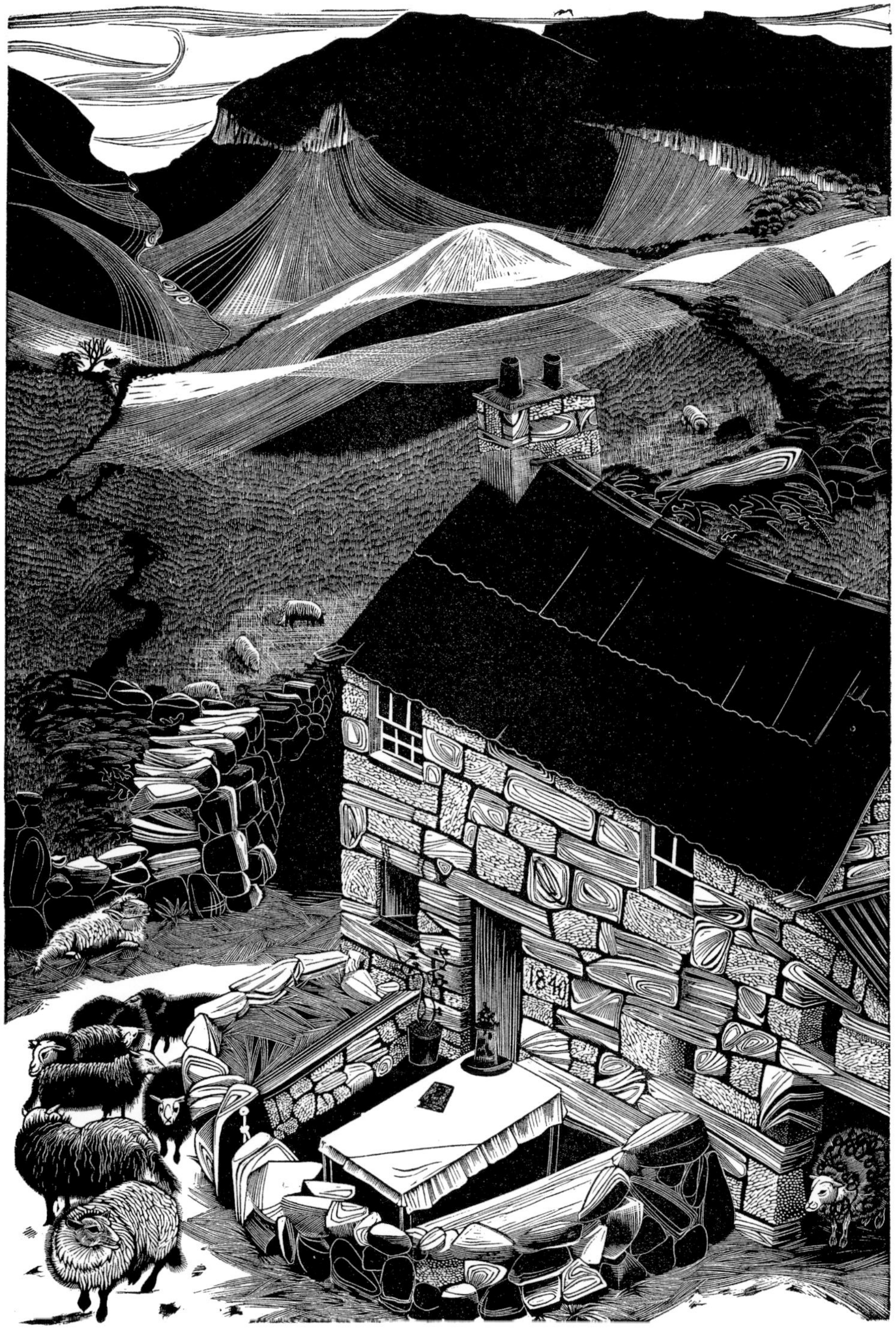
1841

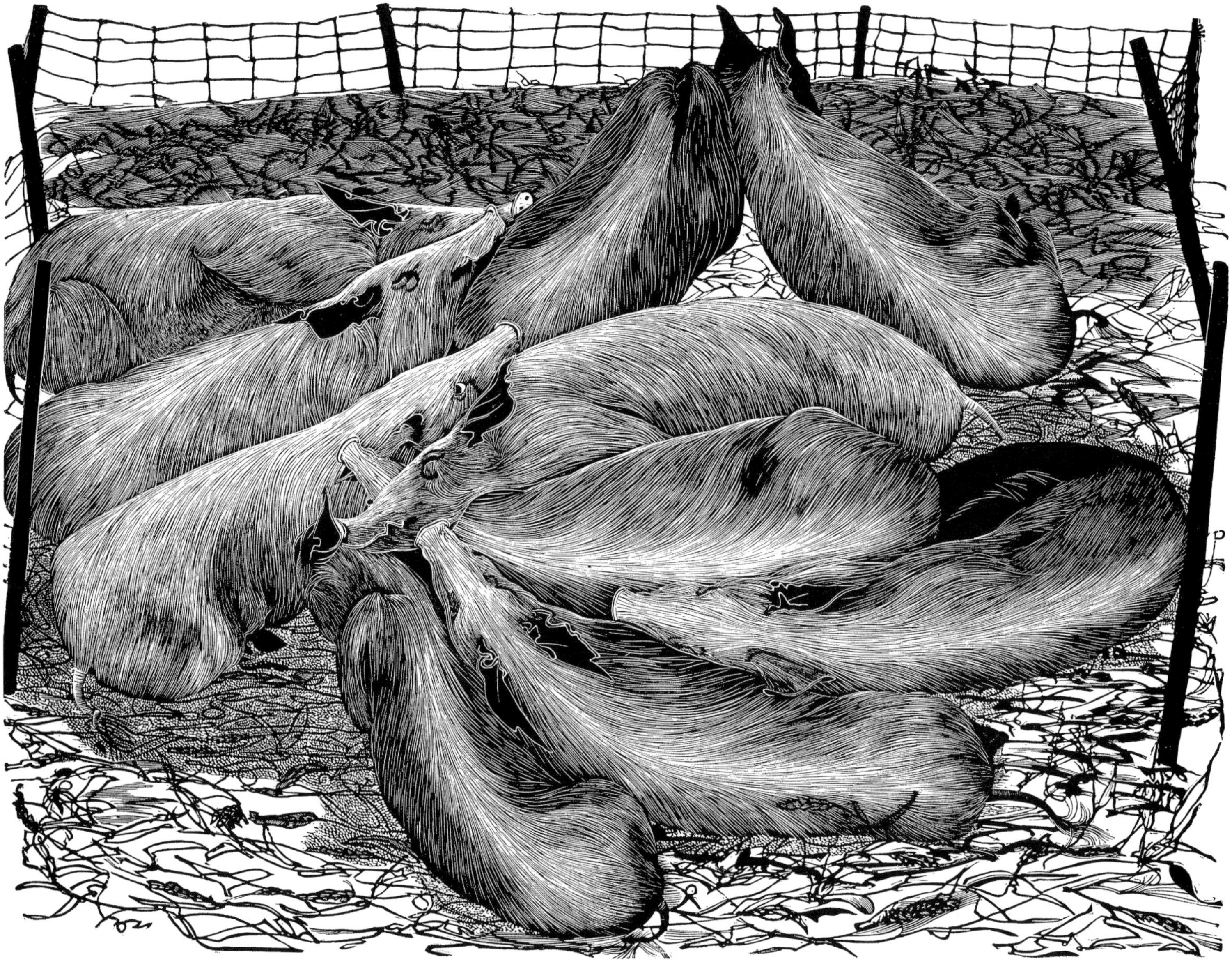

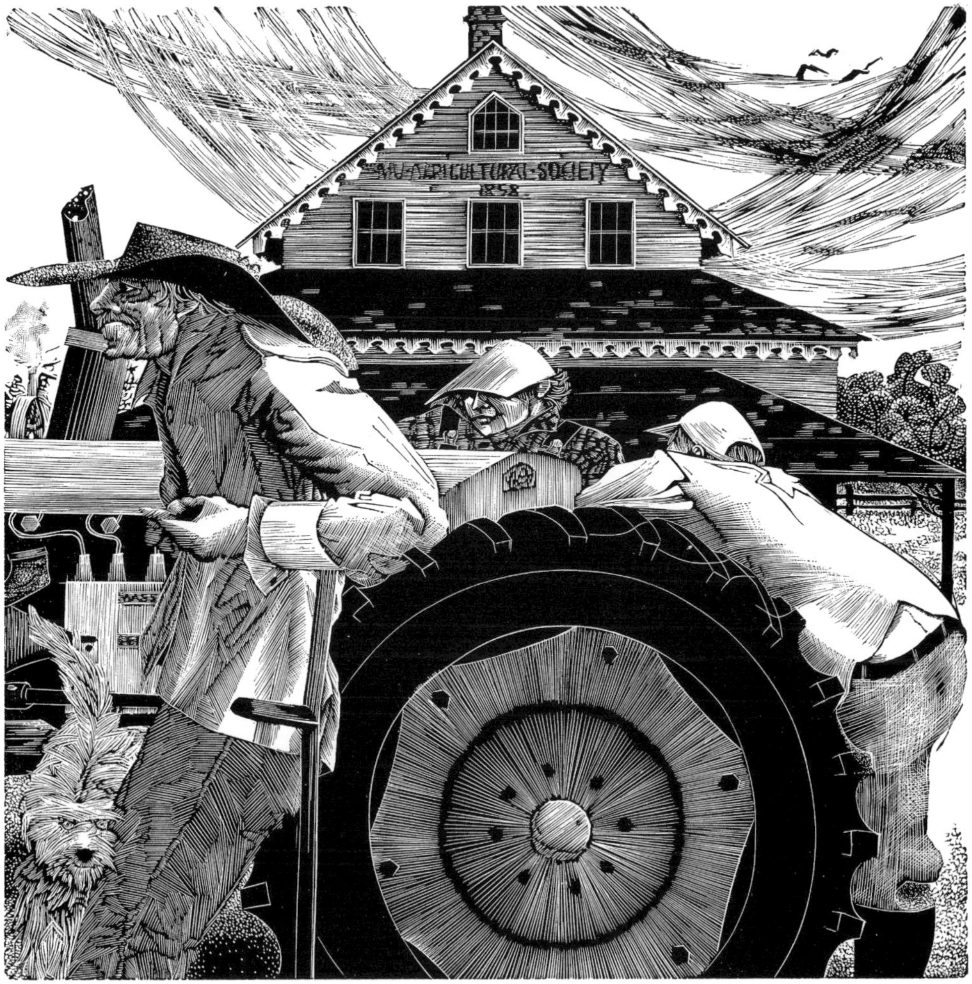

Opposite: Mr. Henson's Young Tamworths, 1982

This page: The Power Machine Show, 1994

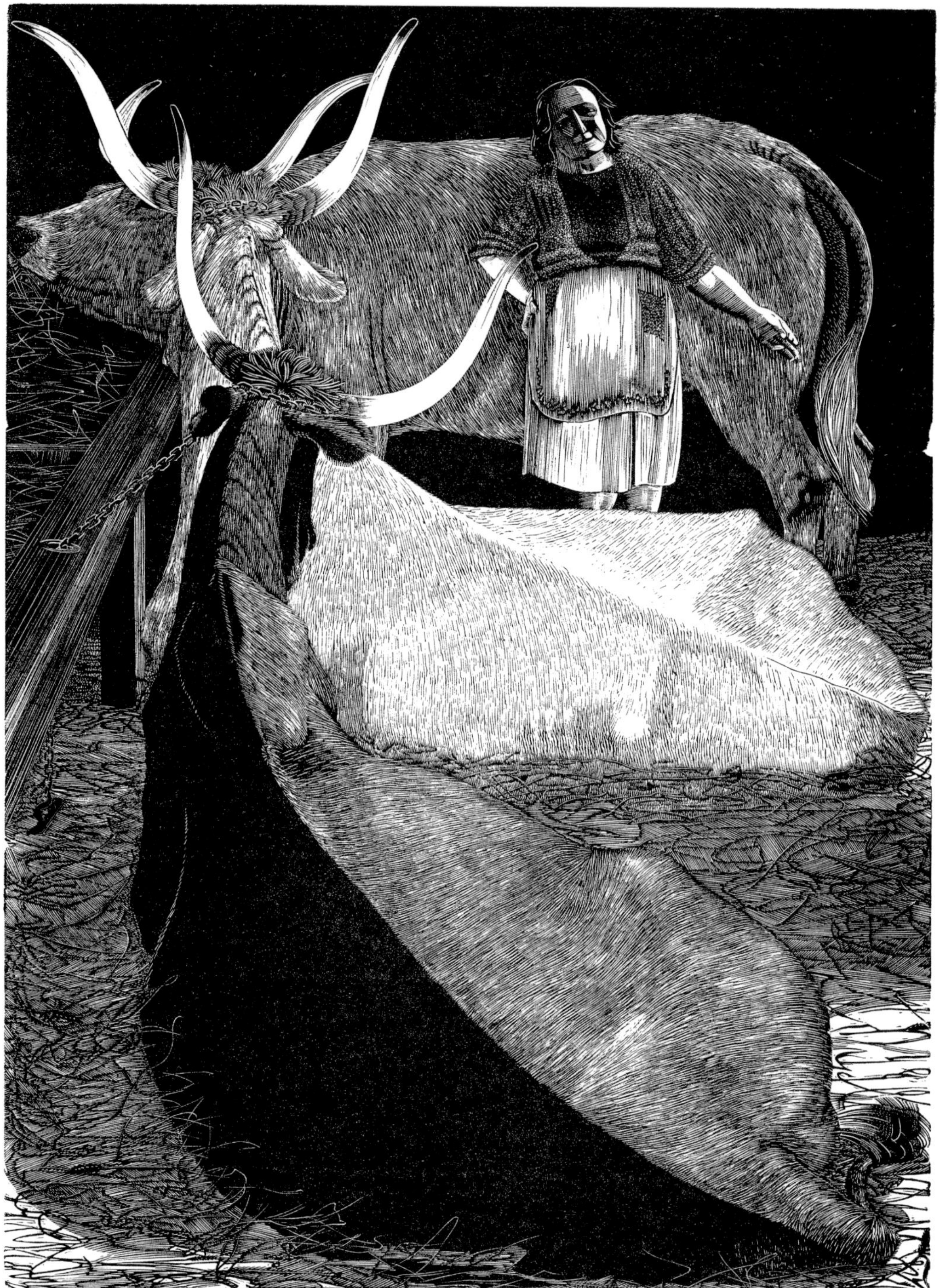

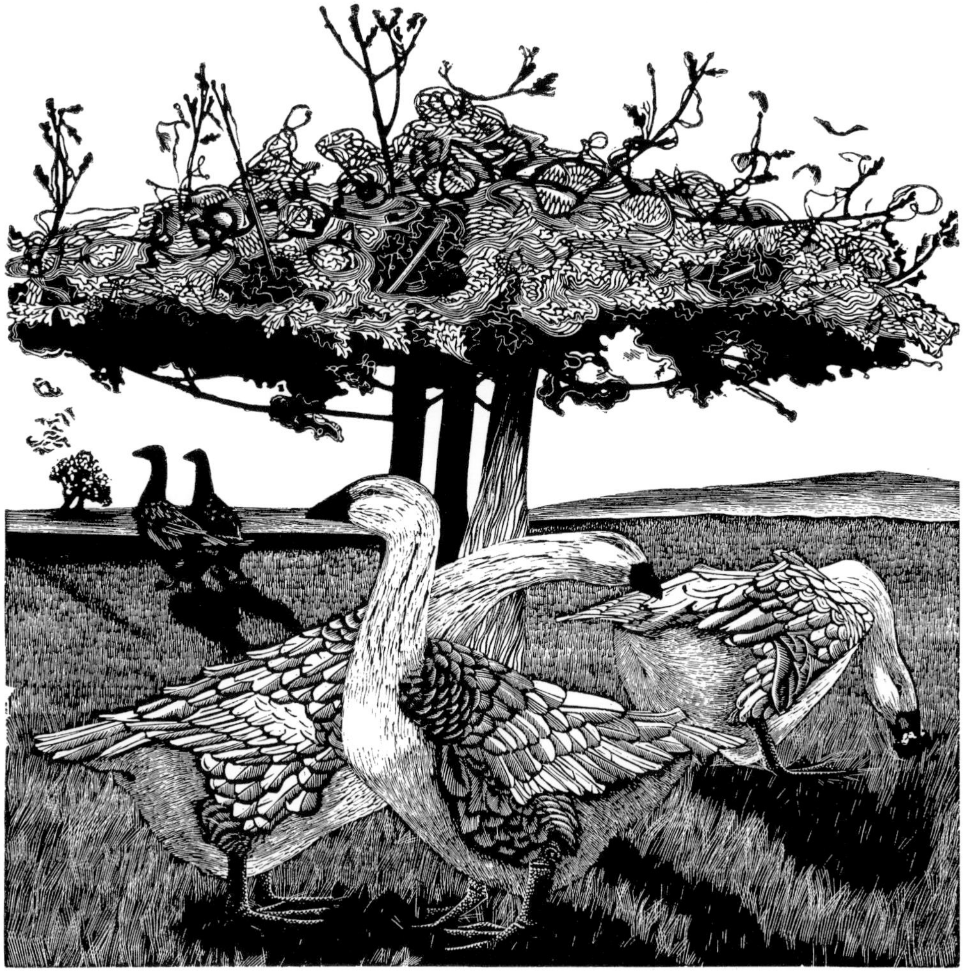

Opposite: Signora Fernando, 1990, 205 × 150 mm

Above: The Family Tree, 1986

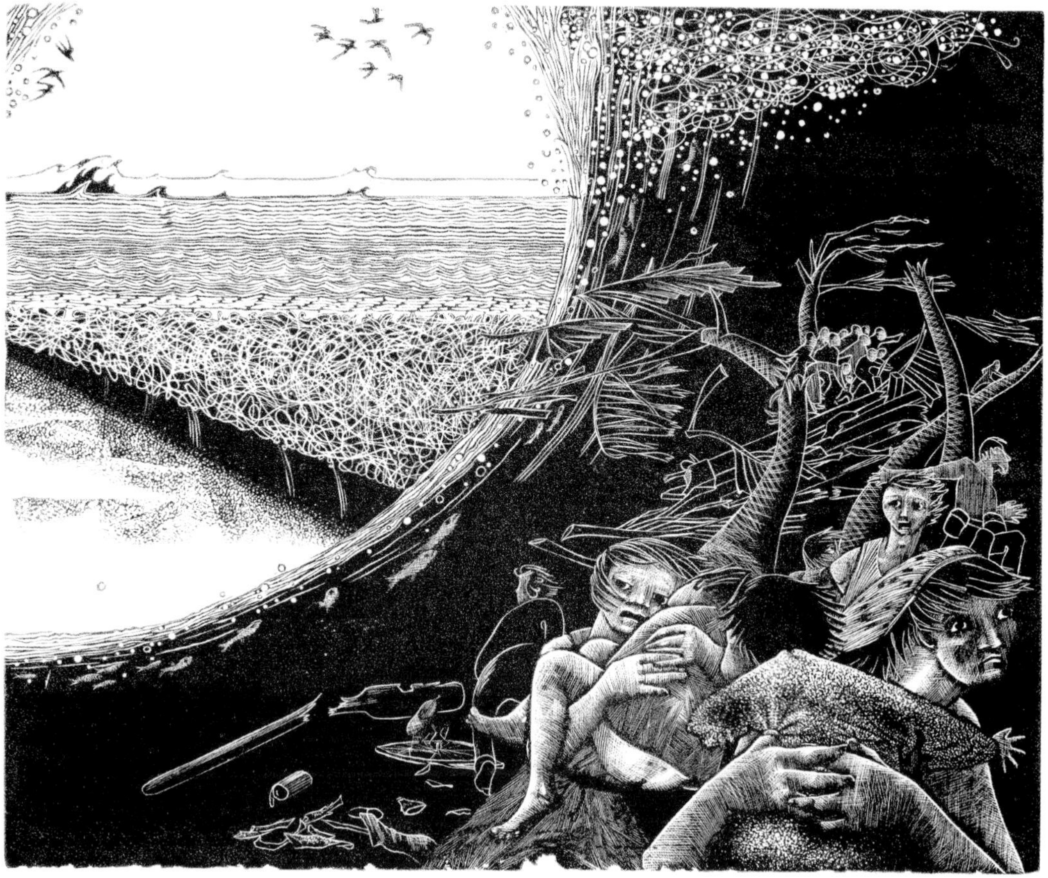

Right: Tsunami, 2005, 127 × 155 mm

Below: The Wind from the Feet of the Dead, 1992, 75 × 243 mm

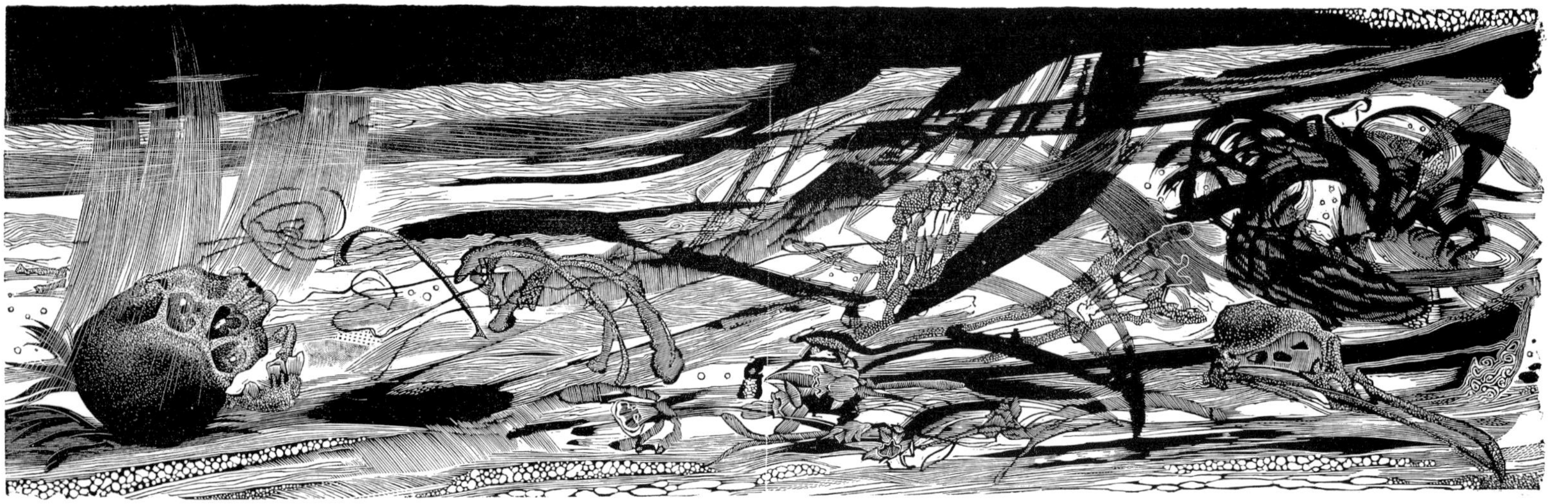

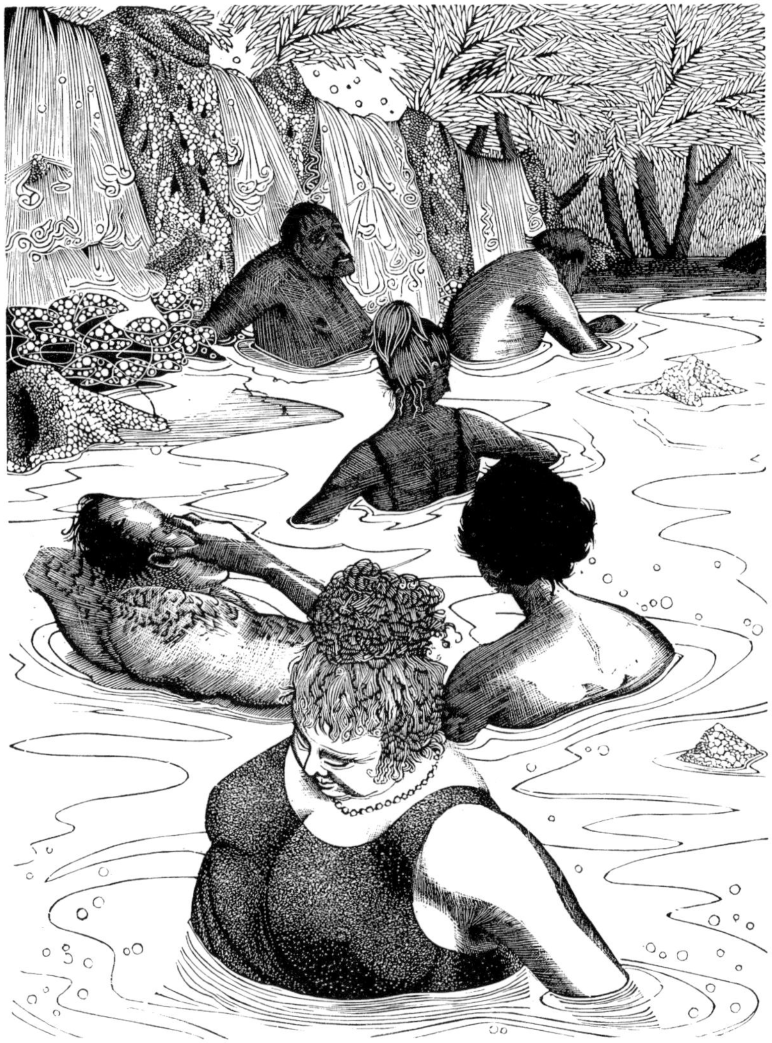

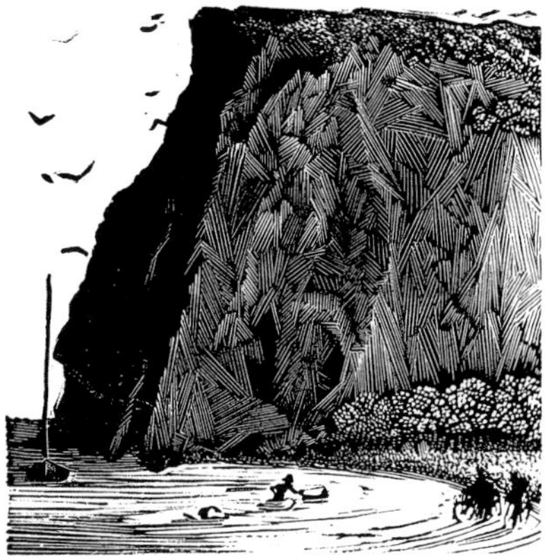

Left: Saturnia, 1991

Above: Carsaig, 1997

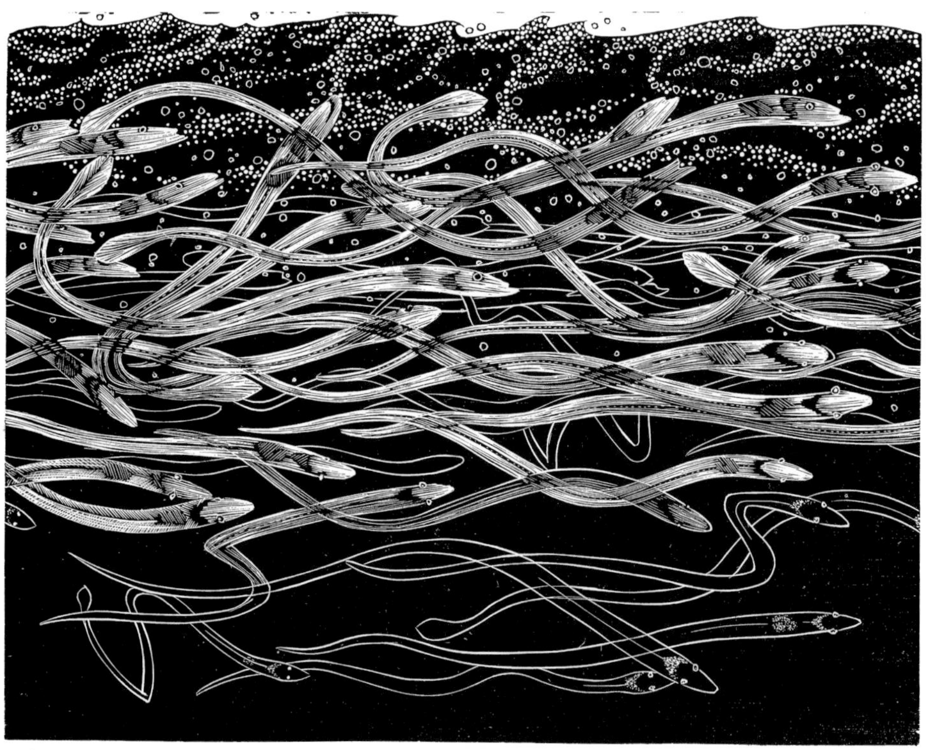

Above: Elvers, 1997

Opposite: Severn Bore, 1994

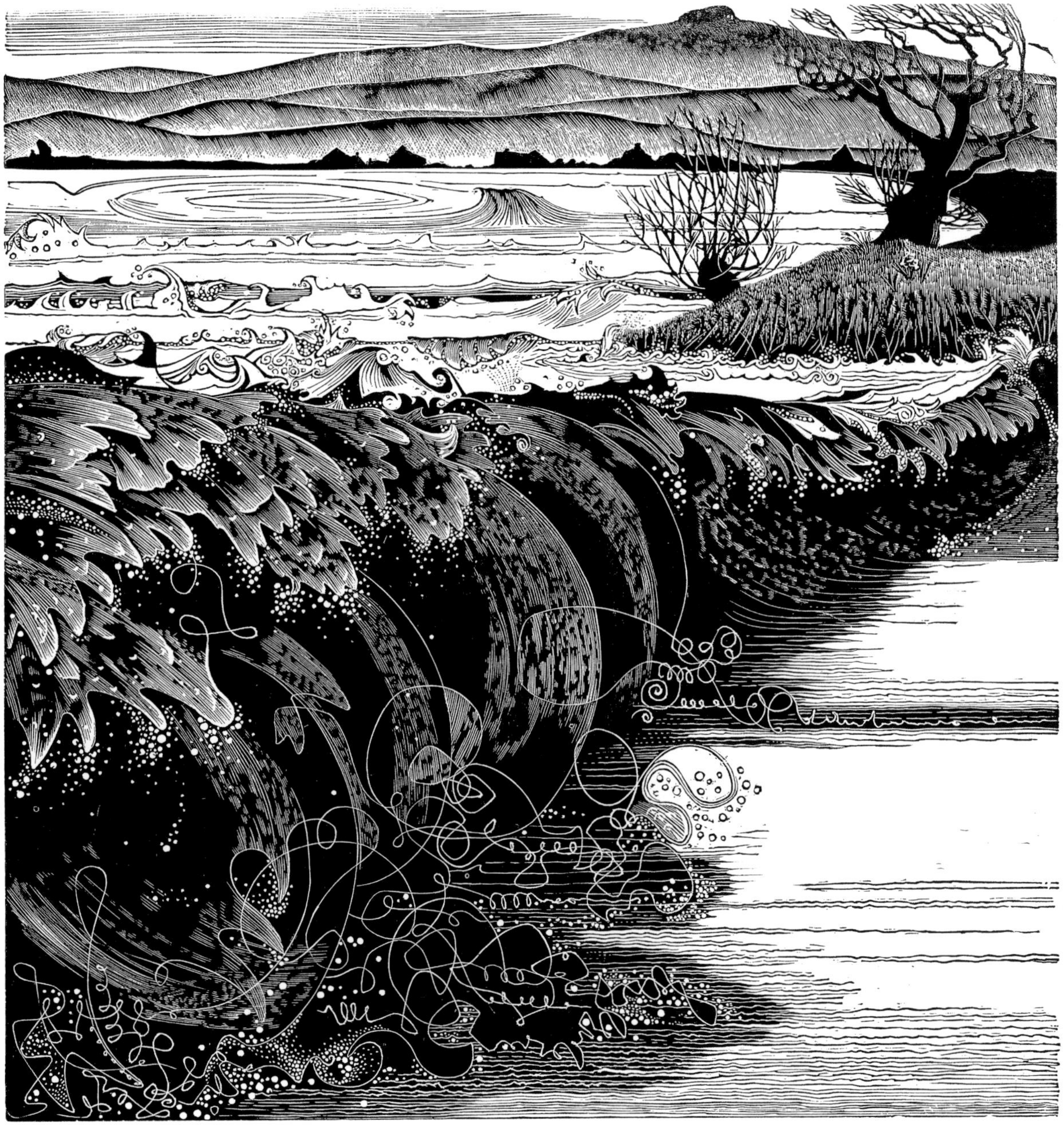

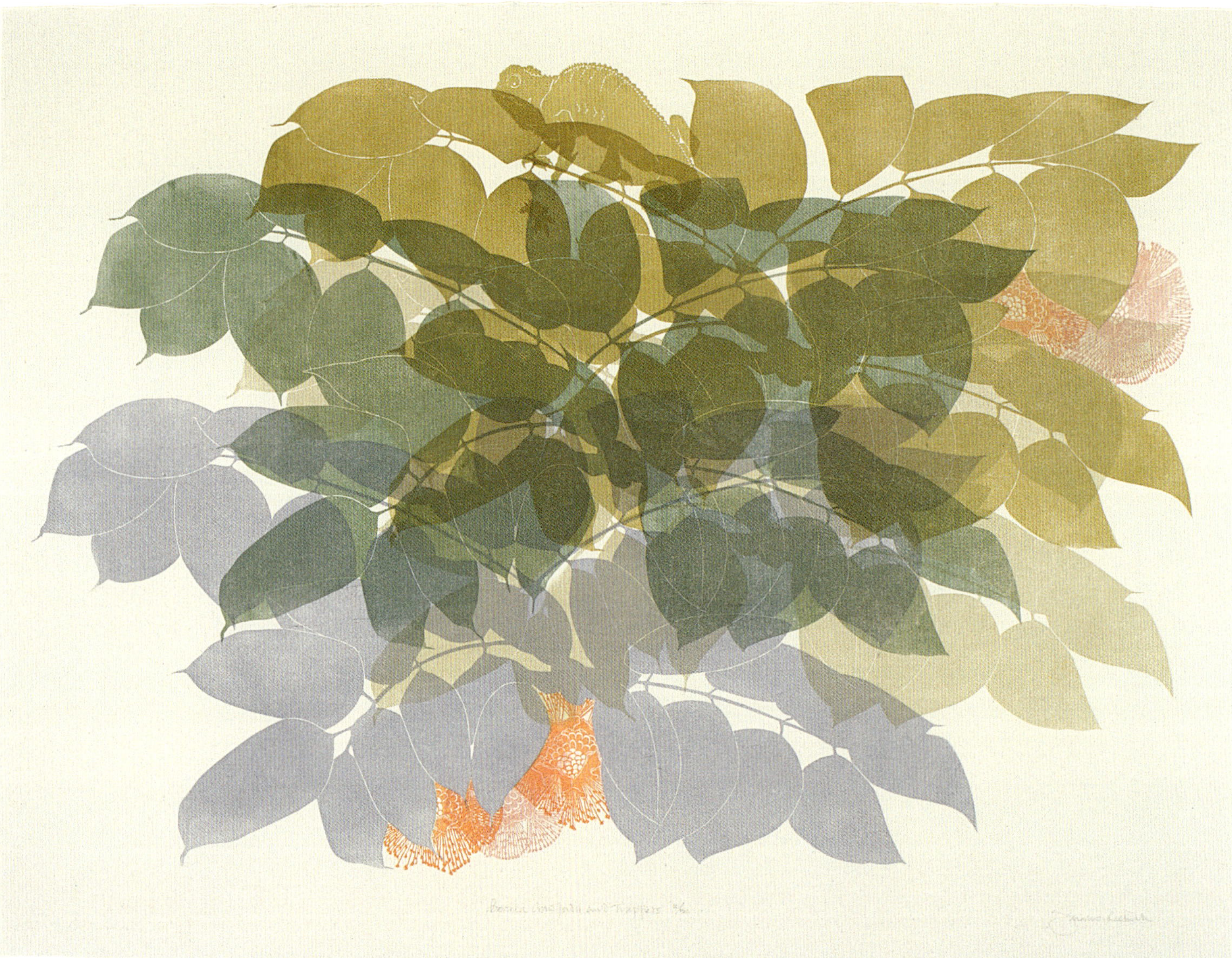

Above: Brownea Crawfordii and Trapfiets, linocut and wood engraving, 1976, approx. 430 × 740 mm

Opposite: September, 1993, 204 × 152 mm

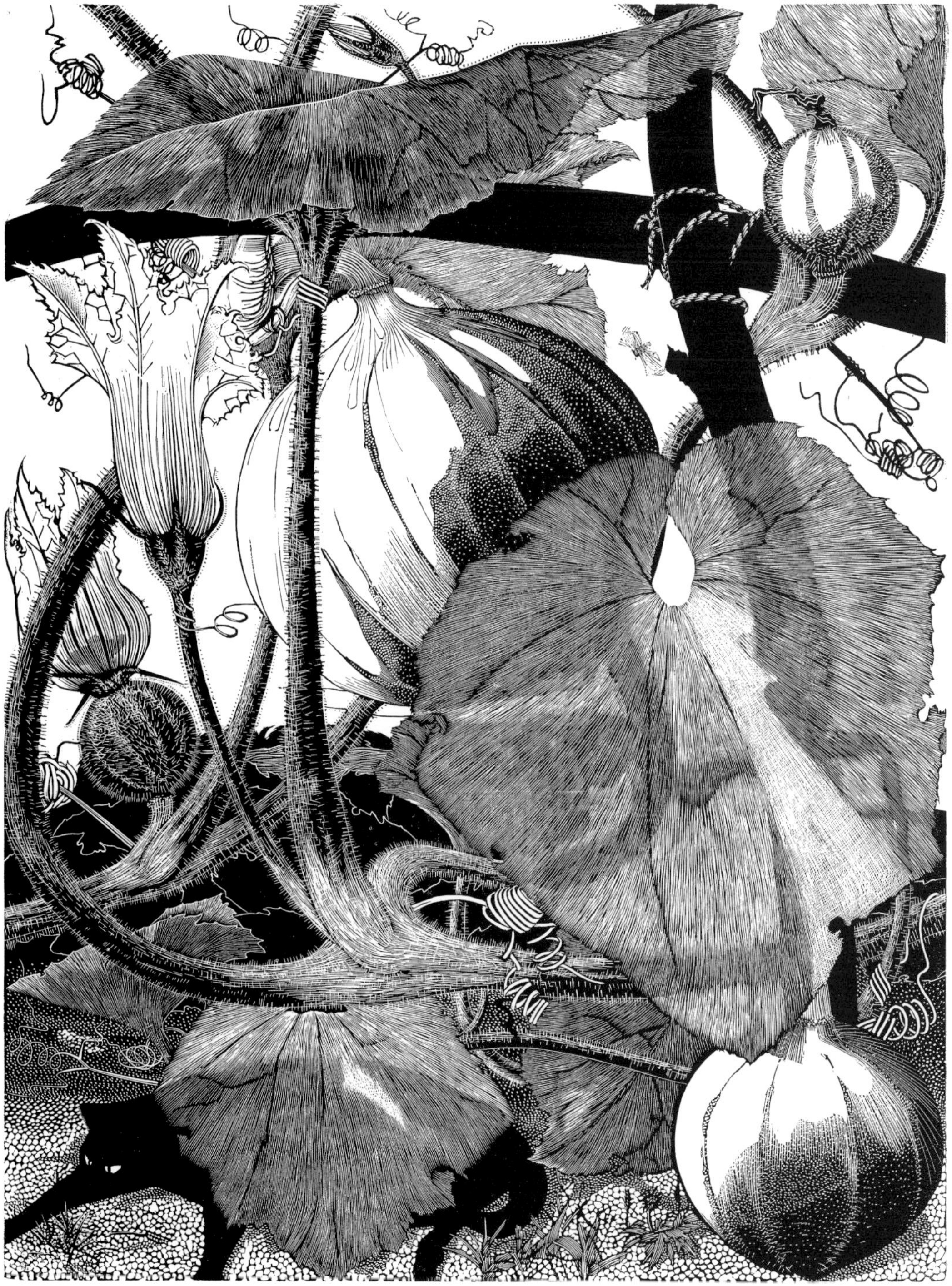

This page: Antipasti, for Leaves from the Walnut Tree, 1993, 193 × 122 mm

Opposite: Olive Grove near Sidari, 1988

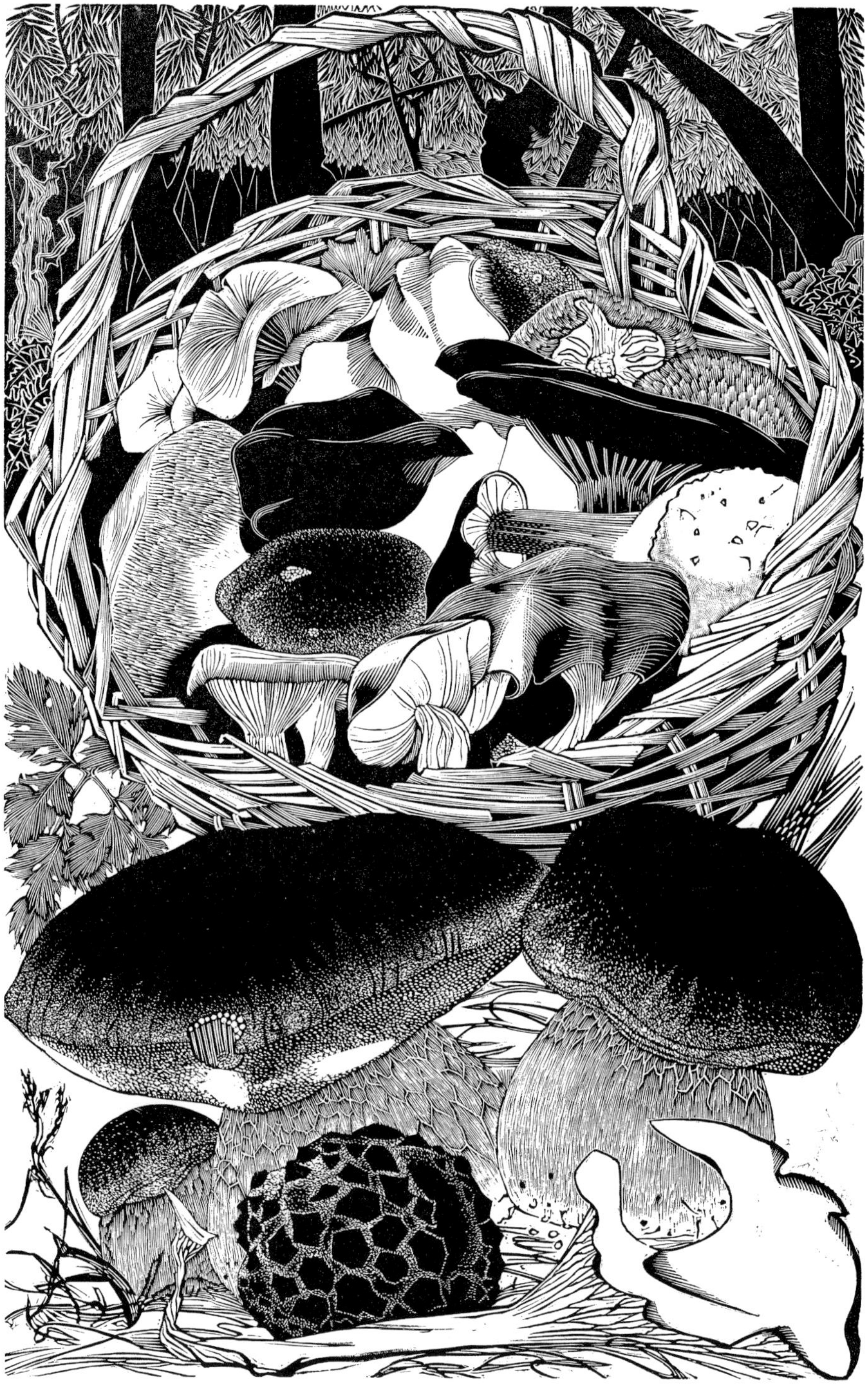

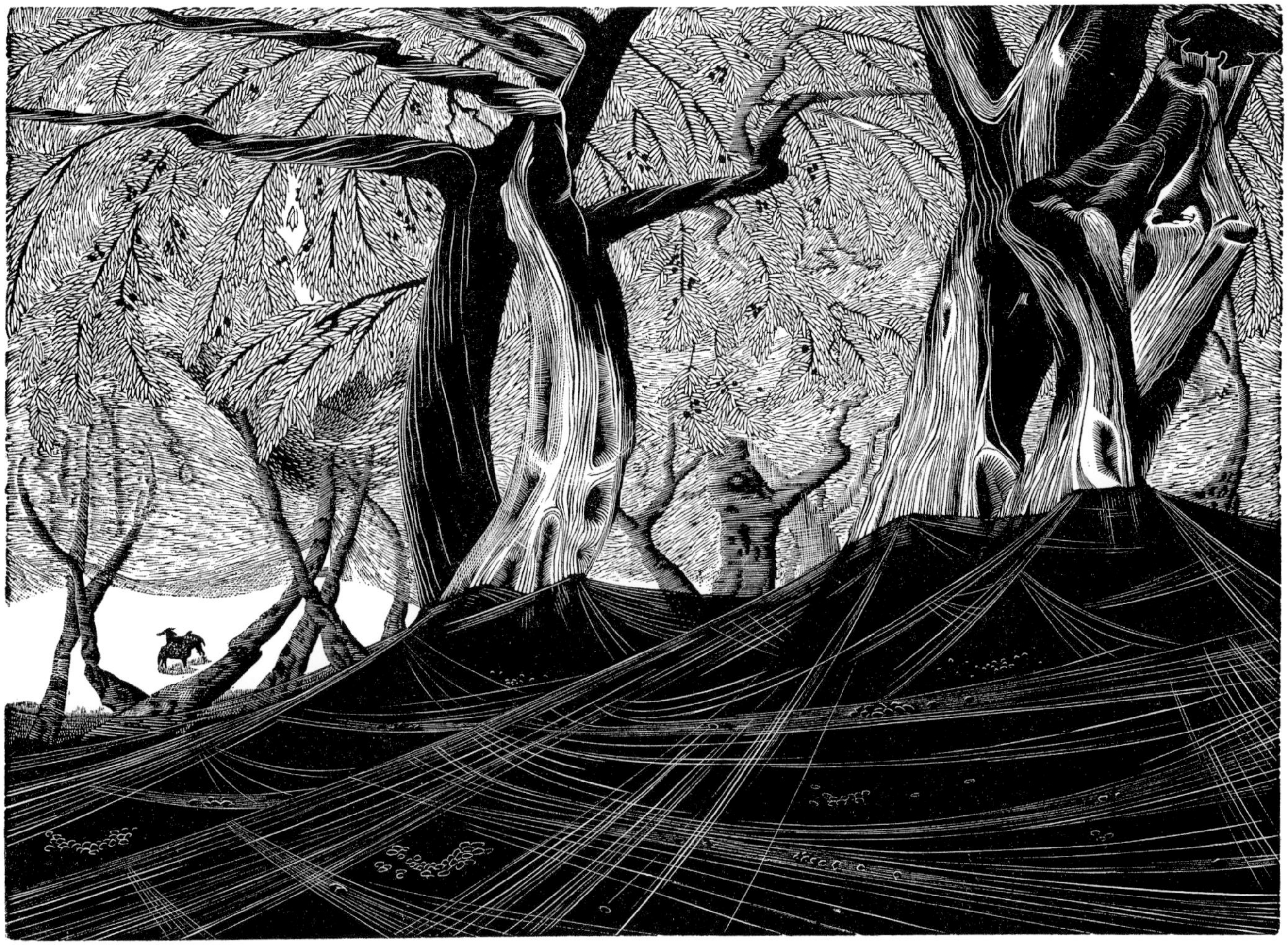

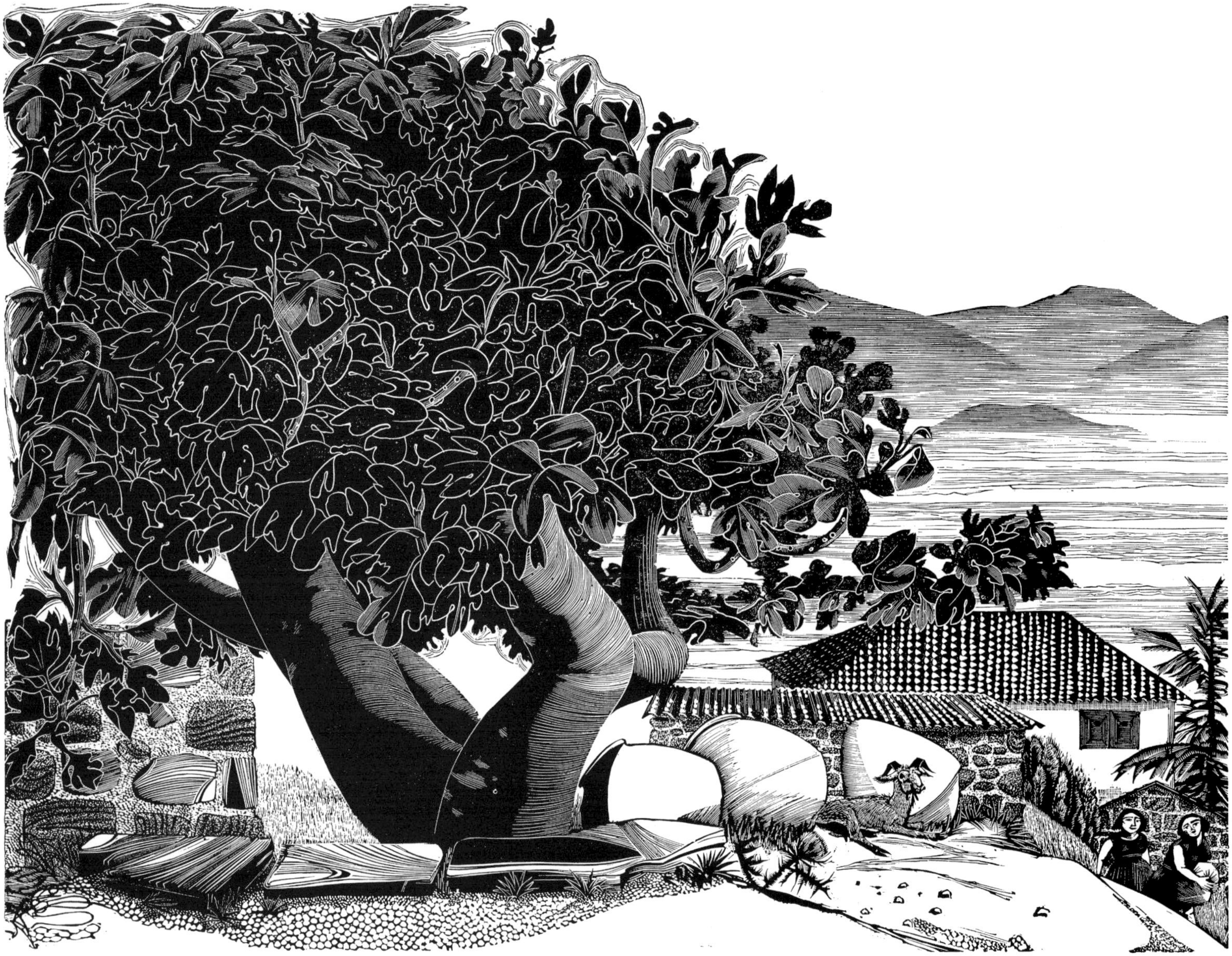

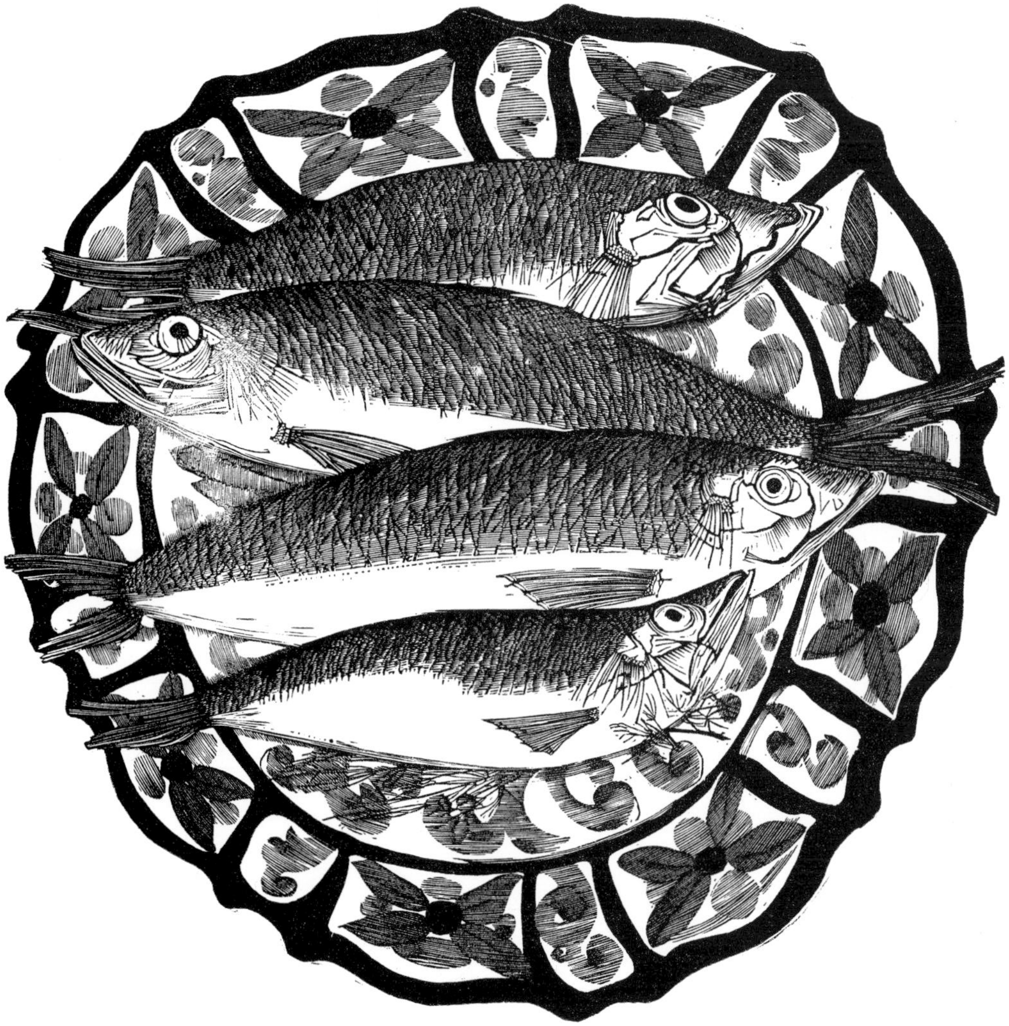

Opposite: Fig Tree in Molyvos, 1985

Above: Sardines, 2006

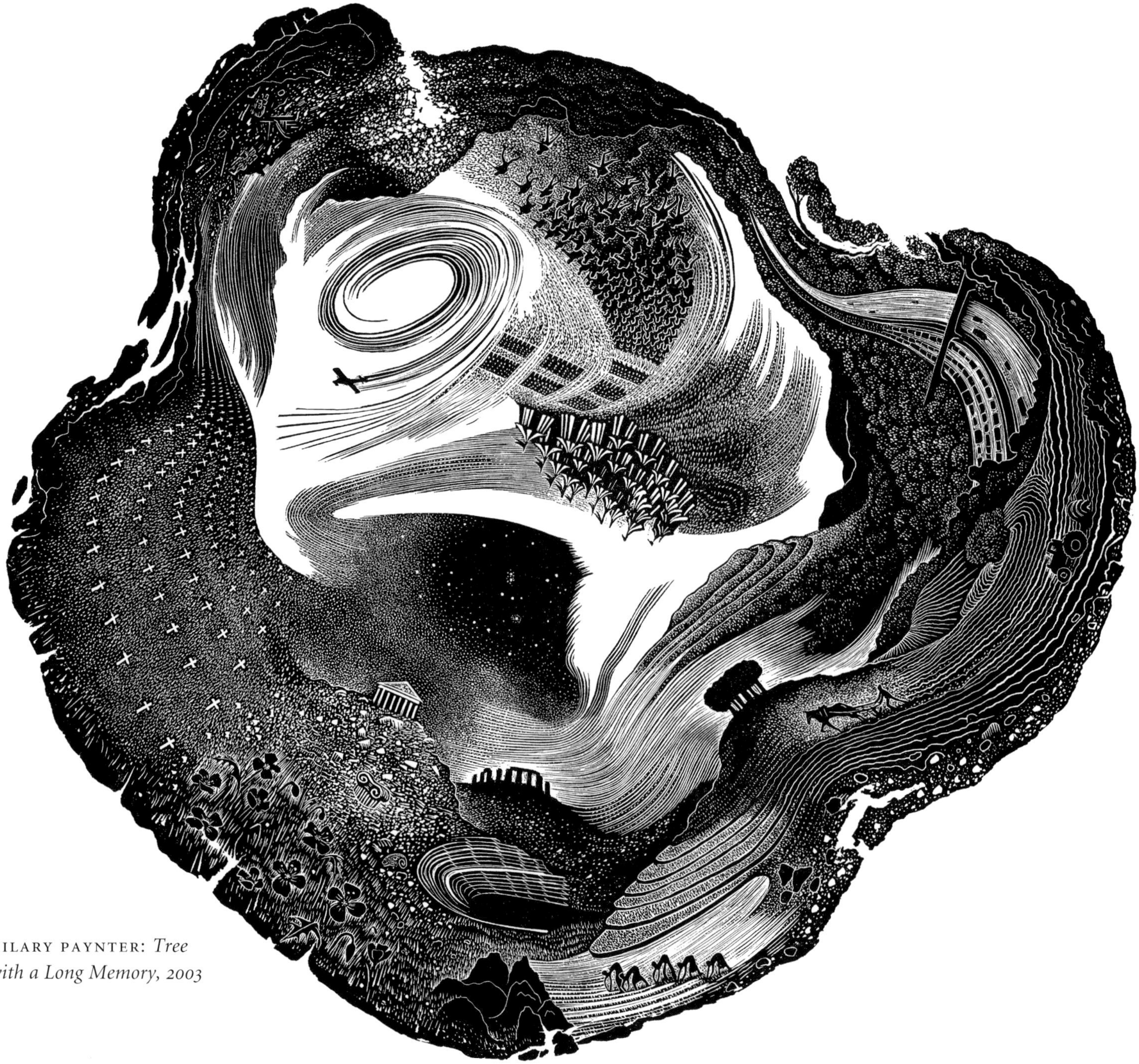

HILARY PAYNTER: *Tree with a Long Memory*, 2003

6. A Statement of Some Sort

Hilary Paynter

Chairman of the Society of Wood Engravers 1998–2006

'I am passionate about wood engraving. Of course I like other kinds of art but it is engraving that drives me.' The constraints of wood engraving – its limitations of size, colour and spontaneity – seem perfectly to suit Hilary Paynter's combative artistic persona. She relishes the challenge of wringing her acerbic images out of the vexations of the medium, using her art to muse on the human condition. Many of her engravings take a sideways swipe at human folly, the victimisation or alienation of the lonely and helpless. Images such as *The Neighbour's Fence* or *The Merry Wives of Windsor* offer sharp satirical comments on British behaviour. But her imagination also has a global reach. *In Exile*, *Crying for Tibet*, *Mount Trashmore*, *The Wall*, and *A Peaceful Protest to the Pentagon* all reflect a wide-ranging concern for the underdog and an indignation at any abuse of power.

In the traditionally pastoral world of British wood engraving, Hilary Paynter's socio-political, polemical imagery is unusual. It owes little to the example of other artists, the nearest in spirit, perhaps, being Kathe Kollwitz. Although she has made hundreds of what she terms 'pretty' engravings, Paynter's real originality and 'bite' is in work based on non-visual ideas. Inner feelings drive her response to the outer world, which is more tactile than visual. Even in her descriptive work, where landscape or buildings are carefully observed, the light is more imagined than natural. Complex ideas that seem to defy expression teem inside her head and she prefers to let them stew for a long time before attempting to give them visual shape. When first starting wood engraving she used her annual Christmas card to make 'a statement of some sort', the anti-establishment nature of her 'statement' invariably irritating her conservative relatives. Alongside straightforward landscapes and

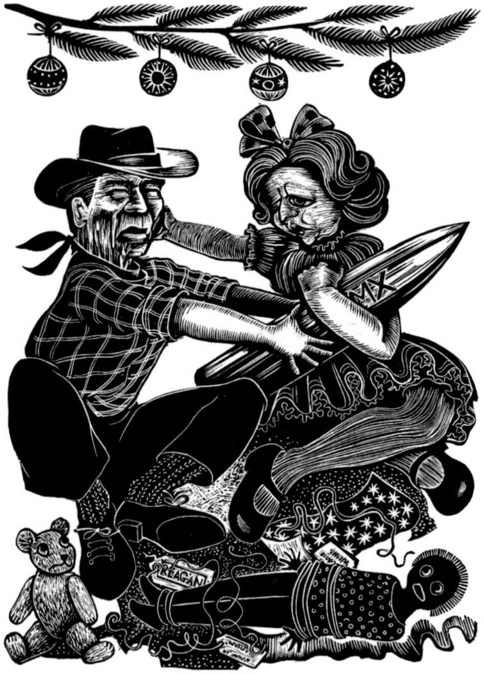

Christmas Presents, 1982, 115 × 82 mm

commissioned work she explored her own individual concerns, usually keeping six or seven blocks on the go at the same time and switching from one idea to another. 'Which one do I use and which is worthy of this lovely block? Sometimes they are very vague ideas and I work them out on the block. I have started engravings with just a couple of hands and no idea what else was going to go on, and then it's grown and I've fitted things in around ... Sometimes I do a sketch but the sketch on the pad is nothing like the block. I prefer to draw straight on the block, not knowing exactly what will happen. Once I know what the final image looks like I lose interest and start a new one.'

Hilary Paynter's imagery was influenced by her early life in different countries and her adult years as a teacher of children with special needs. Her father was an Education Officer in the Navy, and the family moved with each two-year posting. Hilary was born in Dunfermline and moved to Devon during the war with her mother and two older sisters while her father served as a navigator on HMS Dorchester, then after the war lived in Hong Kong. In what were then the very rural New Territories the Paynter family rented a house which had to be approached on foot across three paddy fields and up a lot of steps. The intimidating walk home from school took Hilary through dark bamboo groves, where she once found a hidden shrine and stopped to play with the little offering cups until shooed away by some indignant Chinese. Echoes of her childhood's sense of menace in woods and stone linger in engravings such as *High Force* or *West Moors*.

British postings meant a variety of schools before two wonderful years in Malta, where Hilary's father was jointly headmaster of the naval Junior School and deputy head of the Secondary School. It was a small community and all children of the armed services attended these two schools and knew everyone else and their families. Initially, the family lived outside official quarters, this time on a rocky promontory in Sliema. Much of the day was spent on the beach and Hilary became

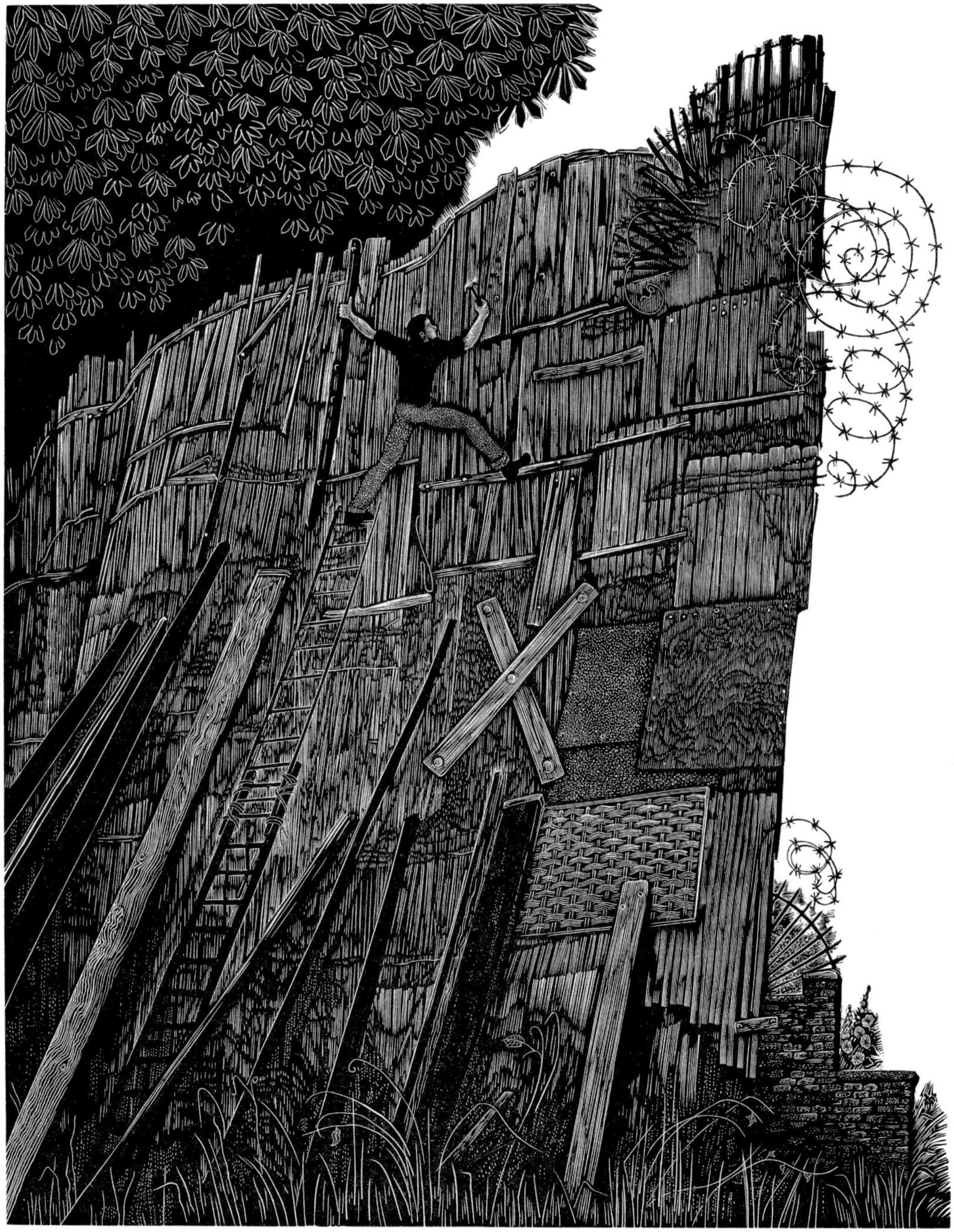

The Neighbour's Fence, 1995,
249 × 200 mm

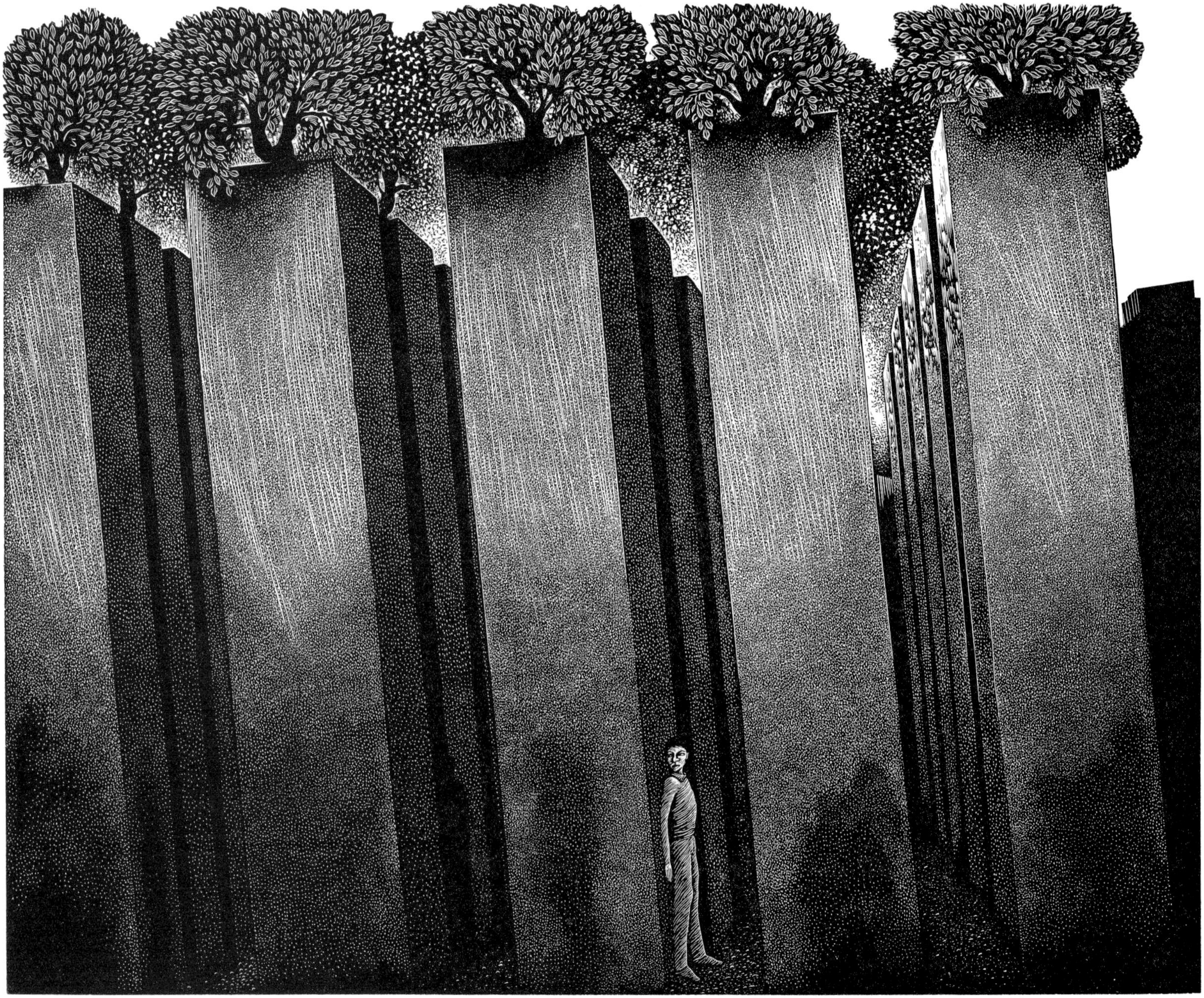

an enthusiastic swimmer, often swimming out to sit on the buoys slung across the harbour. Once she scared herself by swimming out with a snorkel, looking down to see the massive chain holding the buoy disappearing into infinity, and had to be rescued by boat. Her art teacher's drawing club in gardens and rocky coves instilled in Hilary an enduring love of rocks and stone, cliff faces and ancient walls.

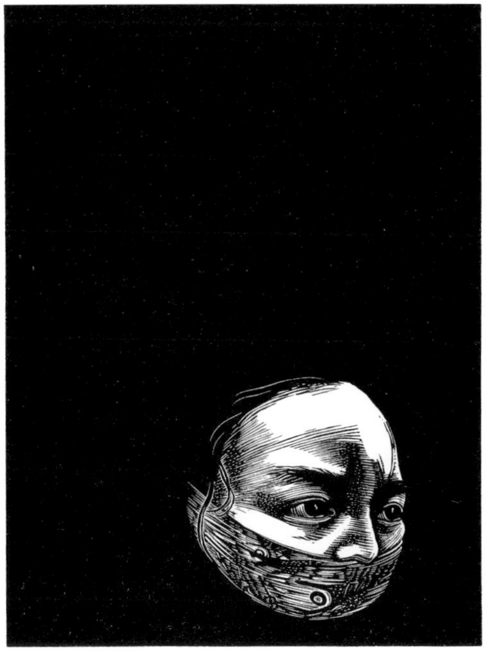

Opposite: In Exile, 1999, 200 × 250 mm

Above: Crying for Tibet, 1995, 103 × 77 mm

At sixteen Hilary was the youngest in her year at Portsmouth Art College, isolated amongst students who, with 'A' levels in English and Art, seemed unapproachably knowledgeable and mature. She chose sculpture as her main subject, carving in stone and modelling in plaster and clay. Her heroes were Epstein and Giacometti, and like them her main subject was the human figure. She chose wood engraving as a secondary subject, ignorant of its methods but in preference to pottery, fabric design and other crafts on the list. Engraving reminded her of an earlier ambition to carve cameos, inspired by a school visit to a Neapolitan cameo factory. She had also coveted her sister's book of Robert Louis Stevenson's poetry, filled with Joan Hassell's wood engravings, but it was not until she started engraving that she recognised the medium.

Teaching was in her blood, and Hilary Paynter followed up her art college diploma with a year's teacher training. Her first job, in a big comprehensive school in Putney with an art department of twelve specialist art teachers, involved a lot of carving and modelling, and she discovered a particular affinity with difficult children. After three years she took a career-break job as a cook at a climbing and skiing centre in Leysin, Switzerland. She packed drawing and painting materials as well as etching plates and a lump of alabaster, which she carved using her Scholl sandals as a hammer. Switzerland was liberating, and after eight months Paynter had to tear herself away in order to help her parents with their new venture running a teashop in Essex. Her father combined this with teaching at a private school in Colchester, and when the art teacher there died he asked his daughter to help out.

There she taught a range of subjects that provided valuable experience when she later worked in a special unit.

Hilary Paynter then spent six months with the family of William Manchester, author of *Death of a President*, in Connecticut, returning to England to marry Gerry Bradley, a student teacher whom she had met at the school in Putney. In 1968 her son was born and, although Hilary had intended to be a full-time mother, a job as a teacher in charge of a unit for maladjusted boys proved too strong a draw. The adolescents at The Grove had been expelled from all the schools in Hammersmith and Chelsea and some were barely literate. Hilary encouraged them to succeed in activities in which they had never experienced failure – Astronomy, Stonecarving, Swimming, Snooker. After three absorbing years she decided she ought to know more about the work she was doing and took a Diploma in Education for Maladjusted Children and, later, studied for a Masters degree in the Psychology of Education. She continued to teach full-time, eventually becoming Head of Special Needs at a Social Priority comprehensive school in Acton, West London.

After her MA Hilary Paynter found she had time to spare. Having accidentally discovered the existence of the Society of Wood Engravers at an exhibition in Piccadilly, she became a member, but despaired at the moribund state of the society. When Albert Garrett, the chairman, died suddenly she and the printmaker John Newson convened a meeting, writing to anybody likely to show interest. 'We trawled exhibition catalogues for wood engravers who might be interested in joining the re-formed Society. All but one agreed to support us. It was exhilarating. Many of these engravers were legends to me from my art college days. We had not realised that there were so many still actively engraving.' The first exhibition that Paynter organised to mark the Society's revival in 1984 was a resounding success and toured to two other venues, and the Society has since gone from strength to strength. Paynter has been its keystone and memory-bank as well as shouldering much of the administrative burden, and her grip on the exhibition circuit has been crucial to its success.

Hilary Paynter rediscovered wood engraving for herself after her marriage. At first she sculpted a series of alabaster babies but, without a proper studio and working in the kitchen, it became impossible to continue and wood engraving took over all her spare time. Sundays became sacrosanct, and as soon as *The Archers* came on the radio the family was excluded and she would set to work, often continuing all day. She still listens to stories on tape, finding that they help her to concentrate by blotting out all those things she feels guilty about neglecting. She has developed rapid techniques, limiting herself to two or three favourite tools. Colour is of only occasional interest to her; she thinks in texture and in the round, needing to feel and depict the hidden structure and forms of her subject matter.

For nearly three decades Hilary Paynter's engraved 'statements' have proved popular with the public, and her prolific output has engendered eleven successful solo touring exhibitions. Her artistic standing was acknowledged when Nexus Art on Transport commissioned her to create the major piece *From the Rivers to the Sea* for the lower concourse of Newcastle's Central Station Metro. The leaflet that accompanied the unveiling explained how the chosen site 'determined the proportions of her prints, providing a public context for her work beyond the conventional frame or printed page. Embarking on a series of journeys around Tyne and Wear, including a flying lesson over the two rivers, she set about recording the area's historical and contemporary landscape. Her final suite of 14 prints, rich in texture, detail and incident, record an astonishing panoramic travelogue. Set side by side, the images run into each other and, reproduced onto the vitreous enamel panels, create a mural stretching from platform to platform, over 22 metres long.'

Equally important was the invitation to become the President of the Royal Society of Painter-Printmakers. This came in recognition not only of Paynter's administrative skills but also of the place she has achieved for wood engraving within the much larger community of printmakers. A packed timetable and a 'driven' approach to life make the *longueurs* of engraving an unusual choice for the expression of her feelings. But in sculpture she would never achieve quite the same sting. In her wood engraving Hilary Paynter succeeds in combining observational and schematic drawing, mixing sculptural form, caricature, slogan, and cartoon to put across her powerful message.

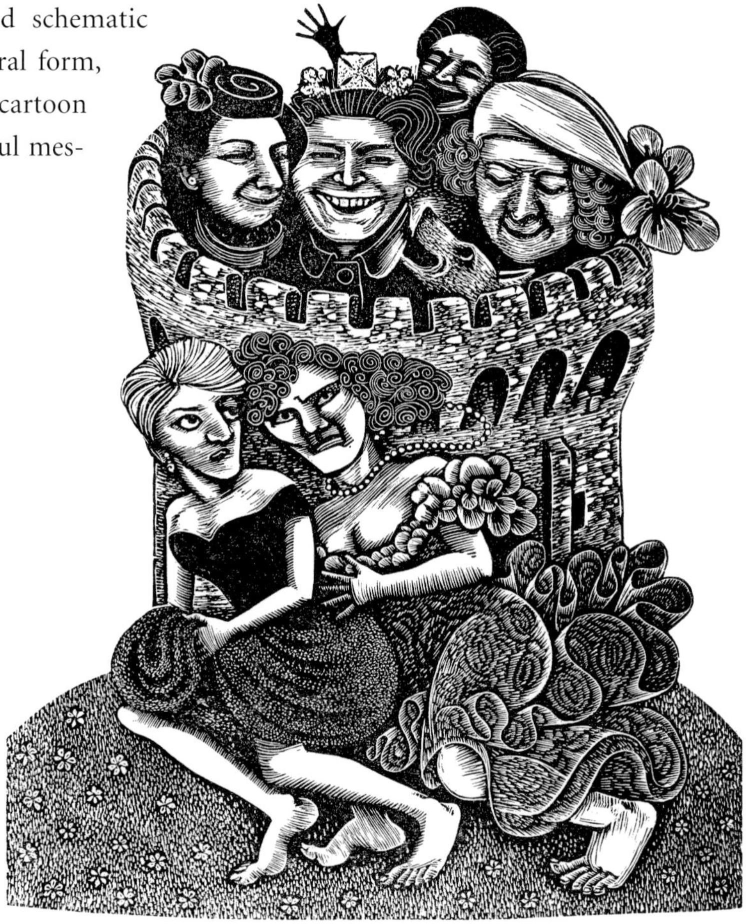

This page: The Merry Wives of Windsor, 1994

Opposite: San Gimignano, 1997, 175 × 250 mm

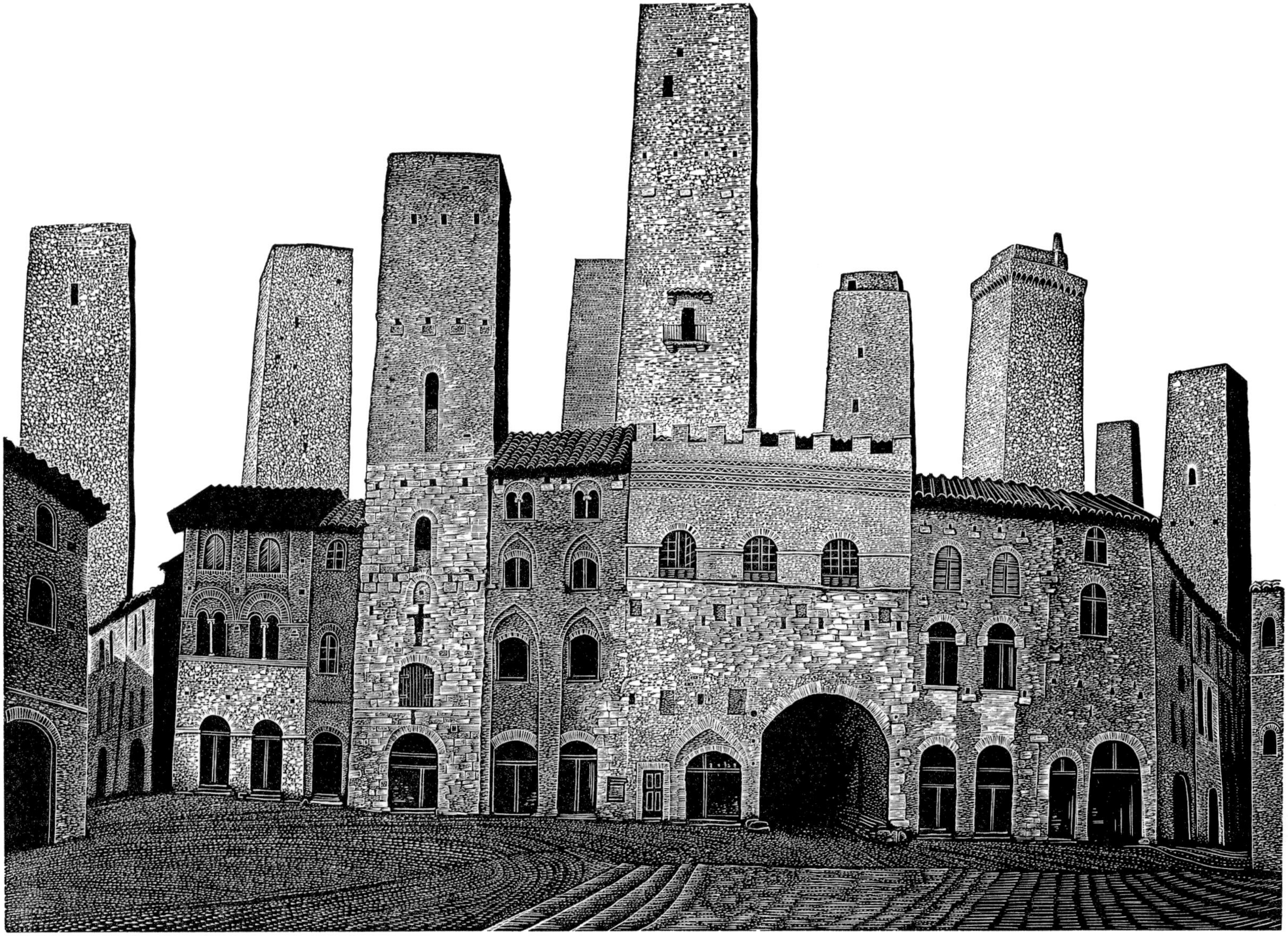

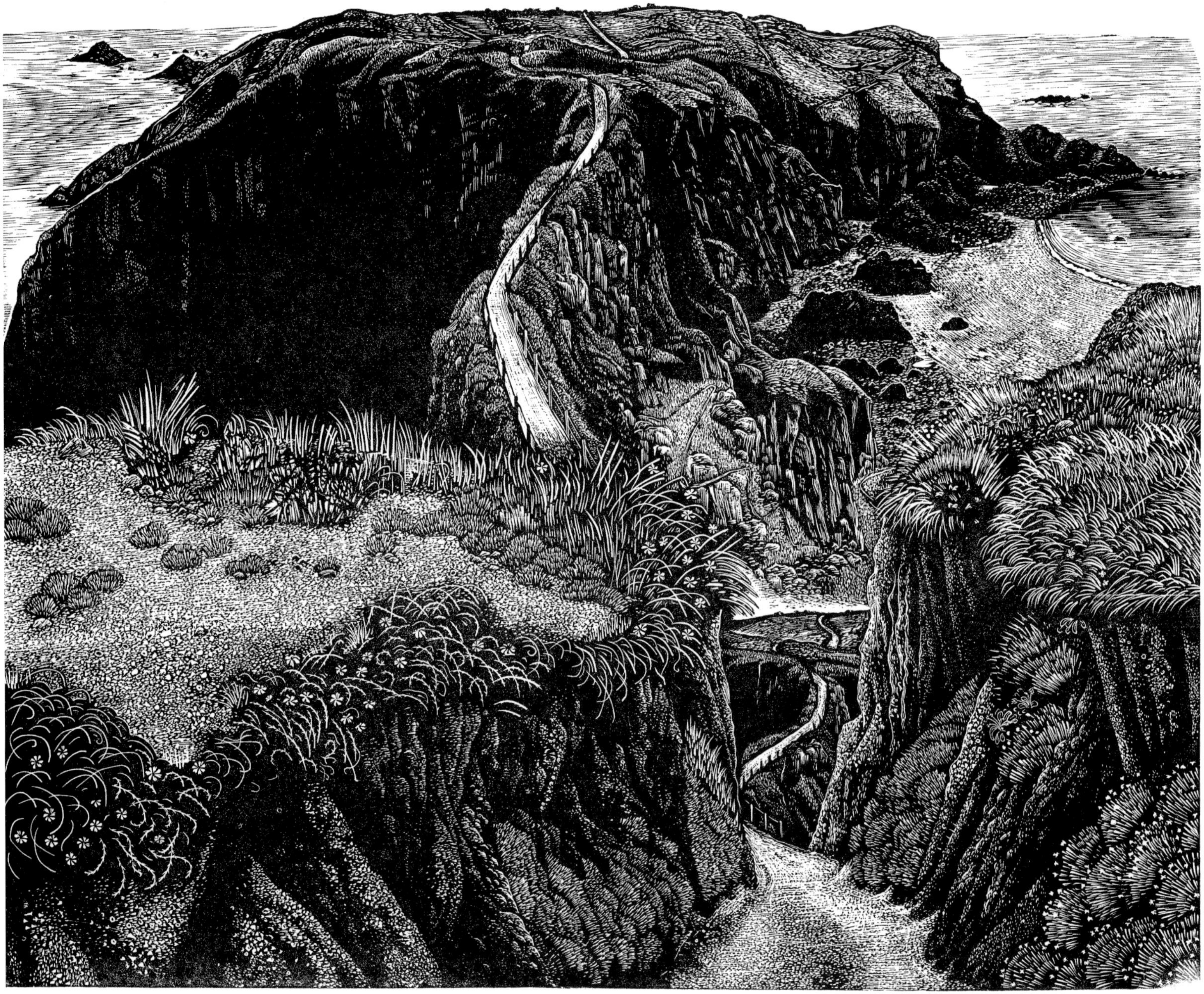

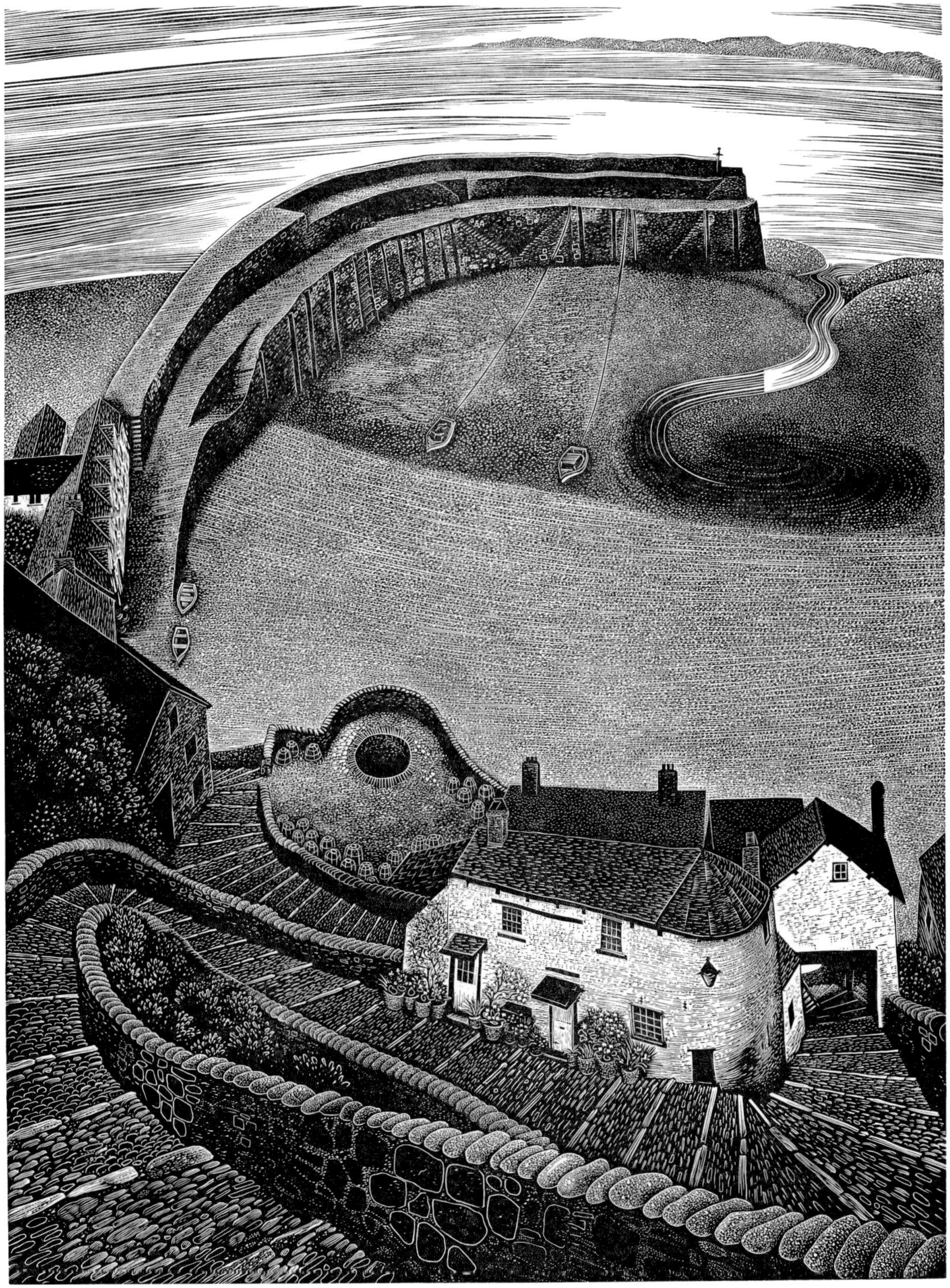

Opposite: La Coupée, Sark, 1983, 200 × 250 mm

This page: Low Tide, Clovelly, 2003, 316 × 240 mm

This page: Paul Kershaw on Skye, 2001, 317 × 241 mm

Opposite: Reclaiming the Land, 1995, 195 × 250 mm

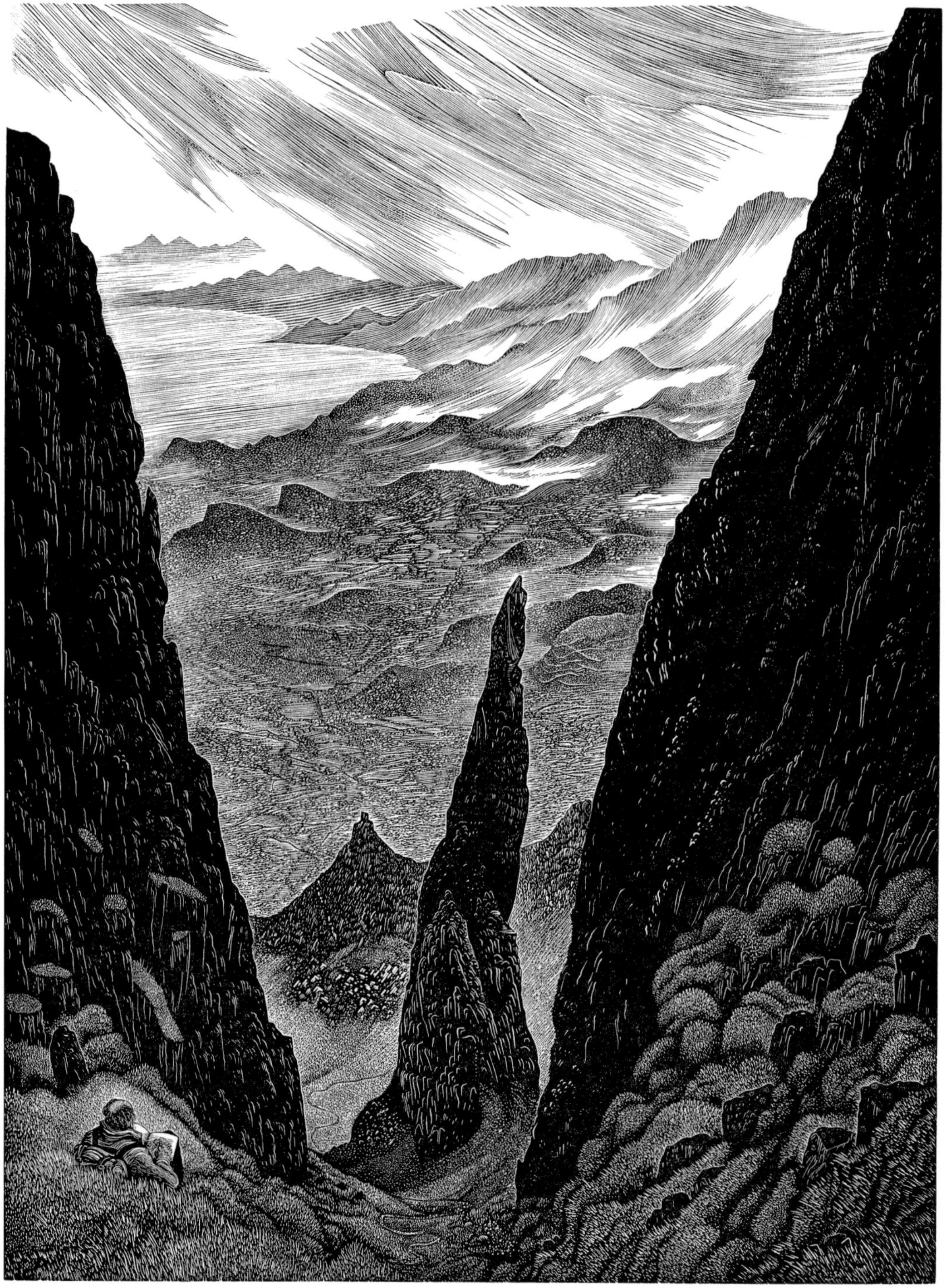

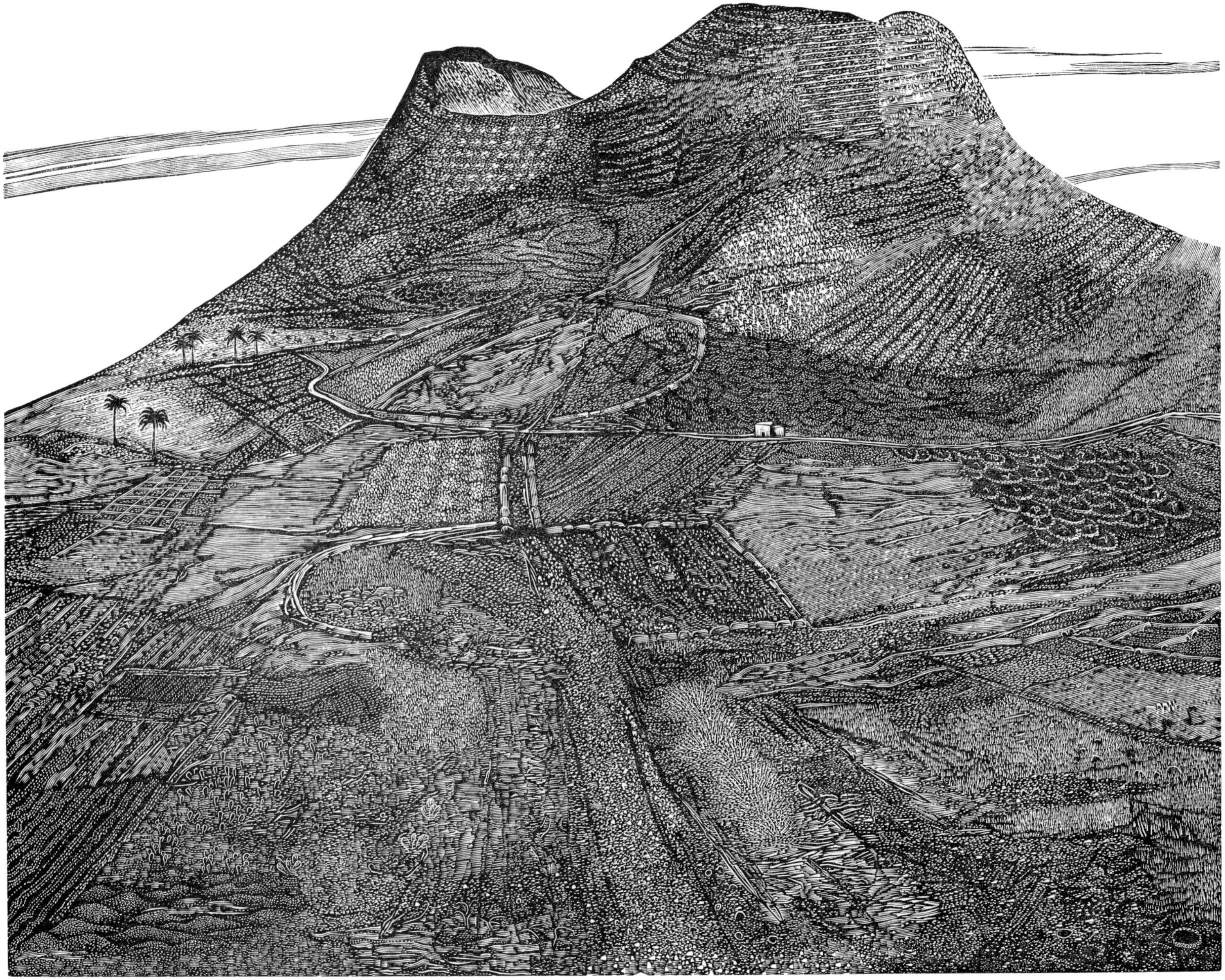

This page:
Wheelhouse,
Jarlshof, 2005,
200 × 200 mm

Opposite:
Rebuilding
Berlin, 1999,
198 × 250 mm

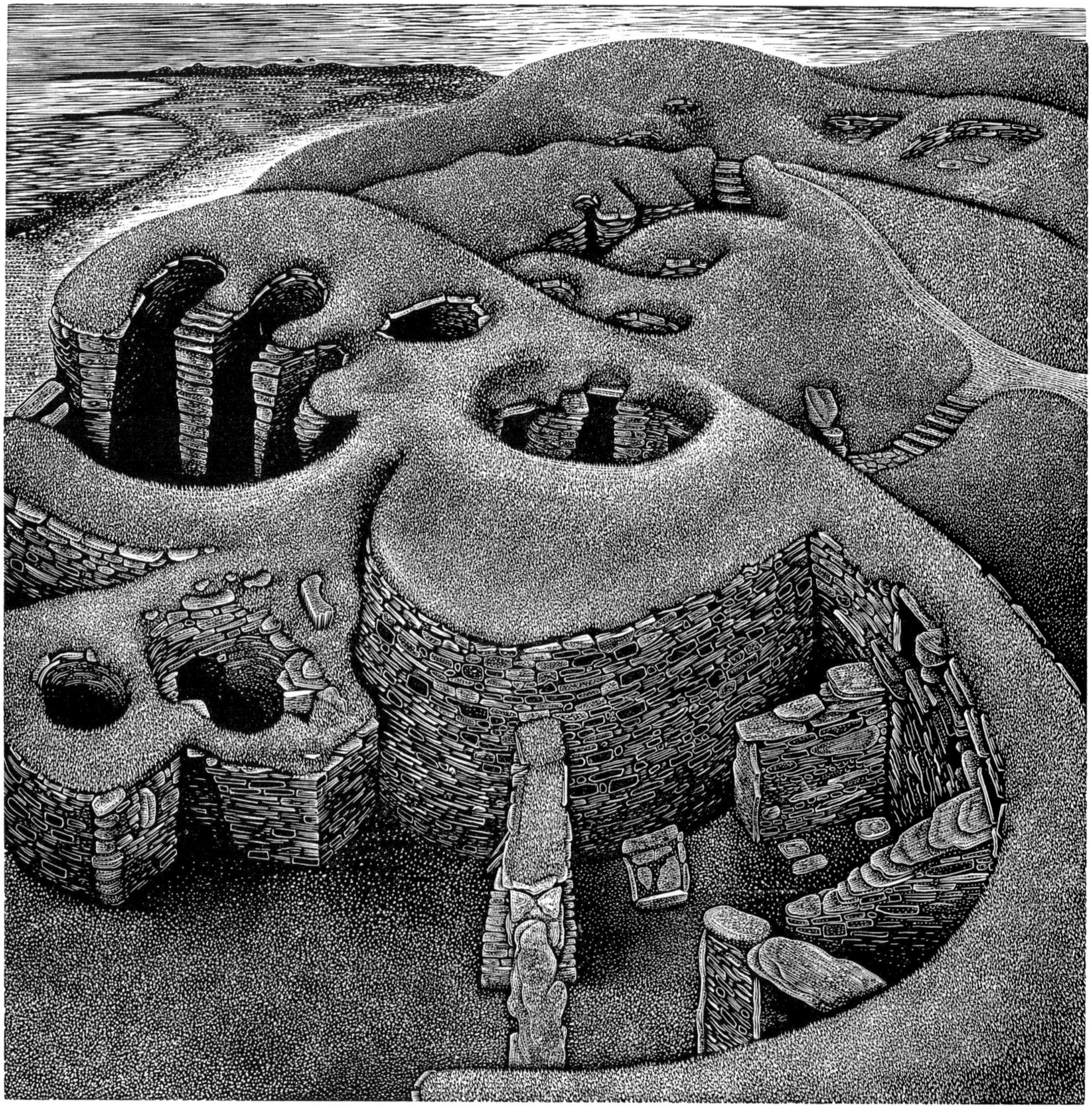

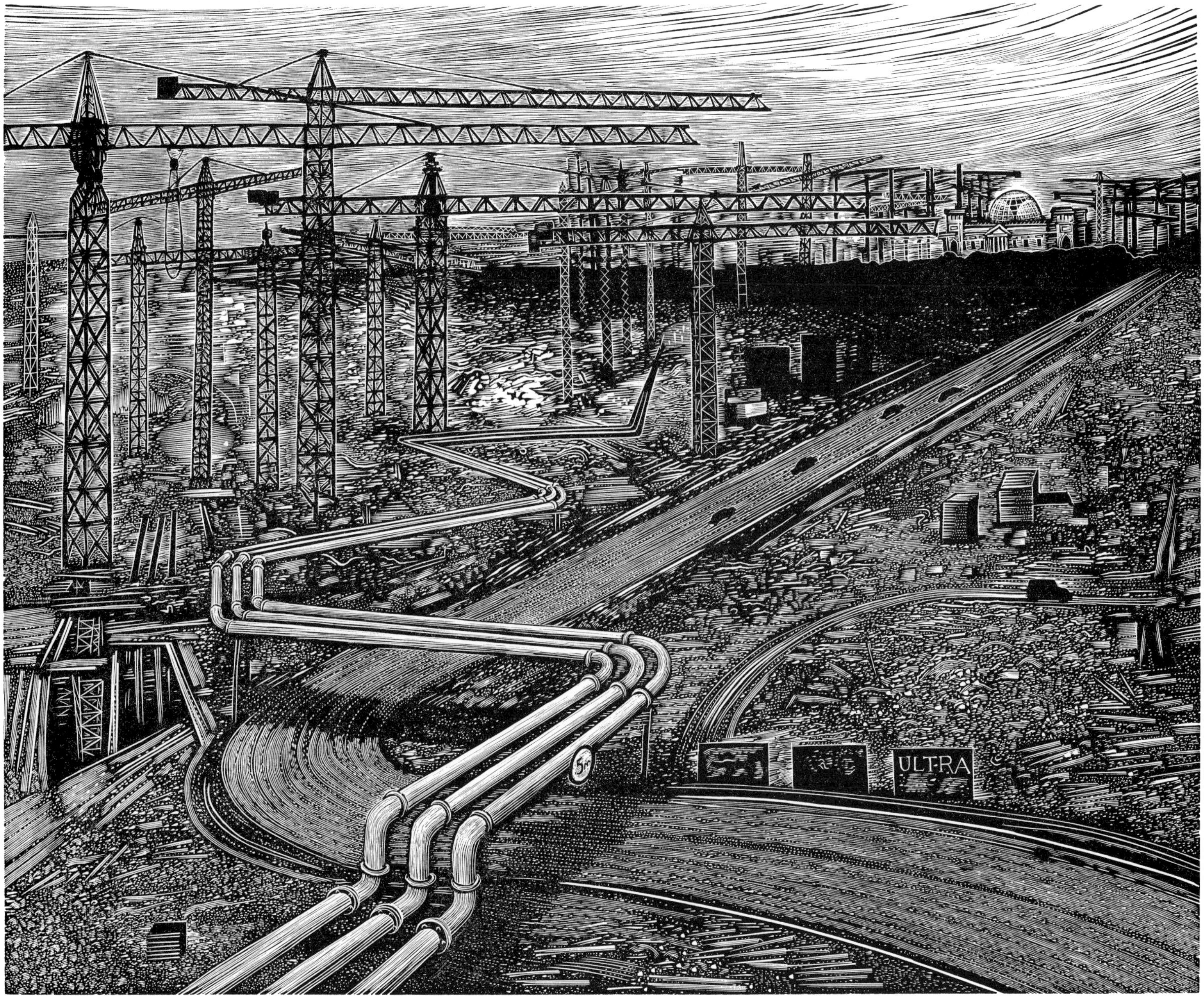
ULT-RA

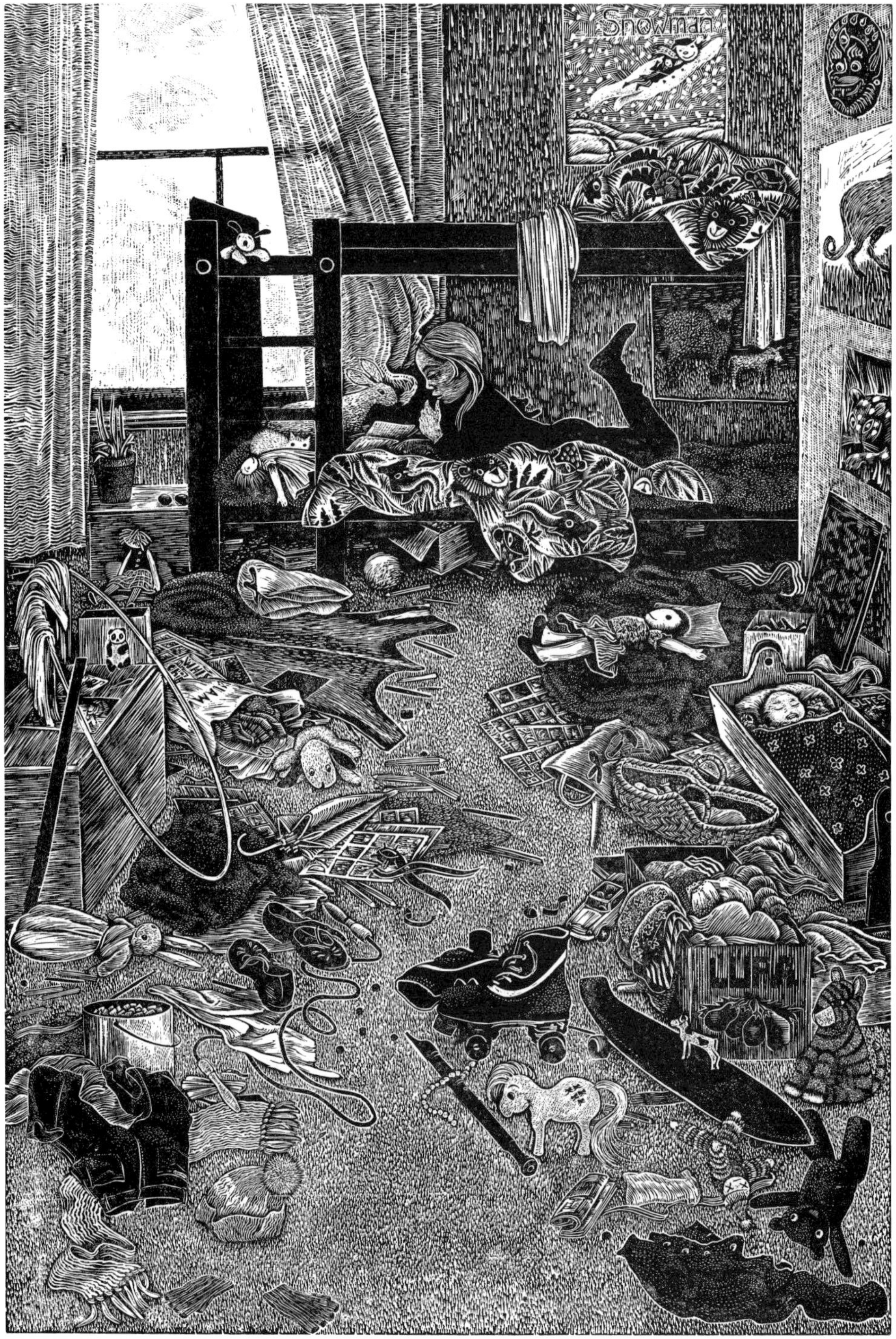

This page: Her World, 1986,
332 × 229 mm

Opposite: 56 Children, 1993,
305 × 305 mm

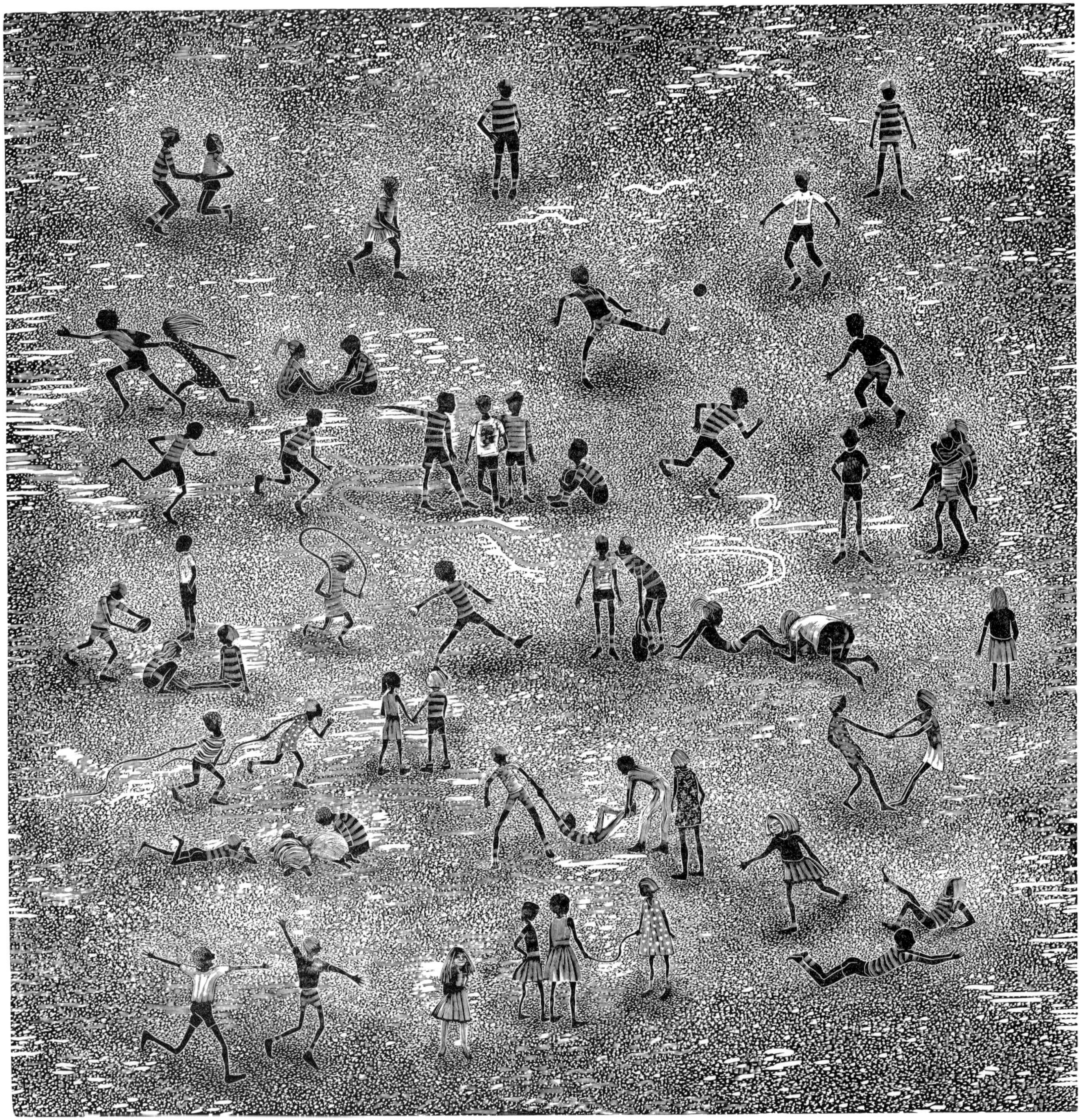

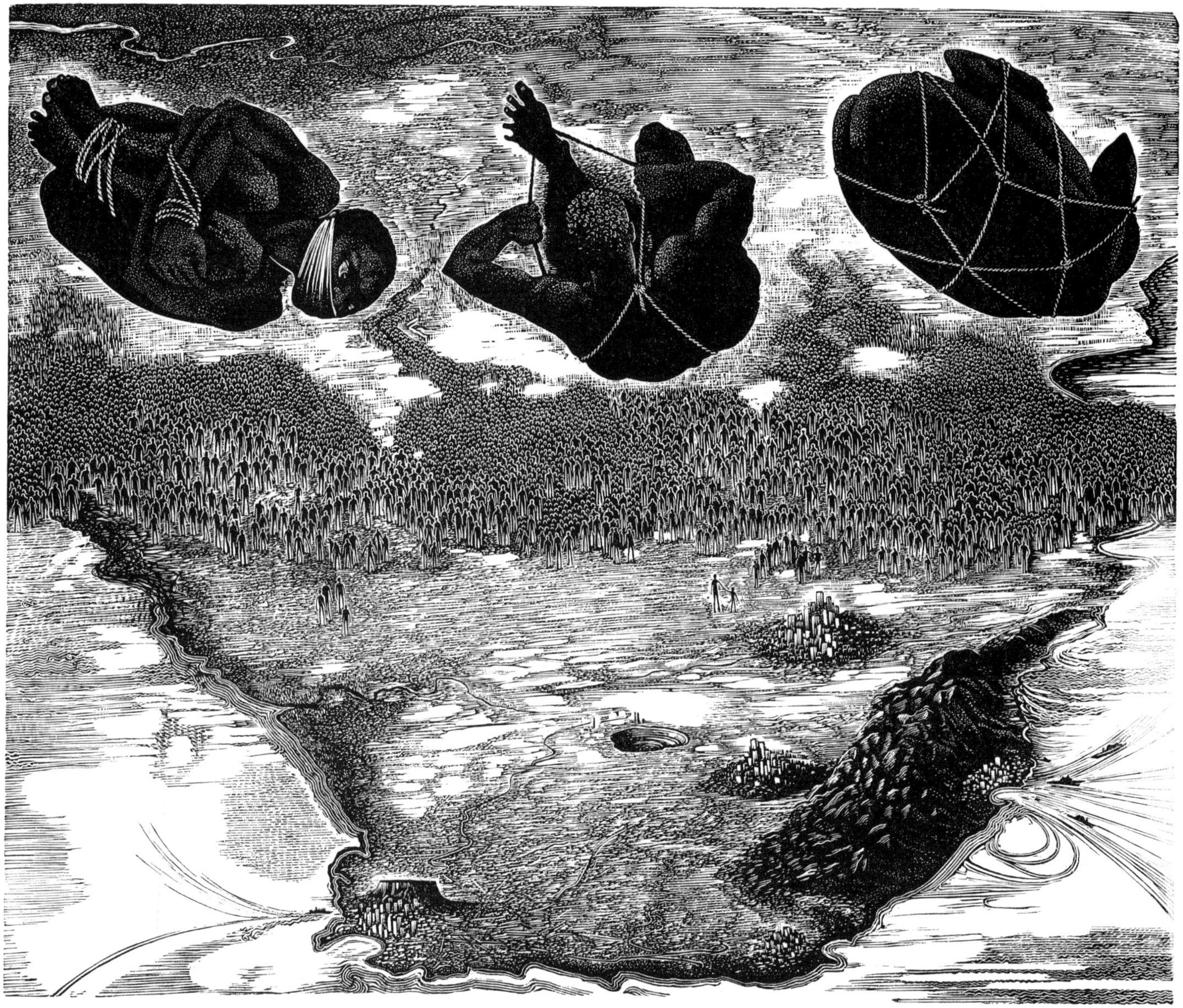

Above: South Africa, 1987, 205 × 250 mm

Opposite: Not on the Itinerary, 2005, 200 × 247 mm

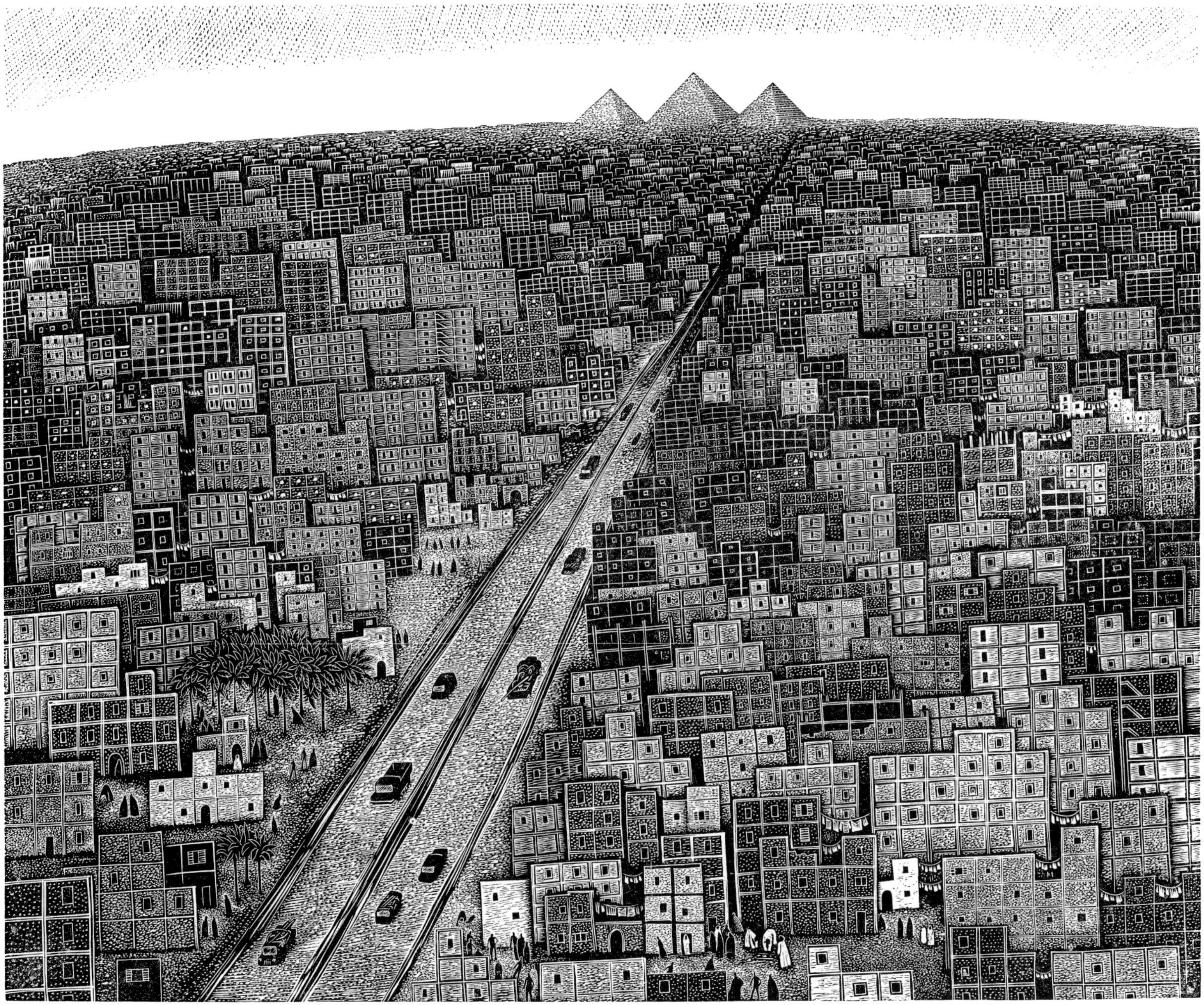

This page: A Peaceful Protest to the Pentagon, 1996, 387 × 303 mm

Opposite: The Wall, 1995, 198 × 250 mm

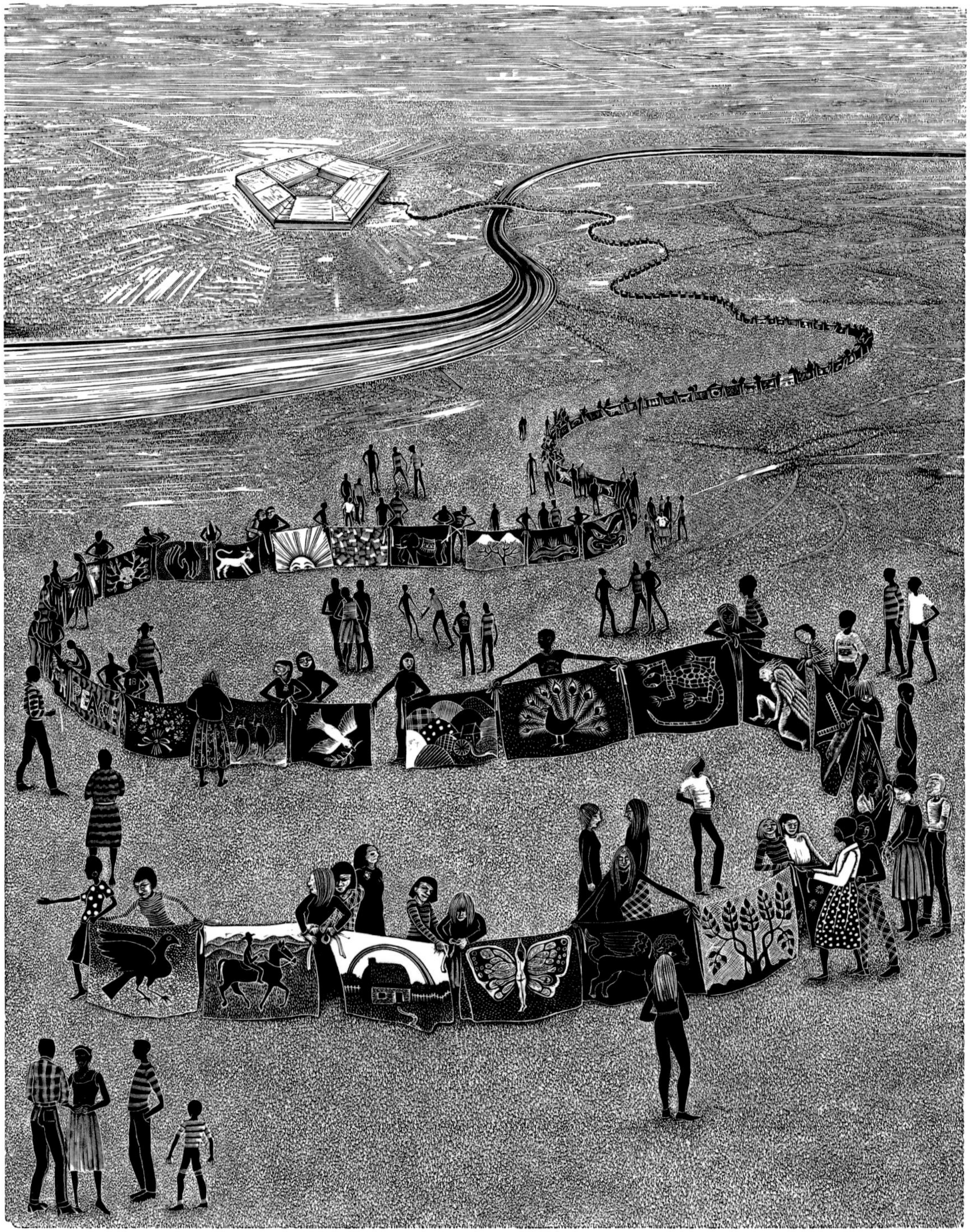

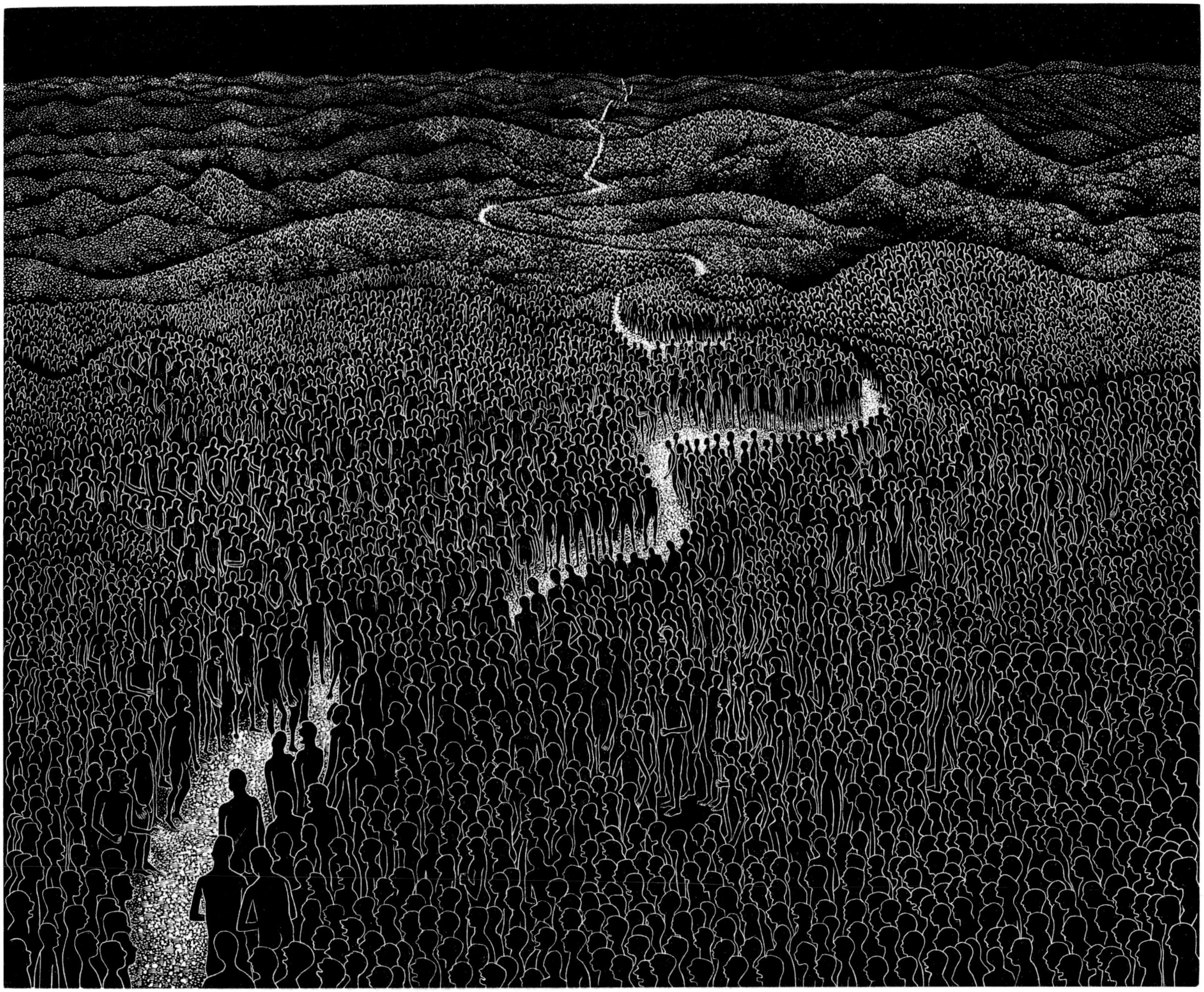

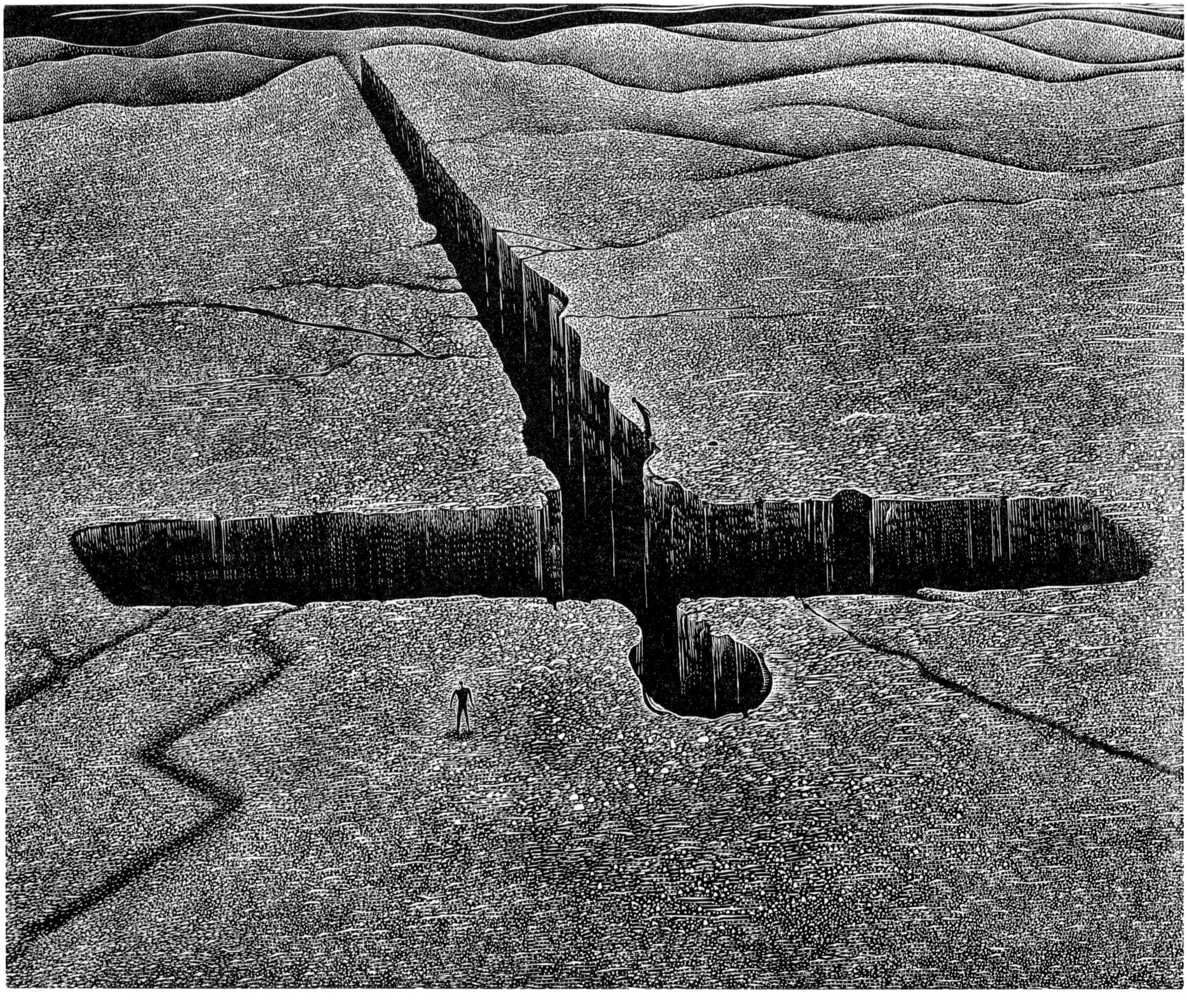

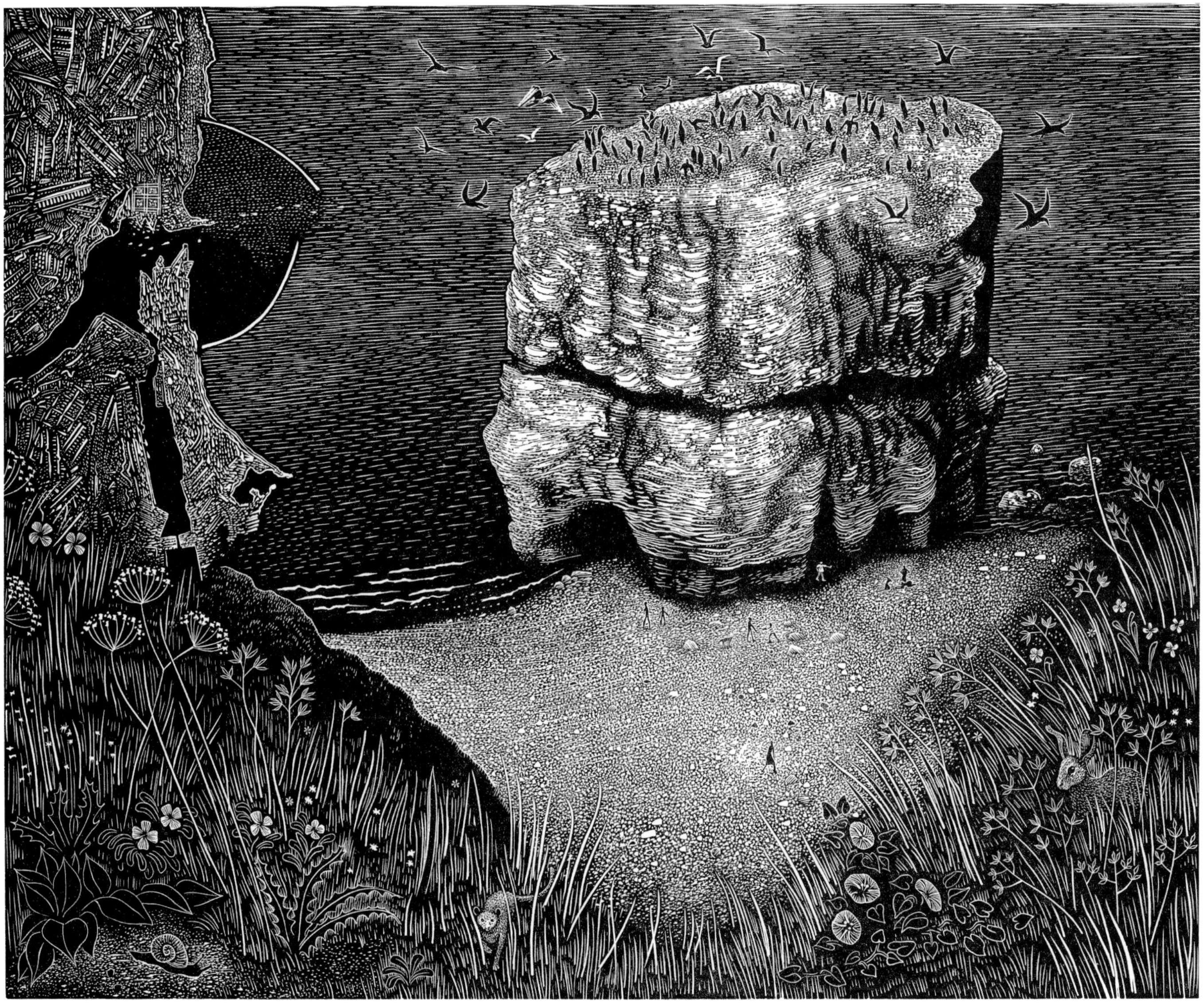

Opposite: Fallen Angel, 2006, 200 × 247 mm

Above: Marsden Rock, 2004, 200 × 250 mm

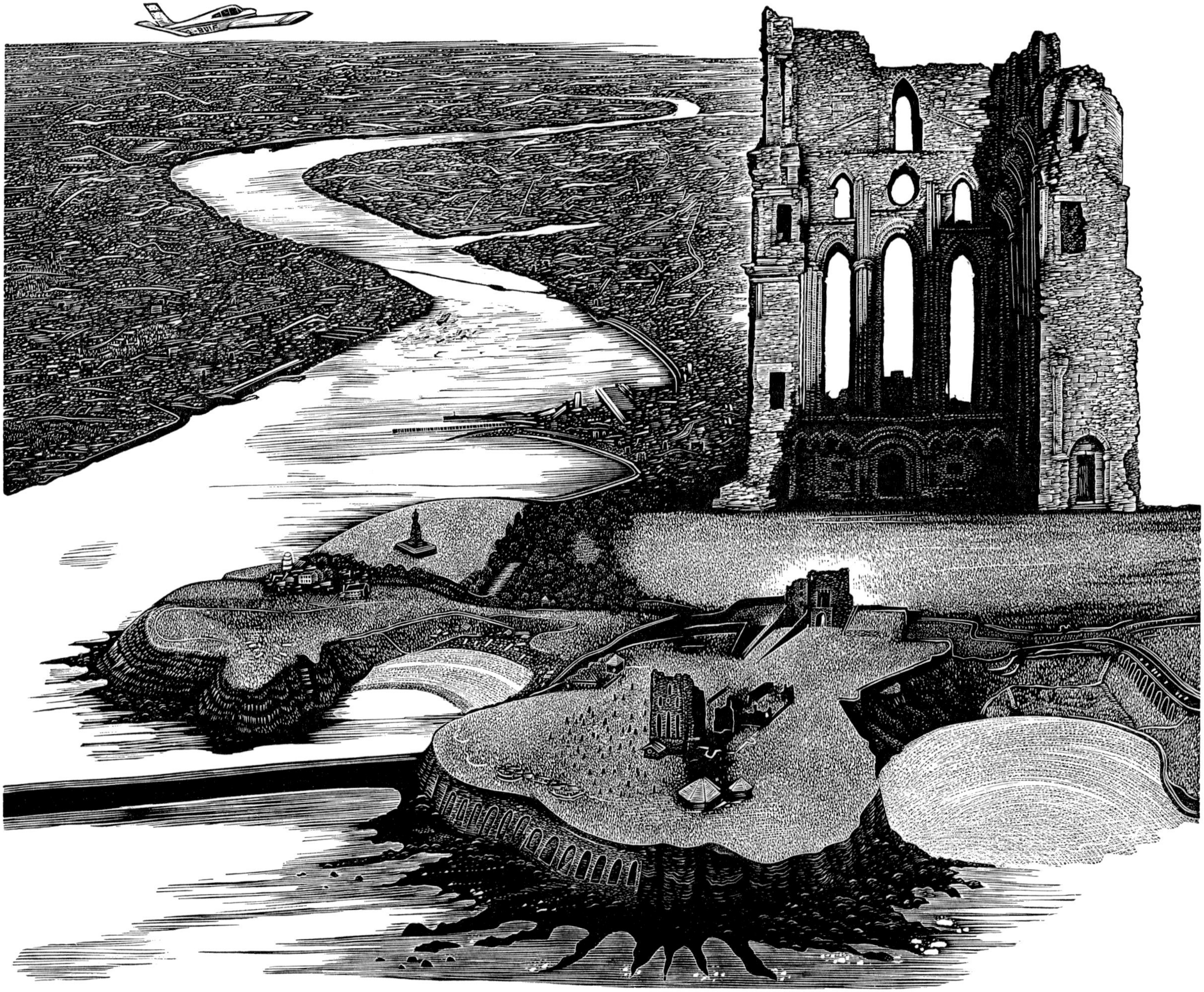

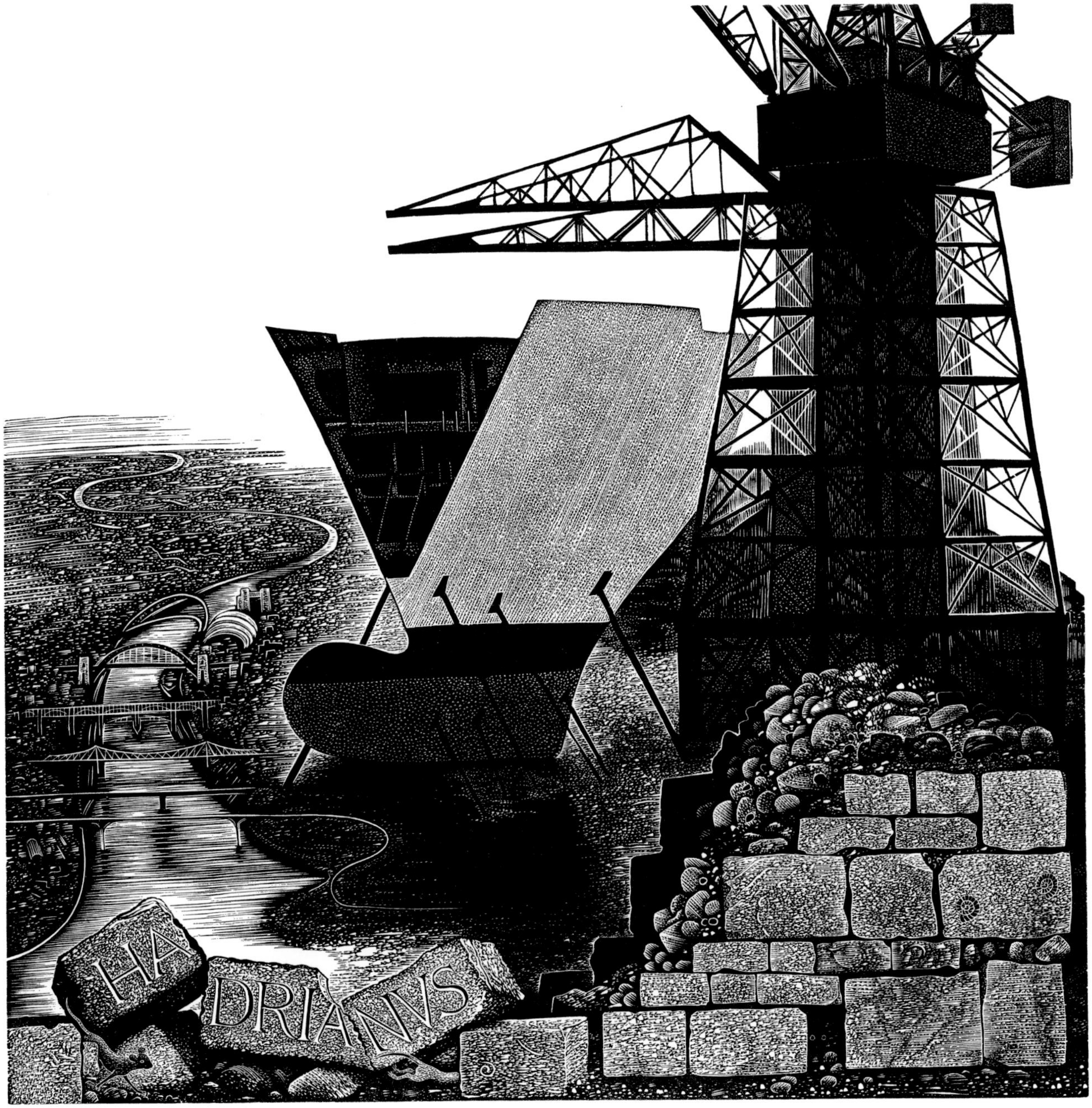

Opposite: Tynemouth Priory, 2004, 198 × 250 mm

This page: Wallsend, 2004, 200 × 200 mm

Tynemouth Priory, Wallsend and Marsden Rock are part of the Nexus Metro commission.

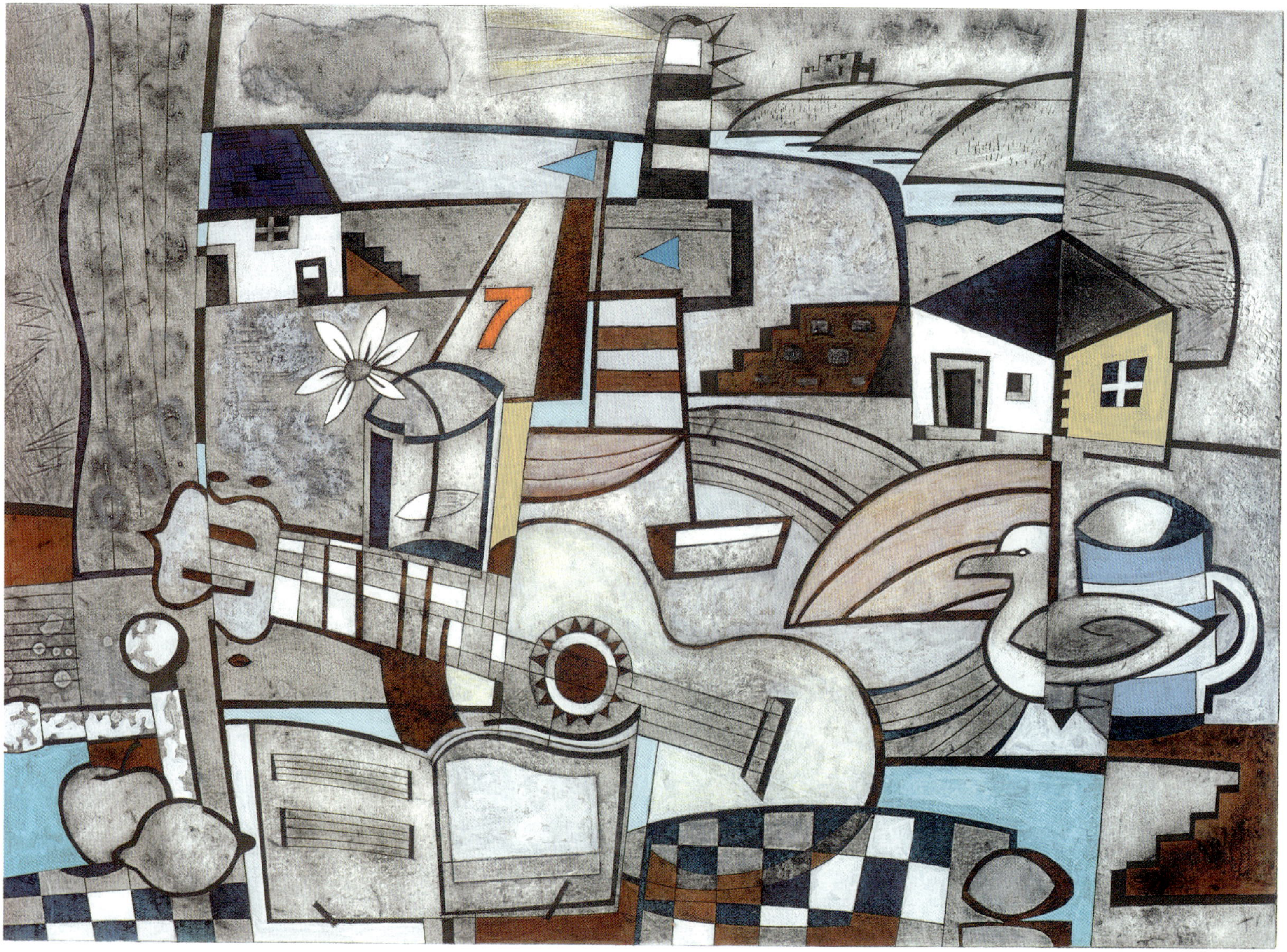

PETER LAWRENCE: *Seven, collagraph and painting, 2001, 300 × 415 mm*

7. Chords, Riffs, and Grace Notes

Peter Lawrence

Chairman of the Society of Wood Engravers 2006–

Dancing lines, stomping blacks, dizzy whites, buzzing greys, wriggling shapes that metamorphose on sight – these are characteristic ingredients of Peter Lawrence's wood engravings. The musical quality of his imagery is so pronounced that ears as well as eyes seem to become involved. Jazz is king here, and the improvisatory nature of jazz lends a contradictory element to this far-from-improvisatory medium. Add to the mixture snatches of Pop Art and Op Art, the clean lines of St Ivesian design, a plethora of symbols for movement and direction as well as crazy typography, and the result is an intriguing collage of shapes that, scrutinised in any order, continue to reveal something new.

'Crikey! No way!' was Lawrence's reaction when his tutor at art college showed him the blocks and tools, and demonstrated the skills necessary for this most painstaking and time-consuming of mediums. It took twenty years for Lawrence to acquire a set of tools to see what he could do. By then the very constraints implicit in engraving presented an interesting challenge, a new way of assembling and compressing different ideas and types of imagery. It also provided the chance to keep up his drawing skills at a time when computers were increasingly rendering hand-skills obsolete. His innate need to make daily marks was as strong as ever, but twenty years as an illustrator and graphic designer spent following other people's briefs had left him no time for personal work. He turned to engraving for private relaxation, experimenting with his own ideas on the blocks. As he had never liked working in three

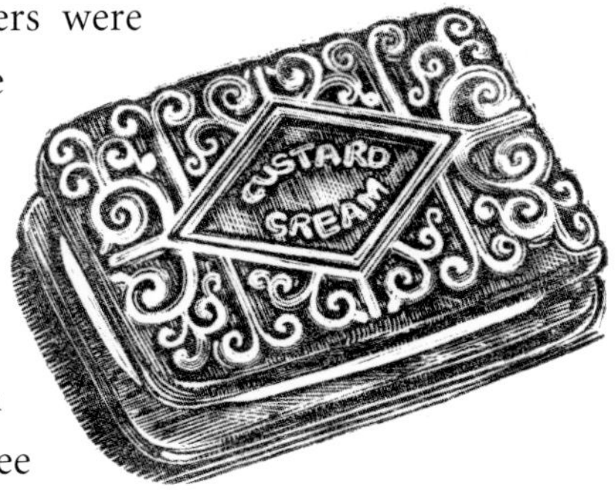

Custard Cream, 1992

dimensions, it was not so much the handling of wood that attracted him, but the crispness of the black-and-white print. He had previously made drawings specifically to resemble wood engravings, and by the time he picked up his tools he already had a large vocabulary of marks to play with.

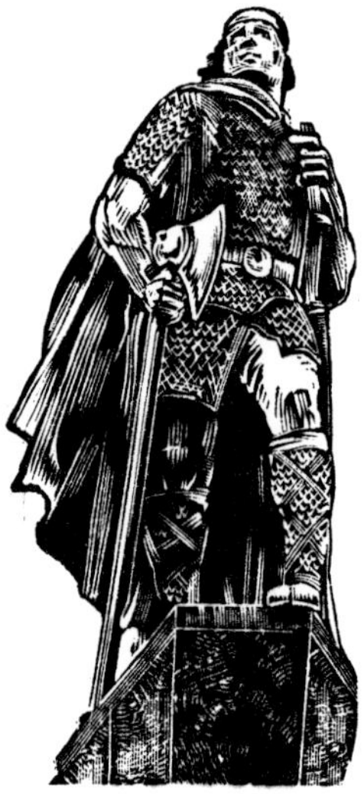

Leifur Eriksson, 1992

Art and music were in Peter Lawrence's blood. He was drawing and writing before he went to primary school, and as a small boy could make sophisticated distinctions between pigments such as burnt sienna and raw umber. His father, a solicitor's clerk, was a keen Sunday painter, and would ask his son to select and squeeze out his oil paints from the Roses chocolate tin in which he kept them. Peter Lawrence's parents came from the East End of London. To escape the grime they had moved out along the railway line to a relatively affluent neighbourhood with tree-lined streets and good schools for their children. Peter was born in Hornchurch, Essex, in 1951, and at the age of eleven ensured parental pride by gaining a place at the Royal Liberty Grammar School in Romford. There were few books at home, so as a teenager Peter spent hours in Romford public library discovering Modern Art – Cubism, Dada, Surrealism, Pop and Op Art. Salvador Dali and René Magritte became his heroes, along with the cartoonists Gerald Scarfe and Ralph Steadman, whose work he imitated in his own drawings. At school Peter designed posters, drew cartoons and made caricatures of the teachers. Teaming up with a like-minded schoolfriend, he joined the Romford and Hornchurch Art Society for life classes and to participate in annual exhibitions, the two being the only schoolchildren amongst the society's elderly members. The pair also frequented London art exhibitions, spending hours trying to make head or tail of blank canvases and piles of bricks. Pop Art, however, struck an immediate chord, and Peter converted his fifth-form art prize into the brand new Thames and Hudson book on Pop Art. They also haunted jazz dives, going to numerous gigs to hear the latest in modern jazz and sitting through whole evenings of improvised saxophone playing. For Peter Lawrence, Pop Art and Jazz became inextricably mixed.

The Royal Liberty Grammar School aspired to university places for all its boys, and when Peter expressed his preference for art college the headmaster hardly spoke to him again. His father sat him down in the kitchen at home and asked 'Are you sure about doing Art? How are you going to make a living?' Faced with his son's absolute determination, however, he was encouraging. A full student grant was available, and in 1969 Peter entered the West of England College of Art. He chose Bristol because he liked the prevailing easy-going attitude, and also because it turned out that his tutor, Peter Reddick, had been at the same grammar school.

After his foundation course Peter Lawrence opted to specialise in Illustration. He had rejected the Graphic Design course because it seemed to involve too much three-dimensional work, but later realised this may have been a mistake. Illustration, which focused purely on specific spaces within book pages, did not offer enough general design scope. Lawrence wanted to control the design of the whole book just as a graphic designer would do, and in his third college year he began to design and illustrate complete books. Looking for illustrative material, he started reading voraciously – Arthur Koestler, Vance Packard, John Berger, Solzhenitsyn, Dostoyevsky – and also children's books, discovering *Alice in Wonderland* and *The House at Pooh Corner* for the first time. He interspersed reading with drawing outdoor scenes of Bristol life, squatting on pavements all around the city.

With a good degree under his belt, Peter Lawrence set himself up as a freelance illustrator. The most enjoyable of the various jobs he undertook was an enormous mural/frieze for a children's bookshop, incorporating all his favourite children's book characters in an imaginary journey around the walls. When similar commissions failed to appear, he took on a full-time job as Graphic Designer to the University of Bristol, designing all the university's prospectuses, posters and leaflets. Those years at the university, learning the detail of preparing material for printing, turned Lawrence into a fully-fledged graphic designer. But, tiring of designing throw-away material, he hankered after designing more traditional books. In 1978 he moved with his wife, a primary school teacher, to Oxford, where he joined Oxprint and its sister company Oxford Illustrators. It is there that he has worked ever since, becoming Managing Director in 1998.

Oxford Illustrators, set up in 1968, specialised in educational publishing, and when Peter Lawrence joined the company the old textbooks were beginning to be enlivened by new designs and added colour. Lawrence loved the work and rushed to get into the studios every Monday morning. As well as designing the books, he illustrated them, working late into the night and throughout most weekends as a freelance illustrator. During the great storm of 1987 he worked right through the night, vaguely aware of the tremendous noise outside, only to find his deadline postponed because fallen trees had stopped all travel. With two sons to support, Lawrence's busy dual life as a designer and illustrator brought in useful extra income. But eventually he decided he could afford to relax. He had already flirted with the idea of wood engraving by going on one of Peter Reddick's weekend courses, where he made a small engraving of daisies. Five years passed before he bought his own tools and made another. Working on small boxwood blocks, he started engraving semi-humorous images – custard cream biscuits and Marilyn Monroe heads, or puffins and Viking statues that he had seen in Iceland.

A visit to St Ives, where the new Tate St Ives gallery had recently opened, showing work by Ben Nicholson and Barbara Hepworth, inspired Peter Lawrence to paint. The semi-abstract paintings he produced freed up his engraving, which seemed a more appropriate medium for assembling many different ideas – different styles of illustration, photographic images, lettering, abstract or constructivist shapes, William Morris designs, numbers, humour. 'Like all graphic designers, I have a magpie nature. My son and I collect ephemera – my son picks them up in the street and posts them to me'. Lawrence began incorporating ephemera into abstract or semi-abstract collages and collagraphs, then tried out his ideas in engravings. 'I still have the first abstract engraving I did. It was the most frightening experience. I had this block and decided to do a purely abstract image, not based on anything figurative. I hesitated for ages, asking myself "am I allowed to do this?" When I got over the fact that I did abstract things and that I was not thrown out of the Society I started incorporating more levels, with elements of collage.'

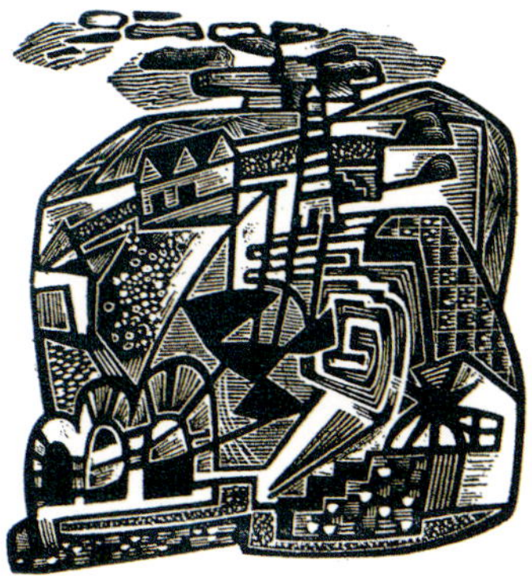

Cornish Quay, 1994

When Peter Lawrence was invited to become Chairman of the Society of Wood Engravers, he felt honoured to be part of a long tradition while still pursuing his own ideas. 'My first love as an engraver was Eric Gill, who was there at the start of the same society. Wow! What I've really enjoyed is the friendship and respect for each other's work that has followed. As Chairman I have tried to attract new members, partly so that we cannot be accused of cliquishness, partly so people can see that they can get recognised, and partly for the Society's self interest. Where are the committee members of the future if we don't encourage participation?' Lawrence's proselytising zeal has also led him into teaching, and while this has increased his admiration for other engravers working in many different styles, it has alerted him to the frequent absence amongst students of a personal viewpoint in their work – a negative that he tries to counter.

Peter Lawrence's discovery that he could assemble multifarious ideas into one small image containing both lyrical flow and the compressed energy of a coiled spring, was momentous. It shifted wood engraving from its illustrative niche and showed what the medium could add to mainstream contemporary art. Images such as *Out and About* or *Free and Unequal* make full use of linear rhythm and positive/negative and derive their strength from the balanced opposition of black and white. Engraving allowed Lawrence's mind to roam freely while deploying all his design skills. 'The placing of one thing against another, the use of counterpoint, whether a block of text against a photo or a big black shape against a small stippled

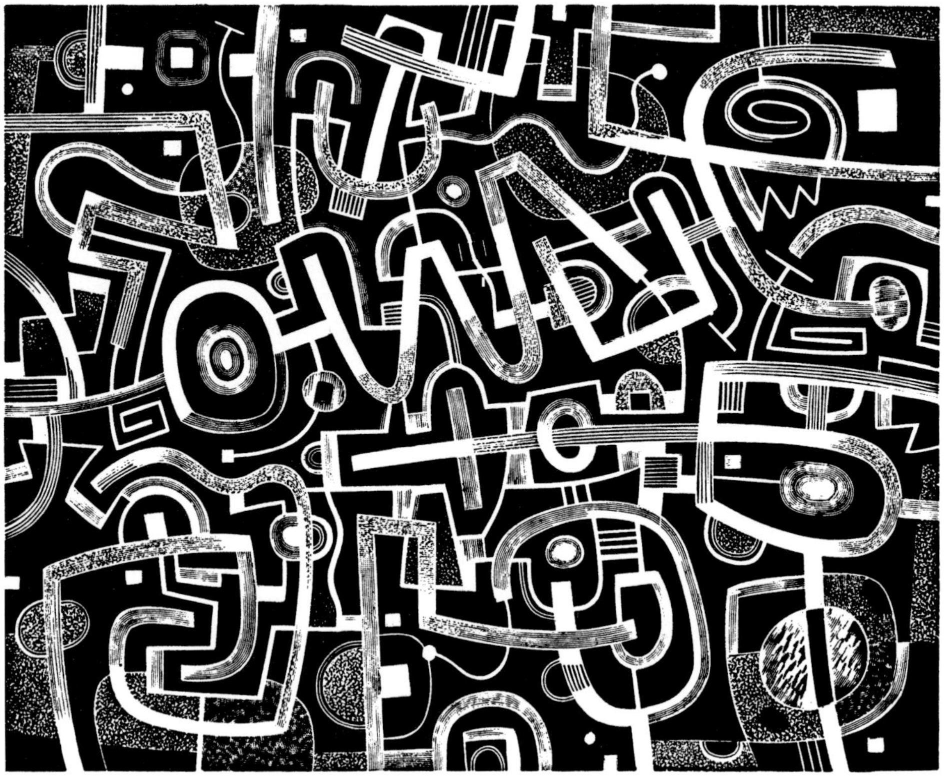

This page: Out and About, 2006

Opposite: Isola Bella, 2003, 160 × 250 mm

one. The importance of the white space between – "creative white space" we used to call it in design. It's like an ensemble of different instruments, where the small "feature" bits are solos.'

For years Peter Lawrence hand-burnished his own blocks, printing his images on thin Japanese paper. Now that the engraver Paul Kershaw prints his work, he is able to work larger and to amalgamate several blocks within one image. He uses Resingrave in preference to wood because it enables him to work on a large scale at less expense. The tint tool is his favourite tool because the line of even thickness it creates most resembles the Rapidograph pen he has used all his life. His engravings, incorporating a myriad different experiences, are about his life, and in making them he relives past pleasures. The complex engraving *Way out West* is based on memories of a holiday in San Francisco and Los Angeles. A holiday in Spain engendered *The Alhambra*, and a trip to Italy produced *Isola Bella*. Making his

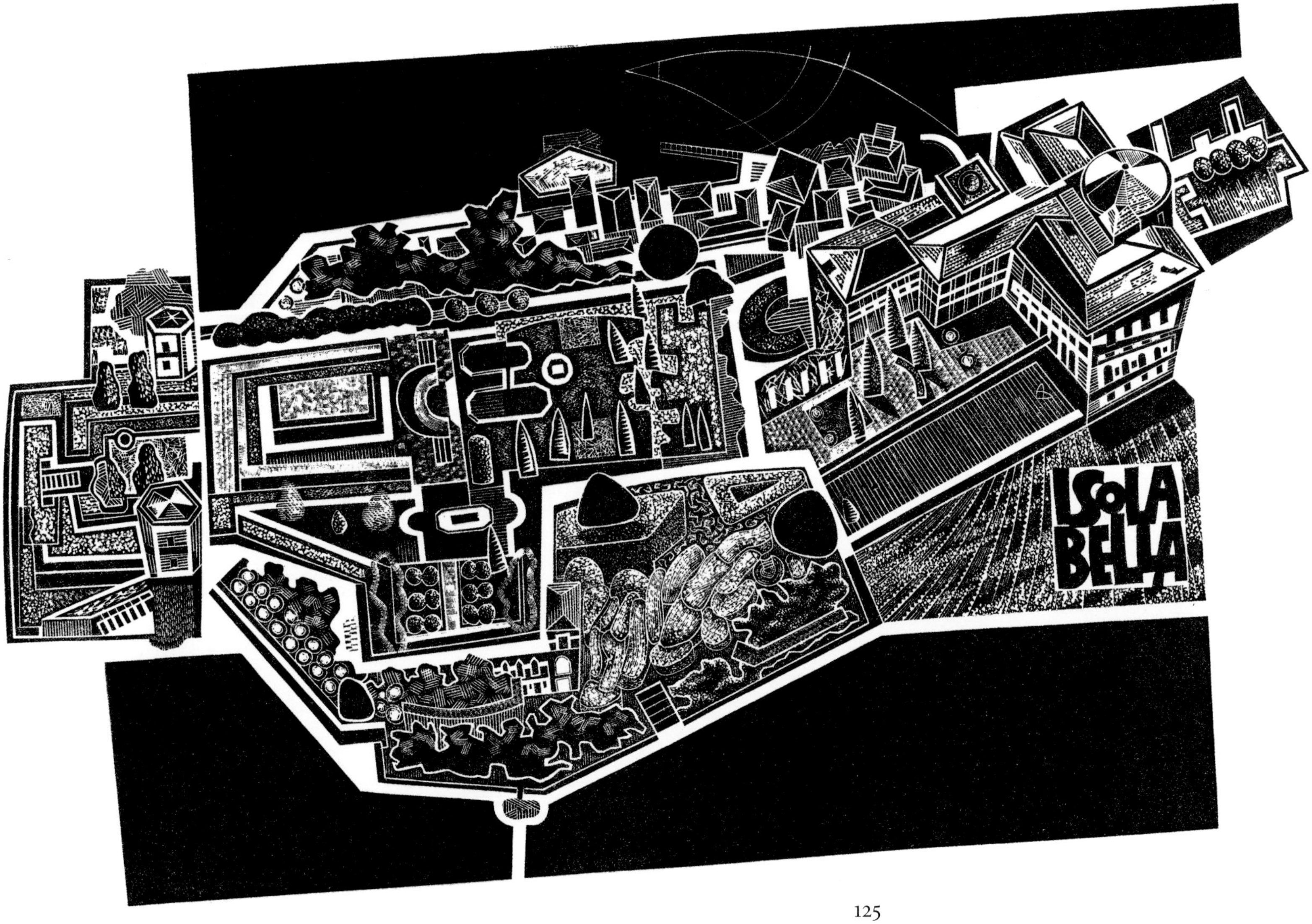

wood engravings gives Peter Lawrence the chance to remember and to dream, mining the deep seam of his interests and experiences while allowing his imagination to wander freely. ‘A combination of structure and control and lack of control is what I aspire to. Engraving is the most difficult thing to do without pre-planning, so I am trying to do something unnatural. I plan the broad outline but allow myself a lot of freedom within the structure, and try to get rhythm into it as I do in the music I love.’

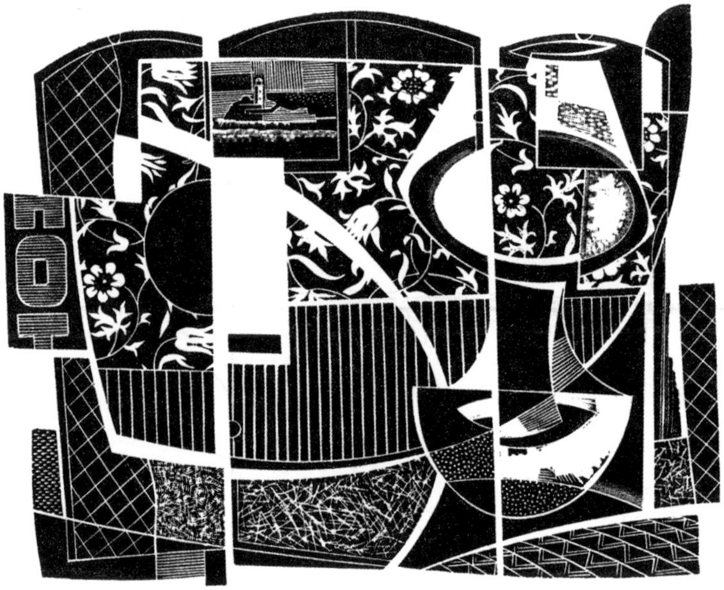

This page: Godrevy Island from Hotel St Ives, 2000, 100 × 130 mm

Opposite: Black Quay, 1998

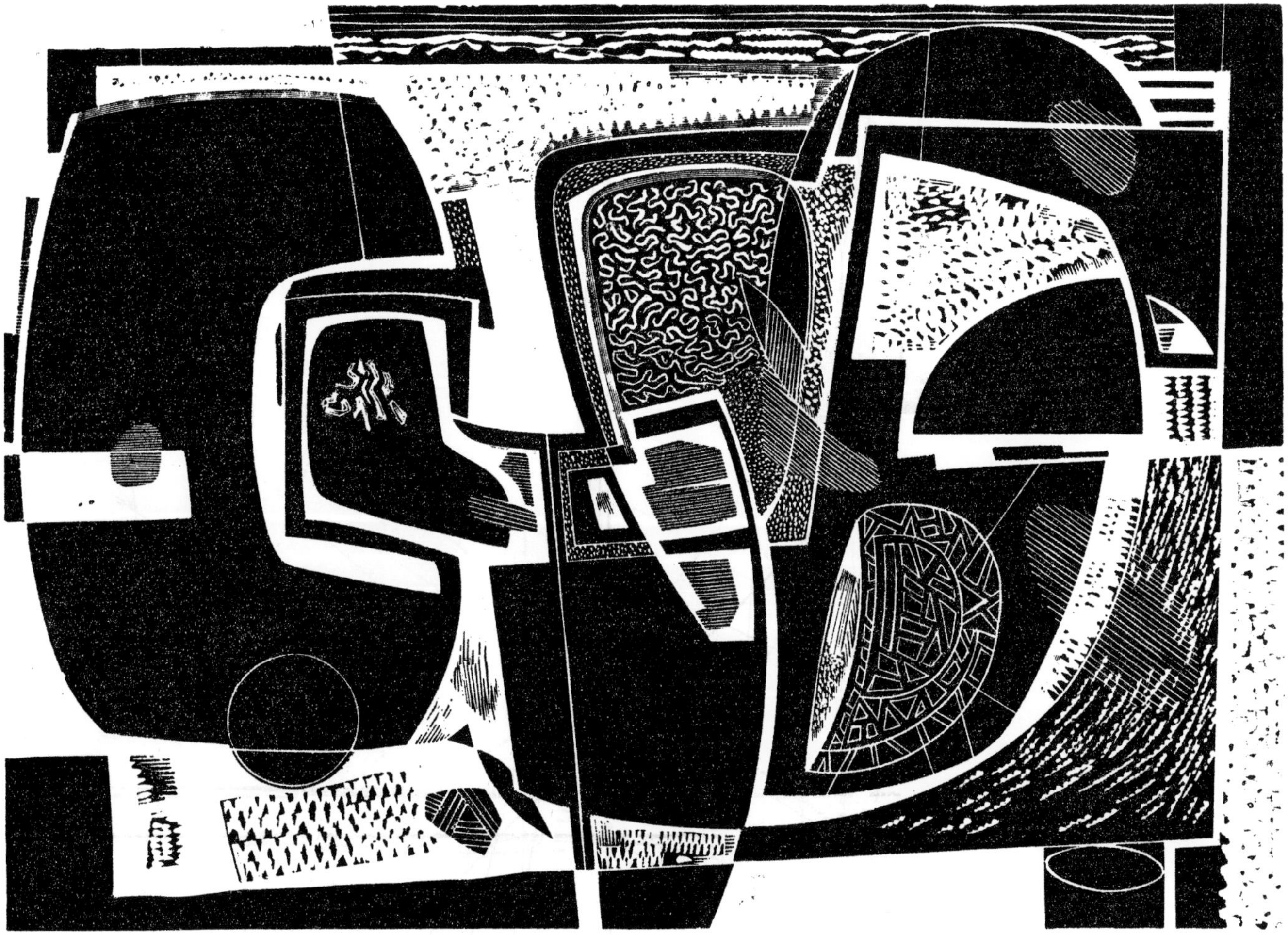

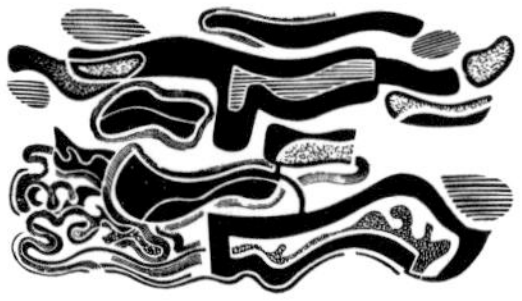

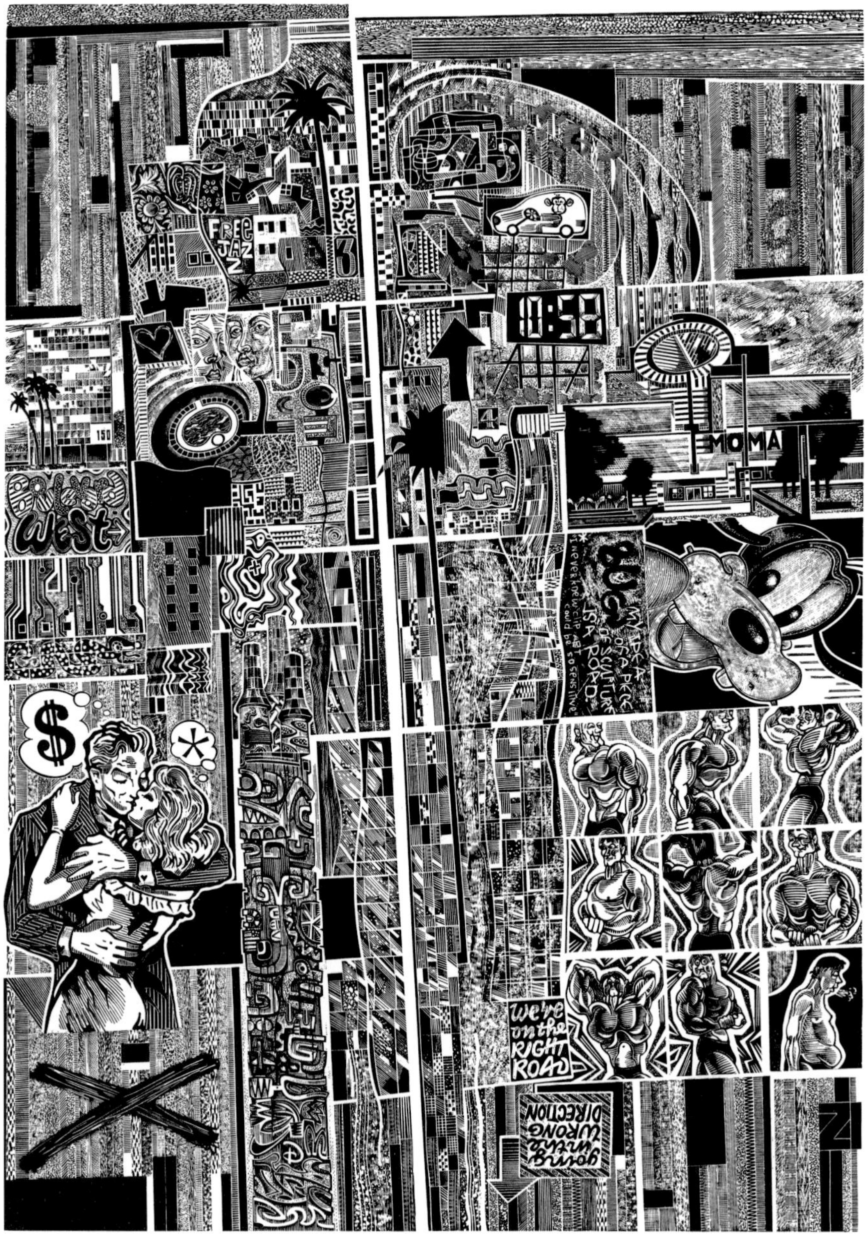

This page: Way Out West, 2004, 400 × 260 mm

Opposite: The Alhambra, 2007, 340 × 255 mm

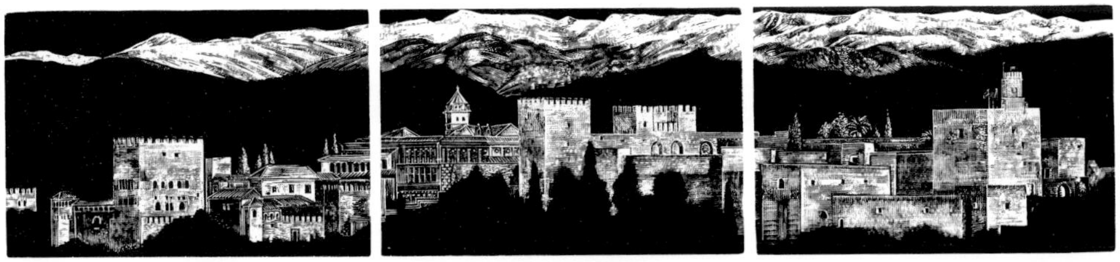

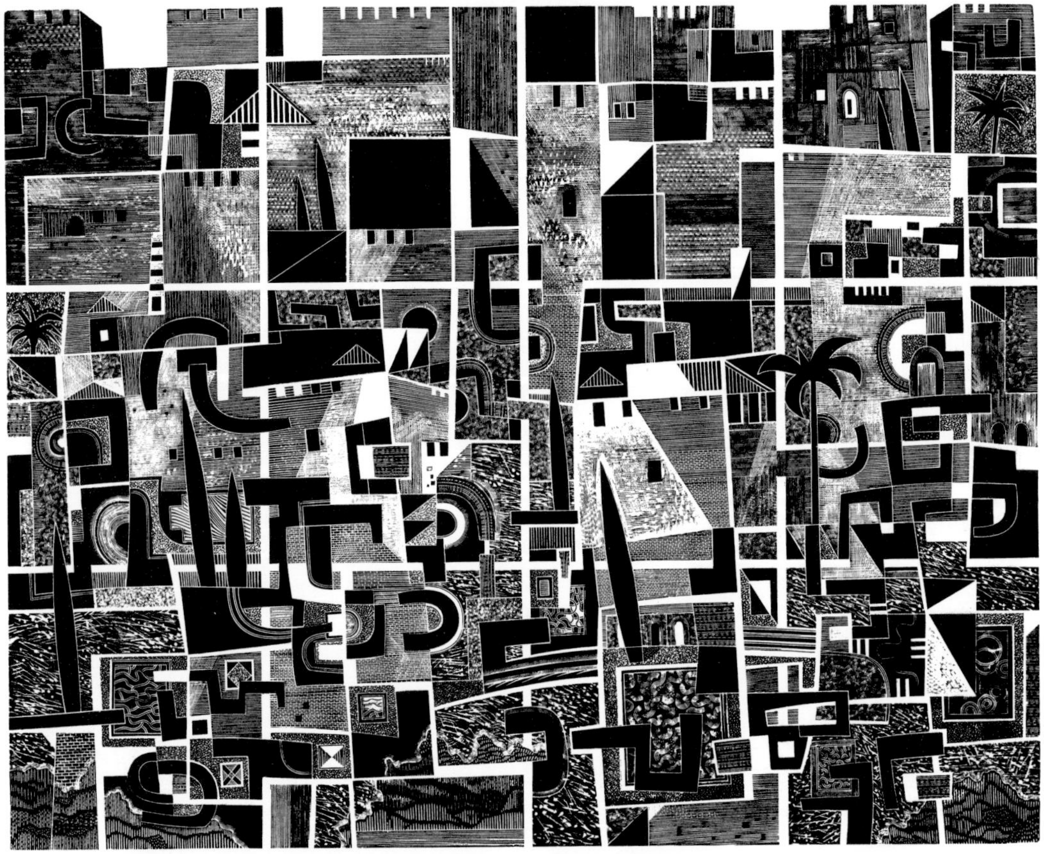

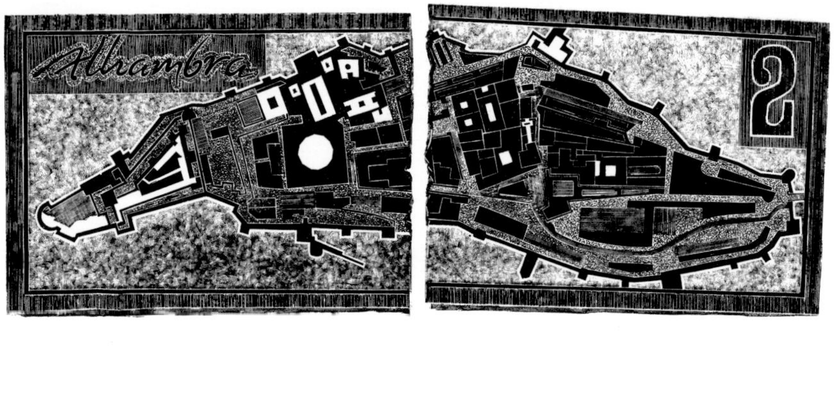
Alhambra

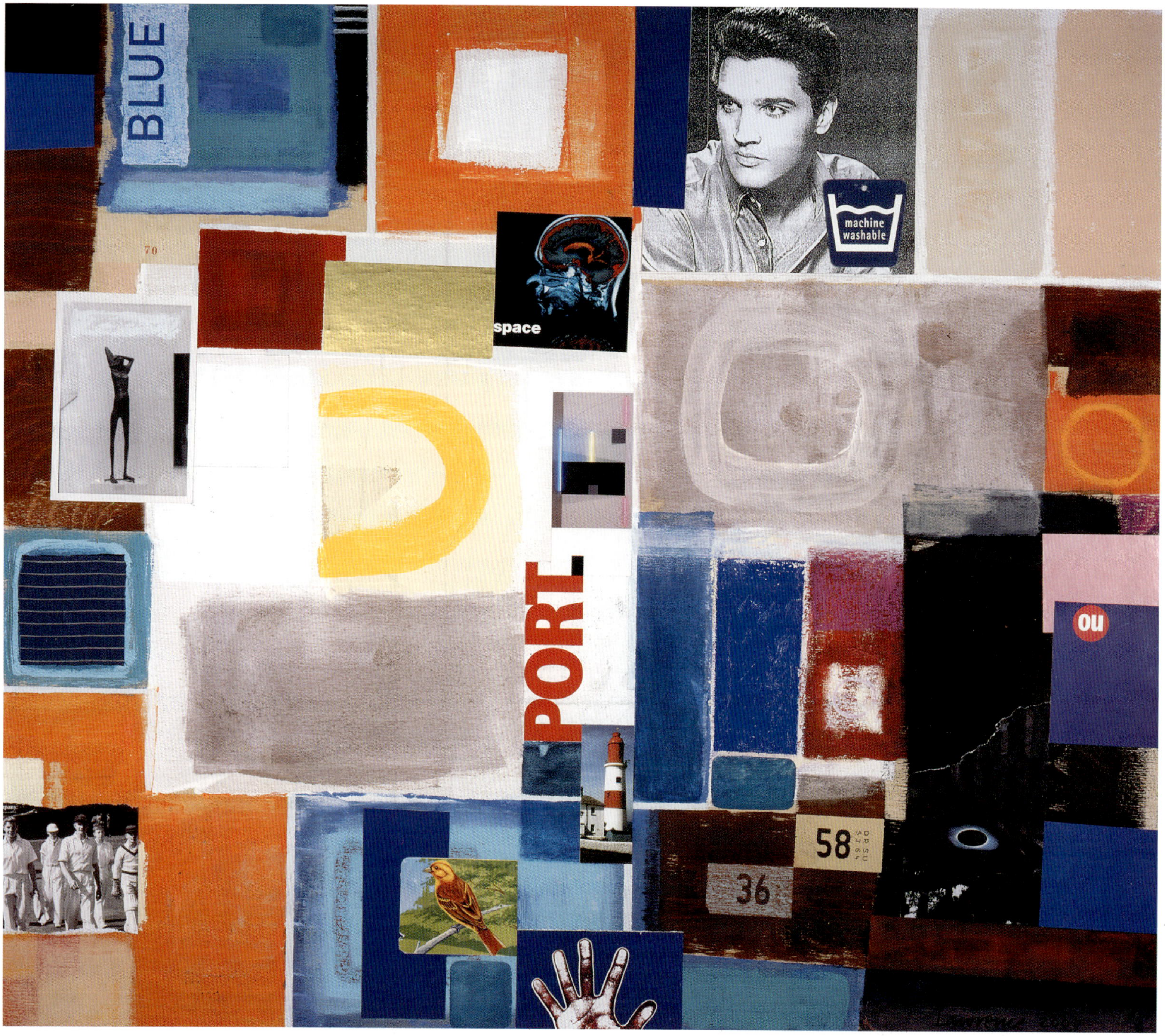
BLUE
70
space
machine washable
PORT
ou
58
36

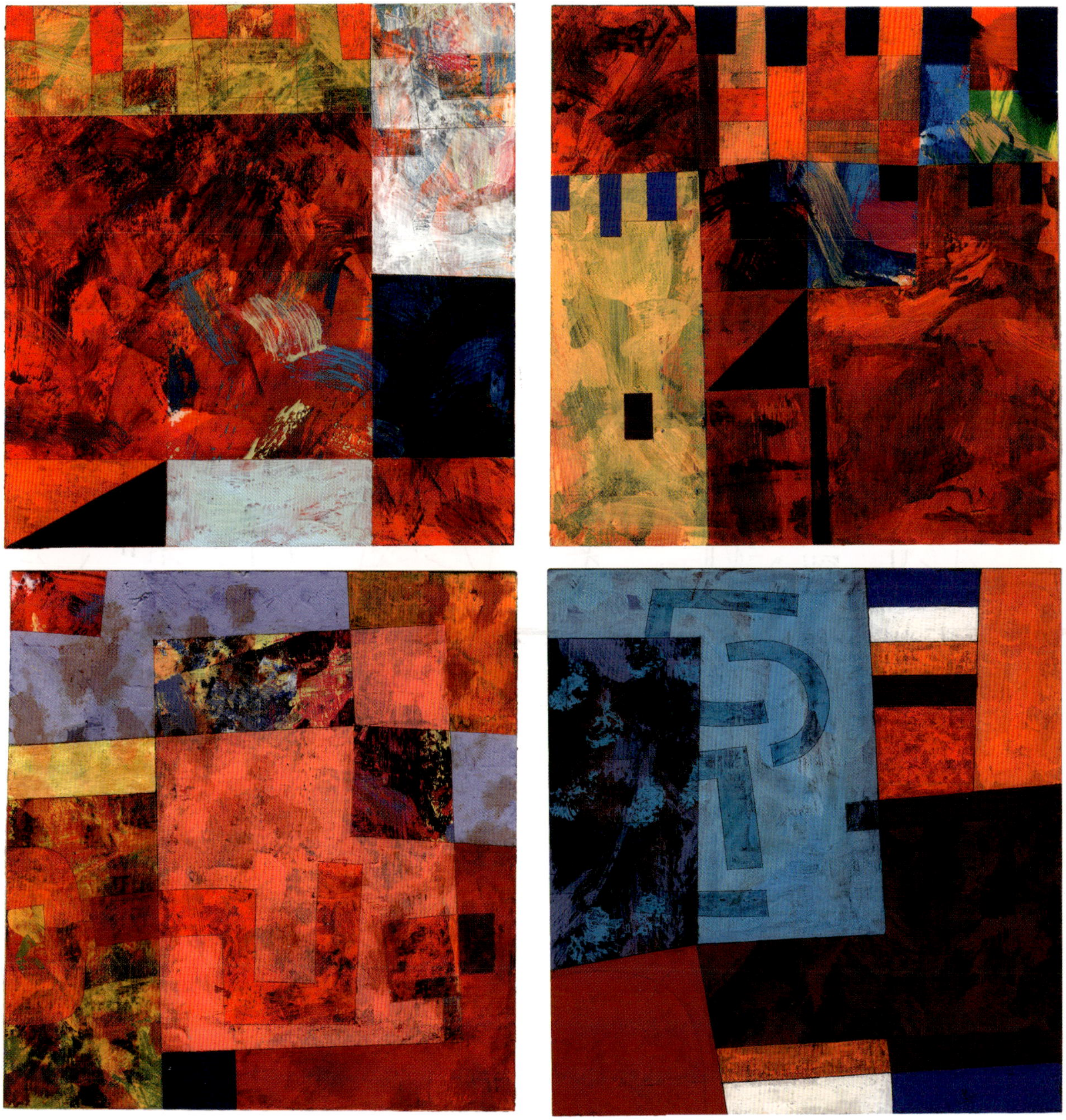

Opposite: Elvis Board, painting and collage, 2000, 640 × 725 mm

This page: Spanish Quarter, gouache and ink, 2007, 340 × 350 mm

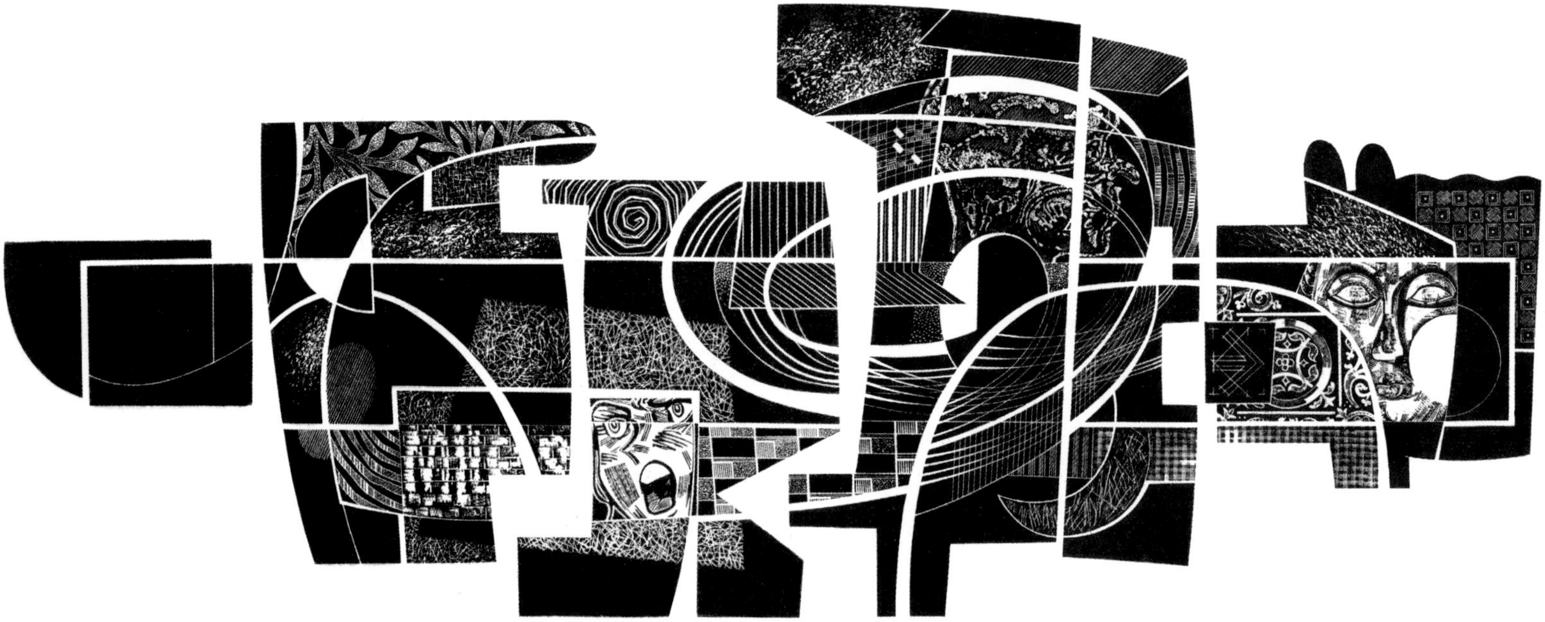

Above: Quintet, 2001, 180 × 450 mm

Opposite: Transform, 2006, 310 × 330 mm

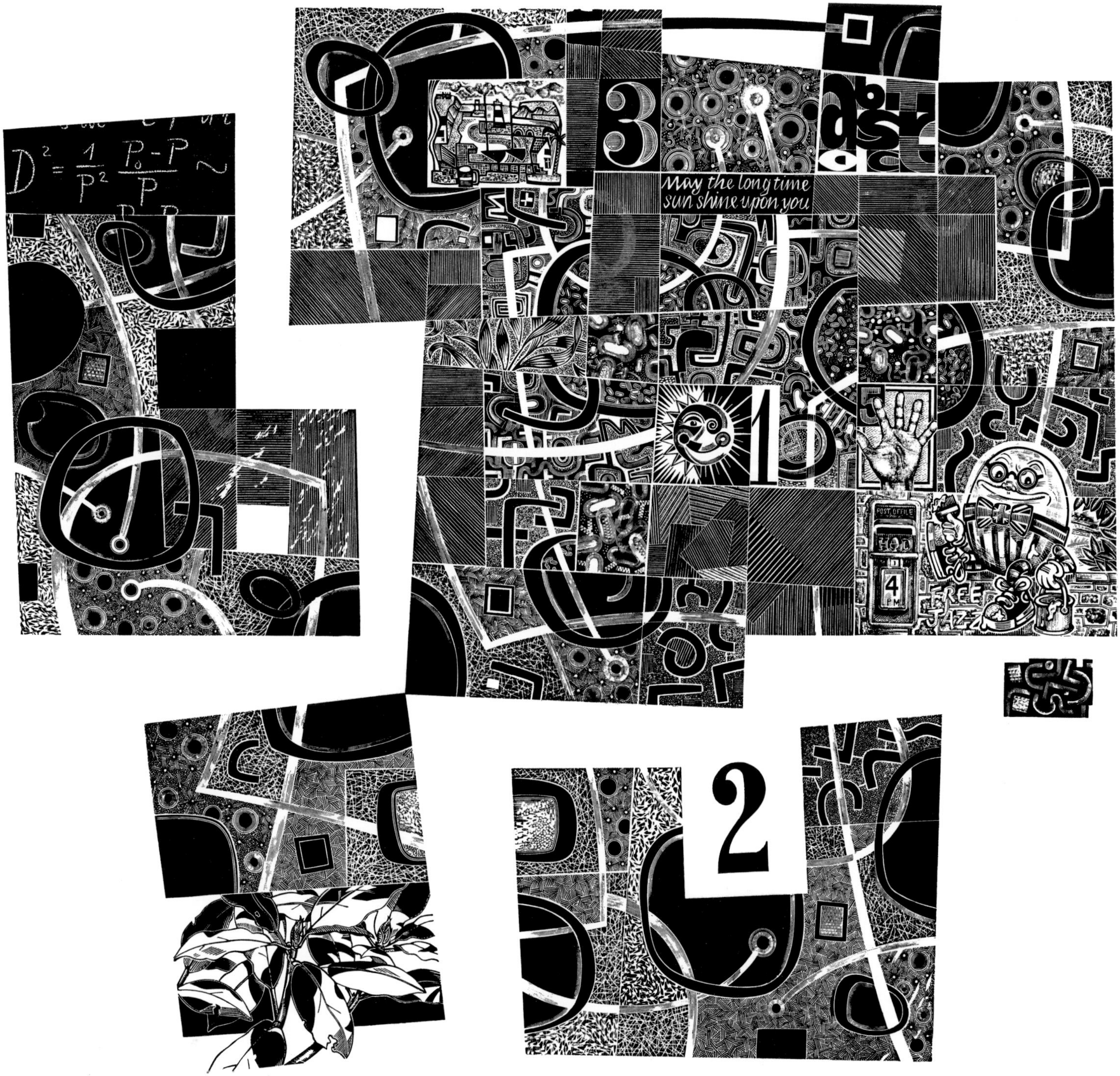

3
May the long time
sun shine upon you
1
POST OFFICE
4
PM
FREE
2

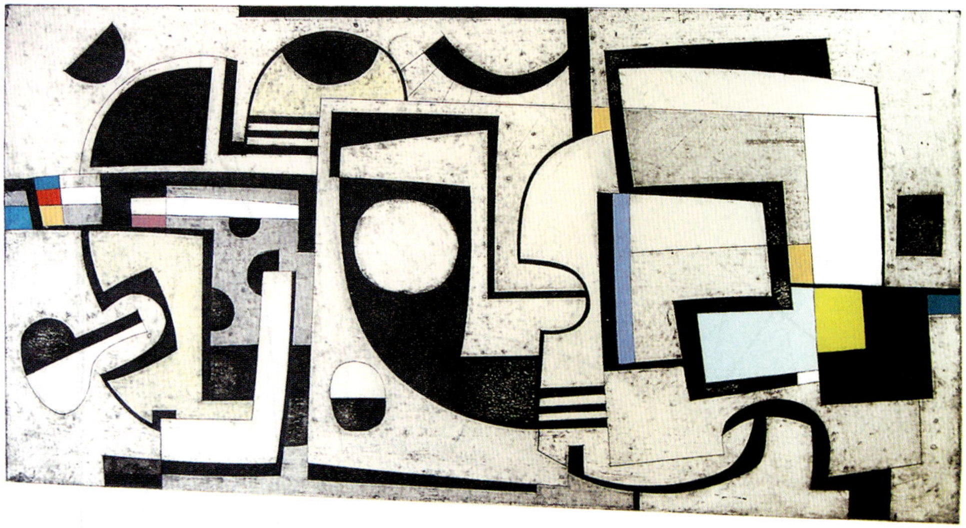

Mingus, collagraph, 2002,
205 × 380 mm

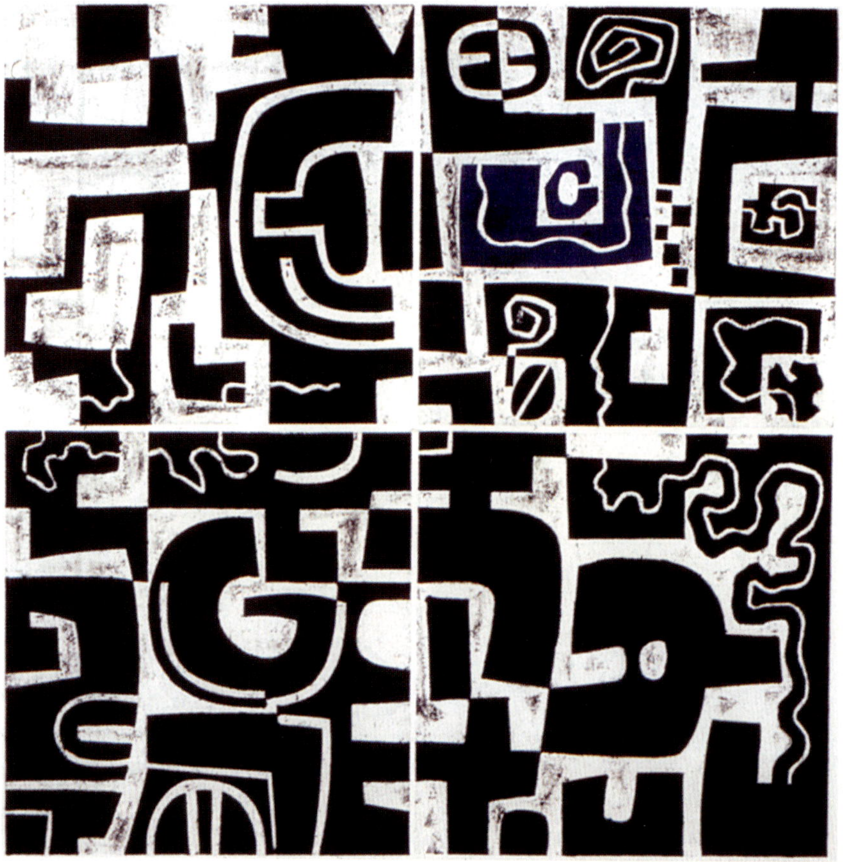

Quartet, collagraph, 2003,
340 × 340 mm

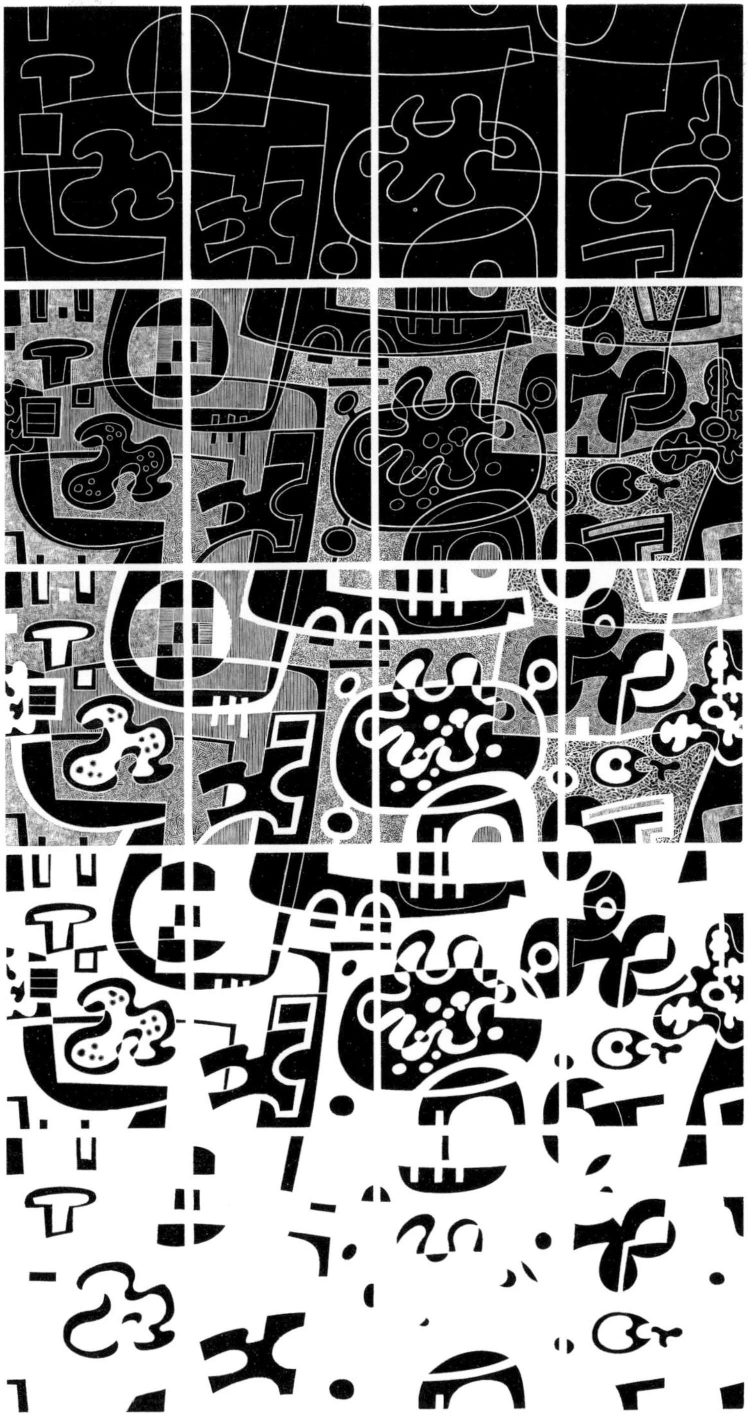

Time & Space, 2009, 390 × 210 mm

Montpelier, 2007, 150 × 350 mm

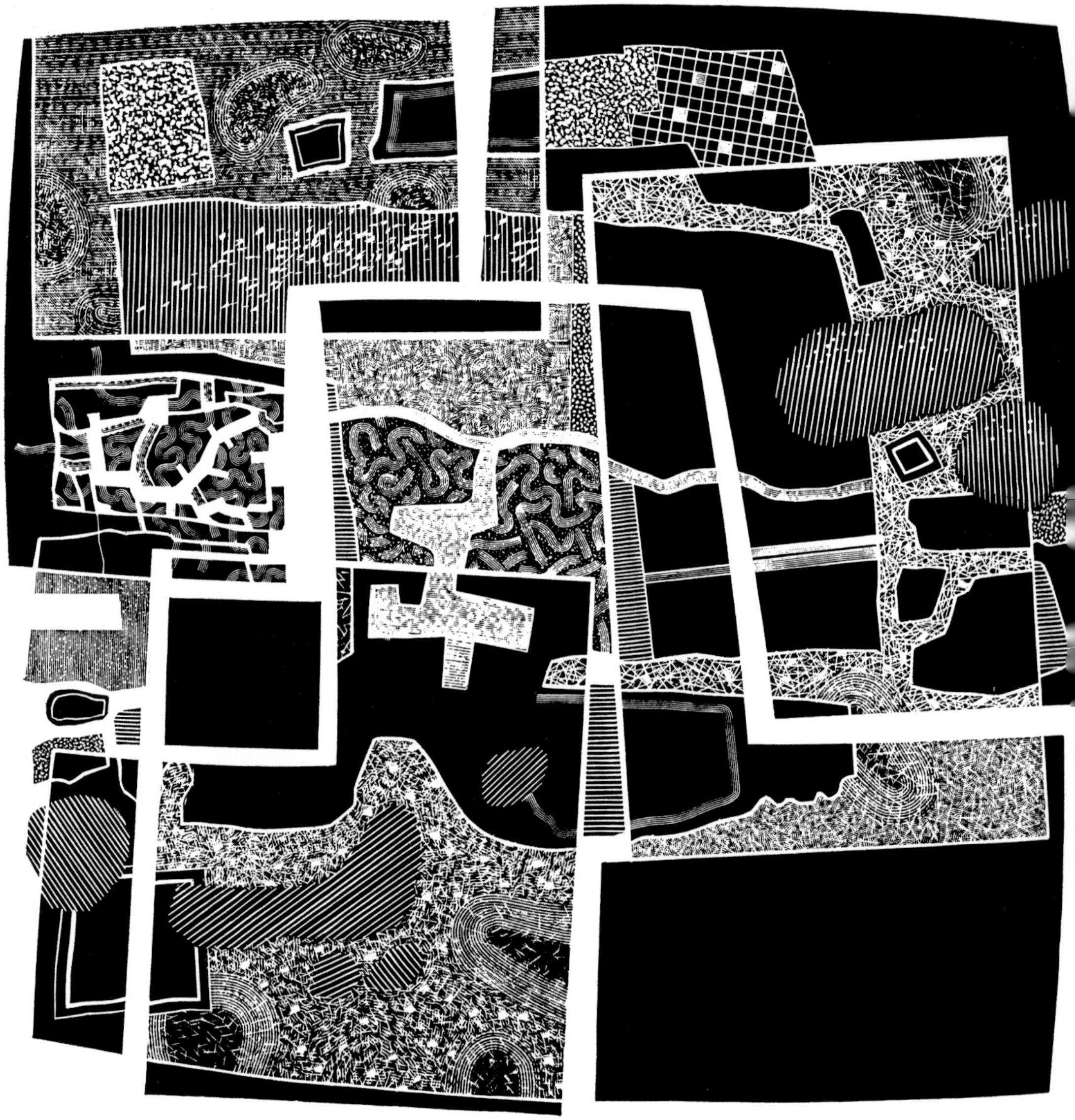

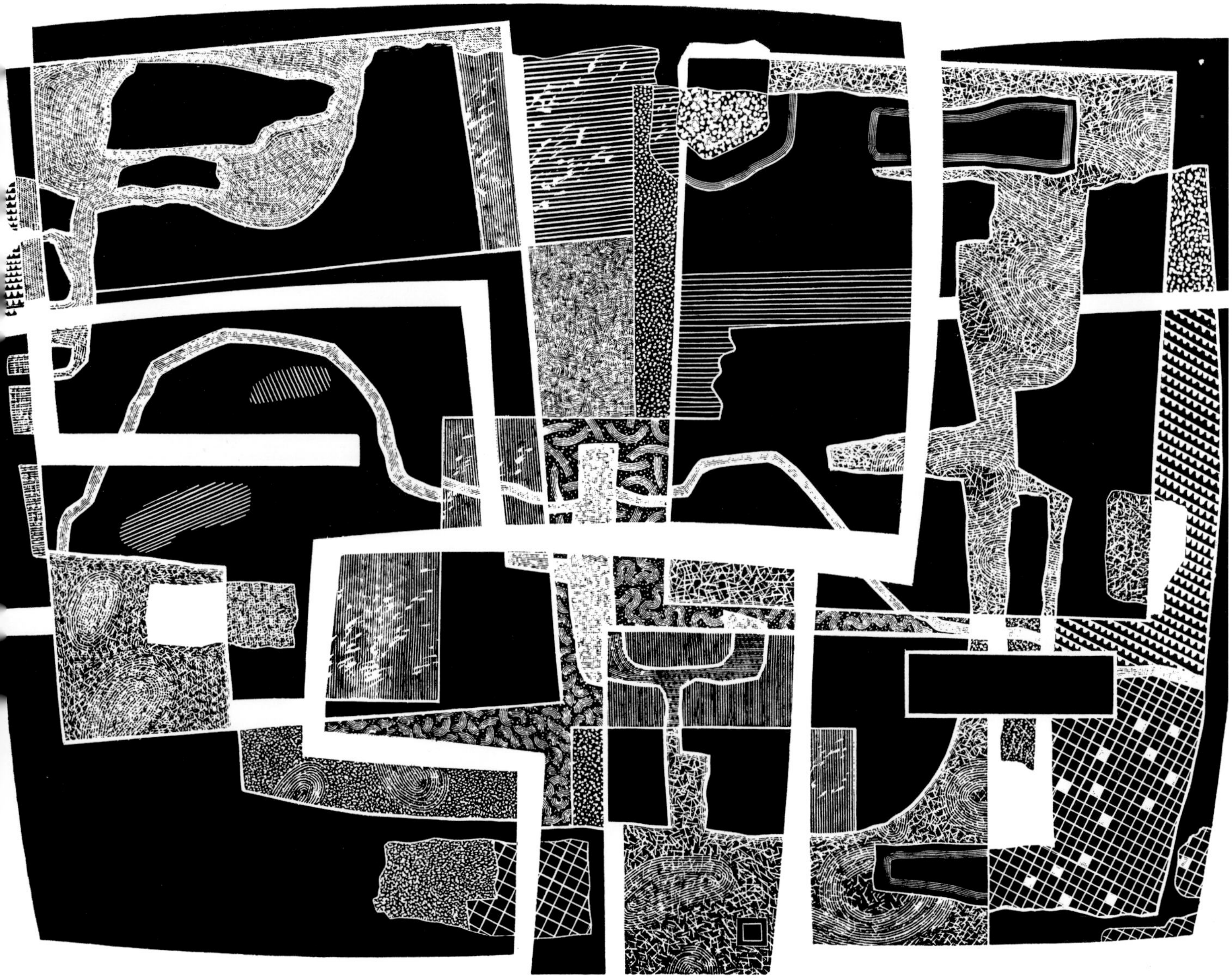

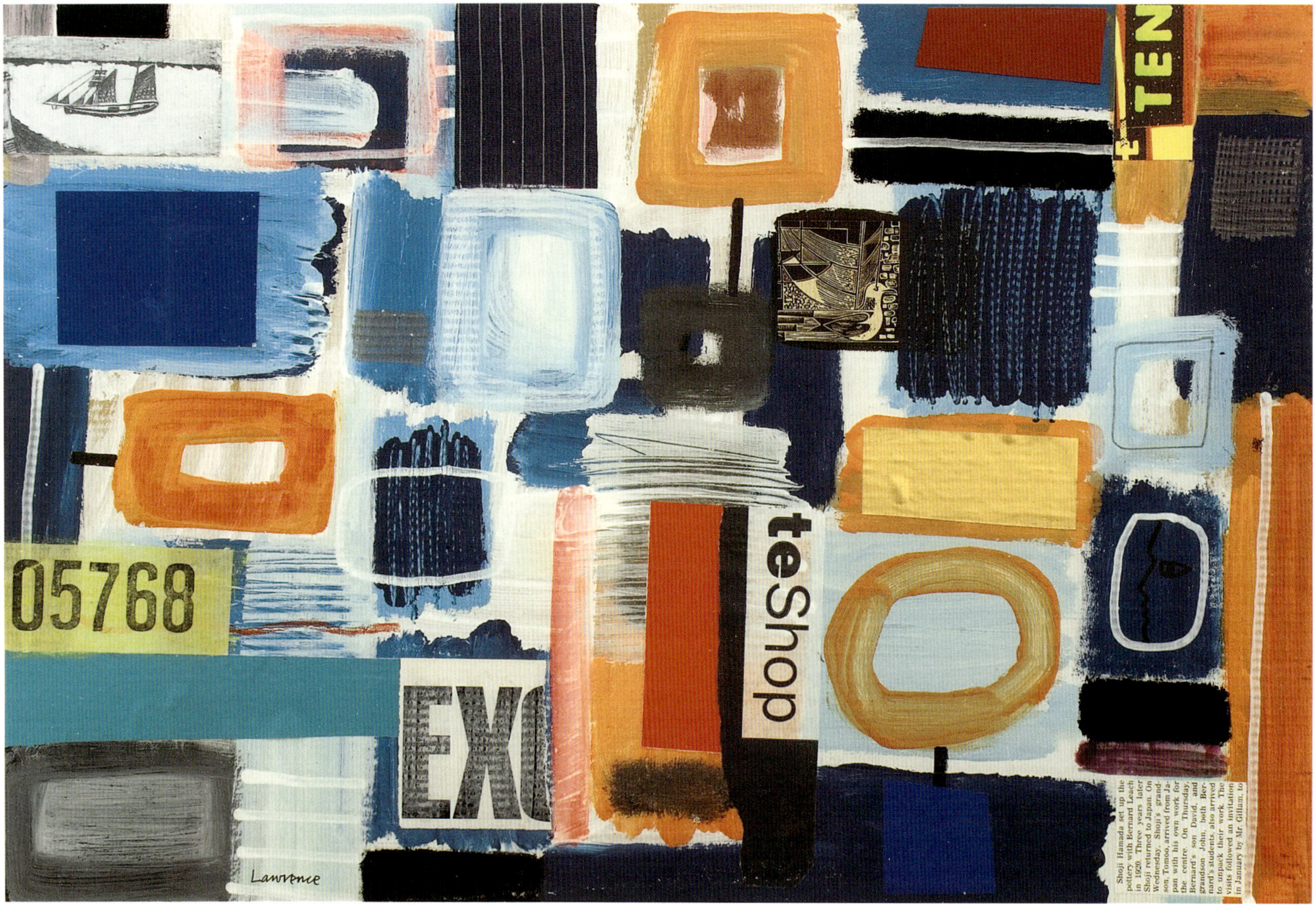
TEN
05768
teShop
Shoji Hamada set up the
pottery with Bernard Leach
in 1920. Three years later
Shoji returned to Japan. On
Wednesday, Shoji's grand-
son, Tomoo, arrived from Ja-
pan with his own work for
the centre. On Thursday,
Bernard's son David, and
grandson John, both Ber-
nard's students, also arrived
to unpack their work. The
visits followed an invitation
in January by Mr. Gillam, to
Lawrence

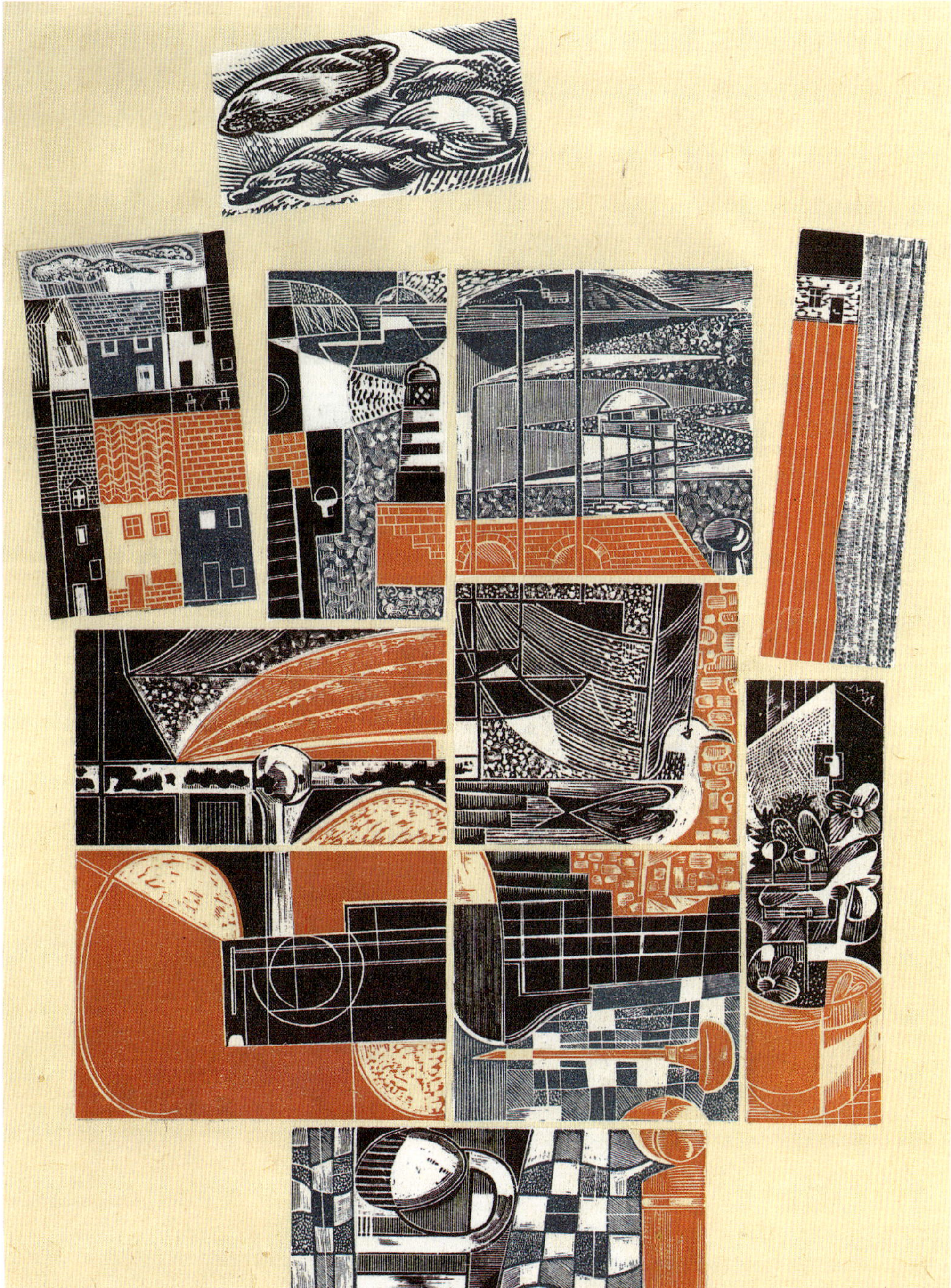

Opposite: St Ives Collection, painting and collage, 2001, 320 × 480 mm

This page: Guitar Collection, 1997, 212 × 150 mm

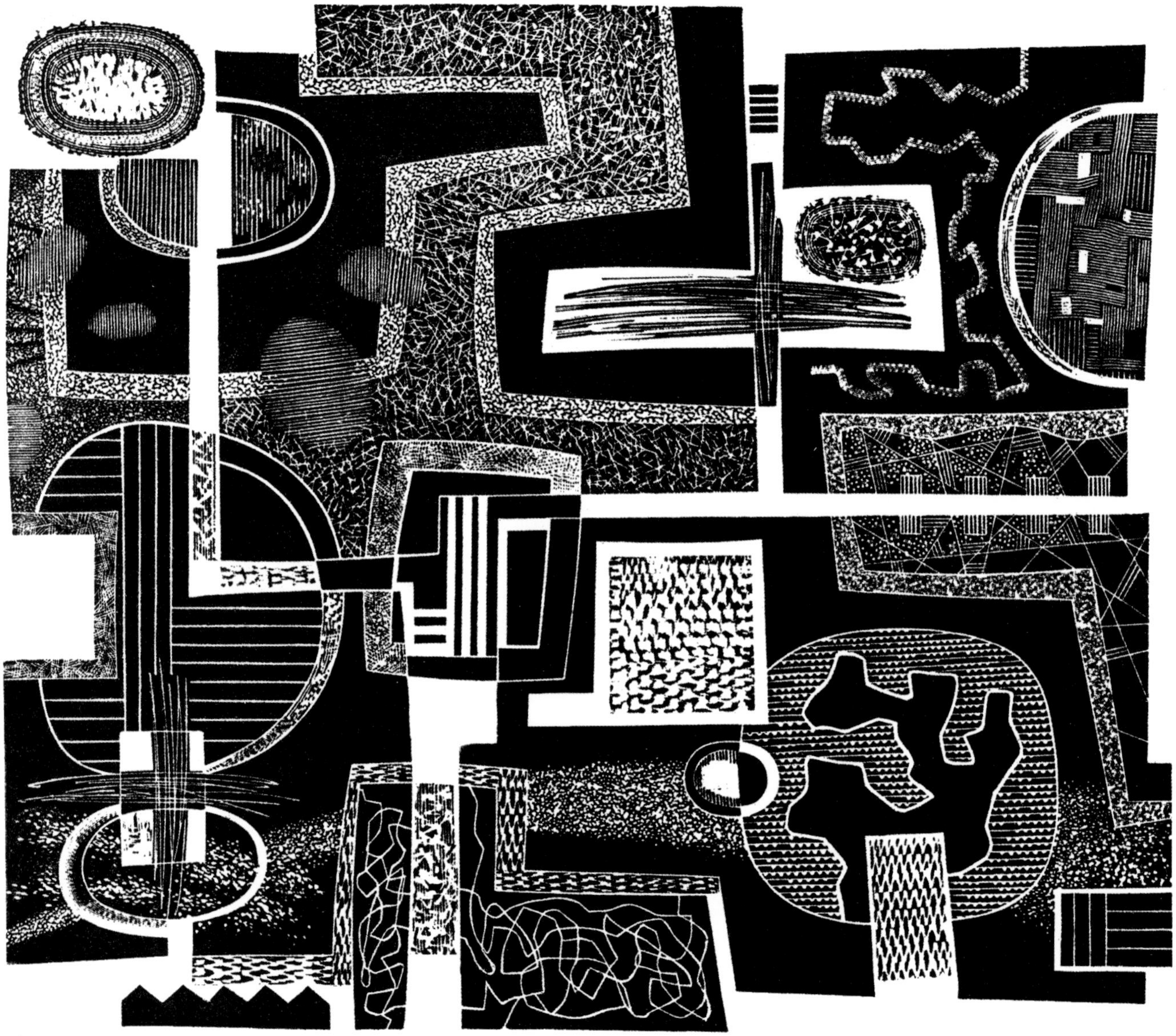

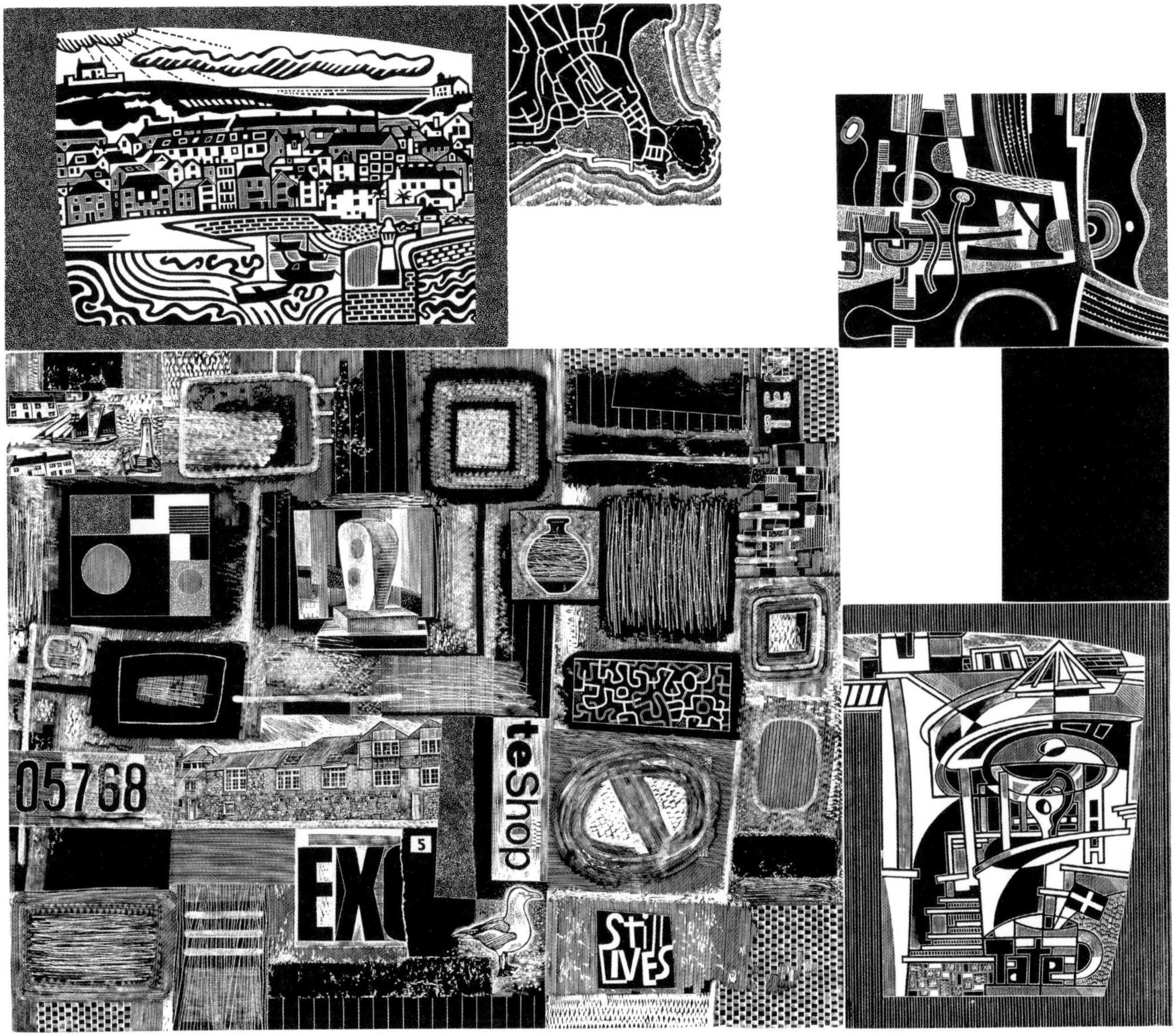

Opposite: Dark Corners, 2002

Above: St Ives, 2008, 305 × 355 mm

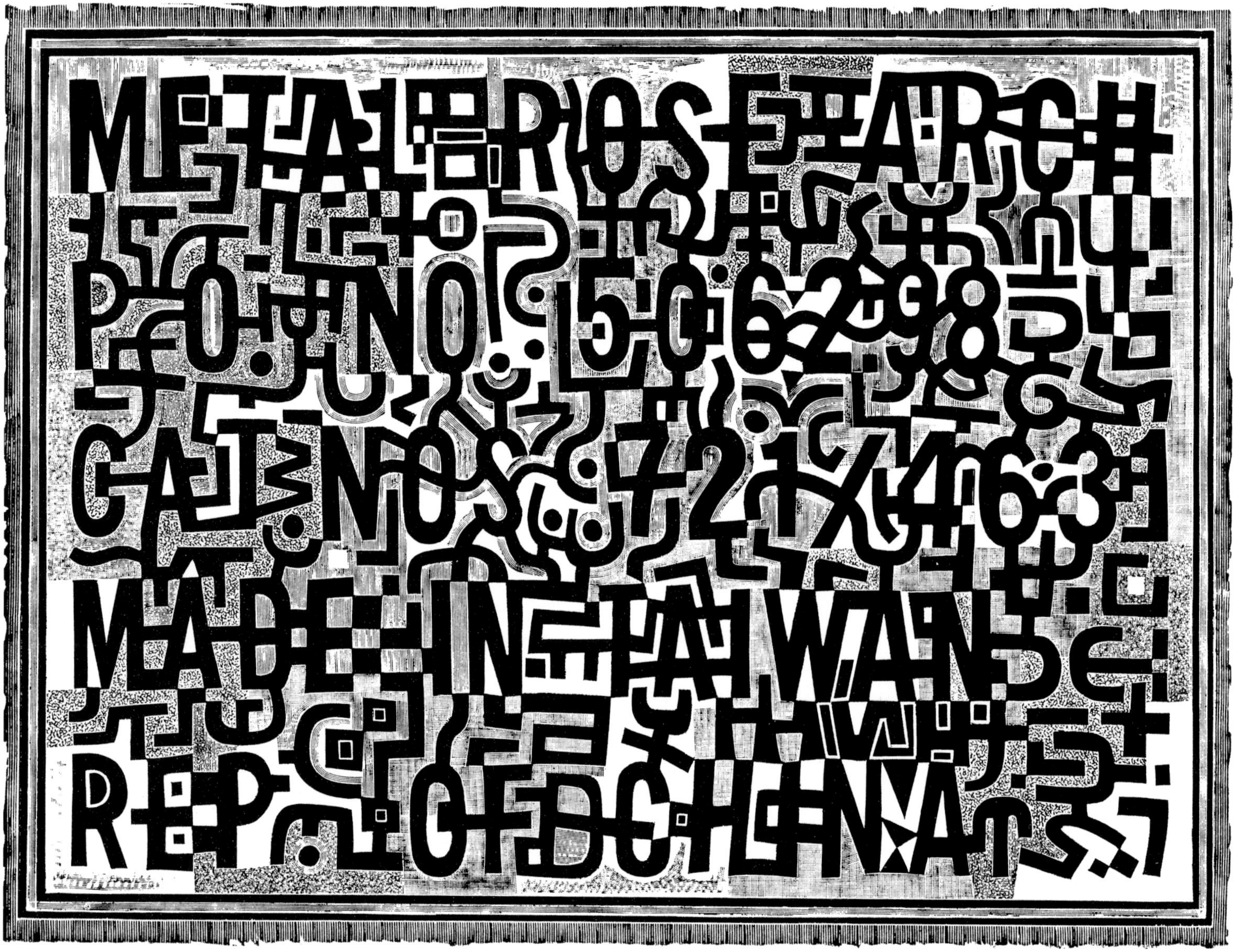

Above: Made in Taiwan, 2006, 155 × 205 mm

Opposite: Square Dance, hand-coloured collagraph, 2004, 300 × 300 mm

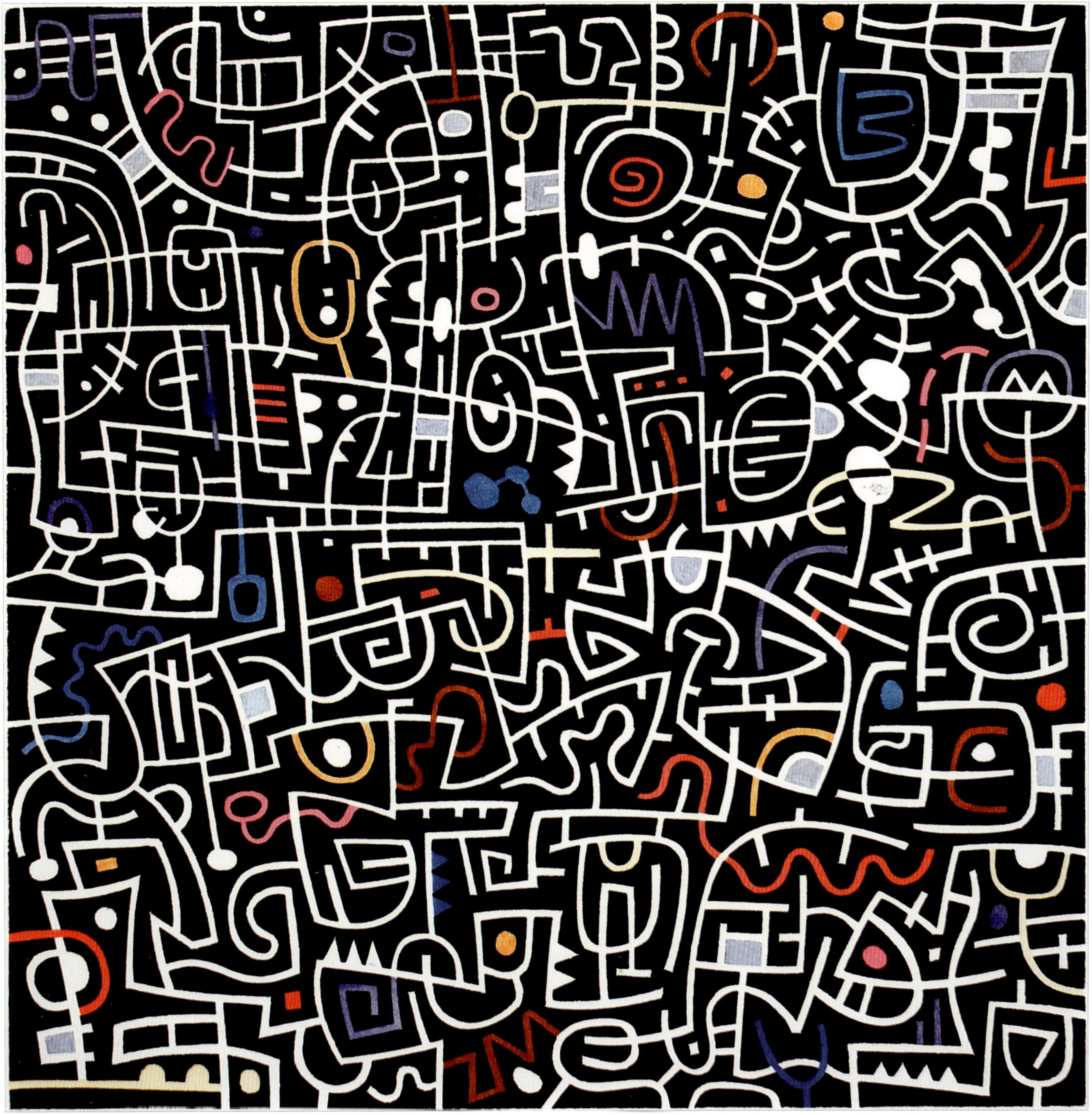

This page: Interior, Brentwood, California, 2000, 200 × 150 mm

Opposite: Take Four, 2004

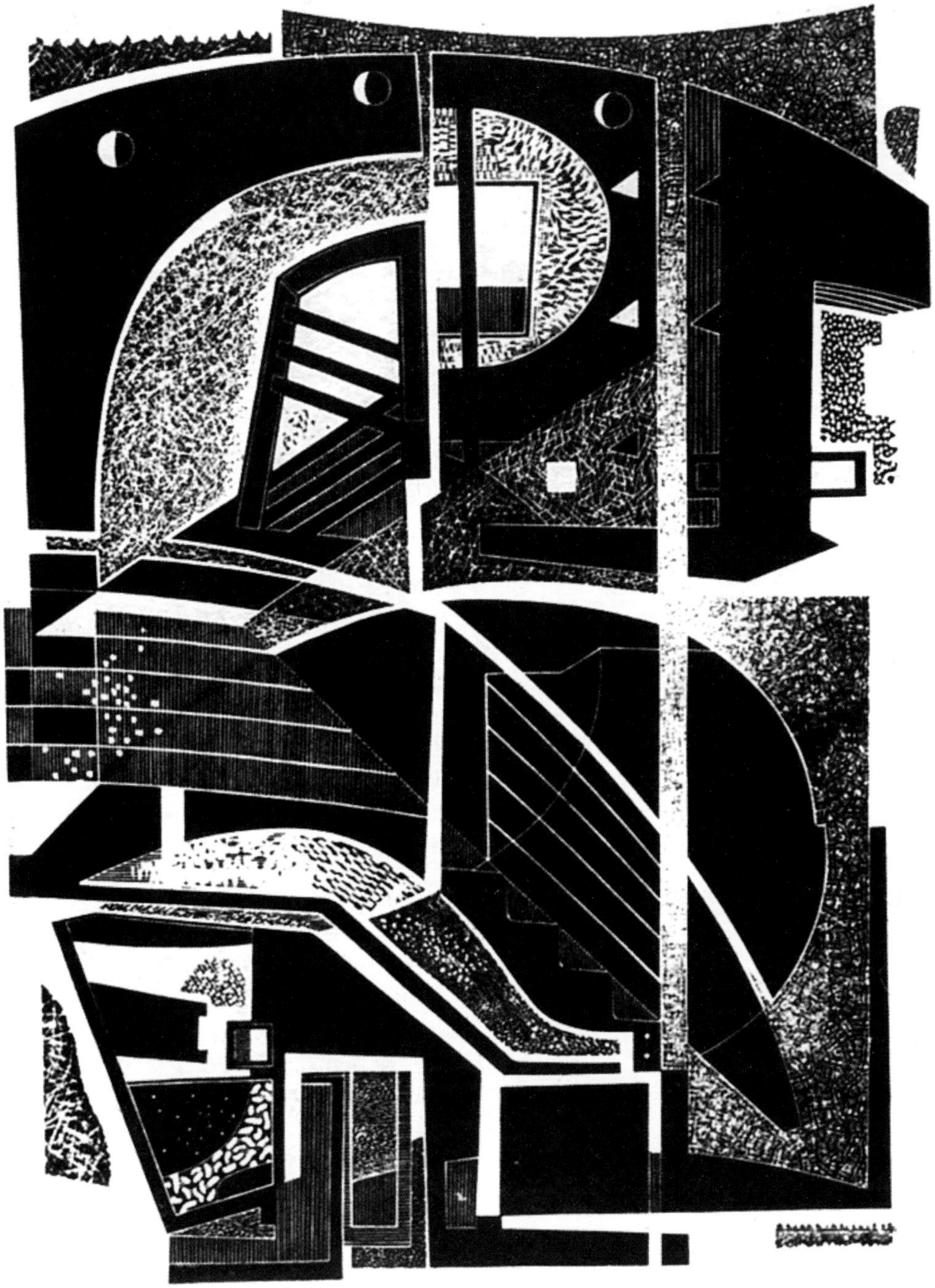

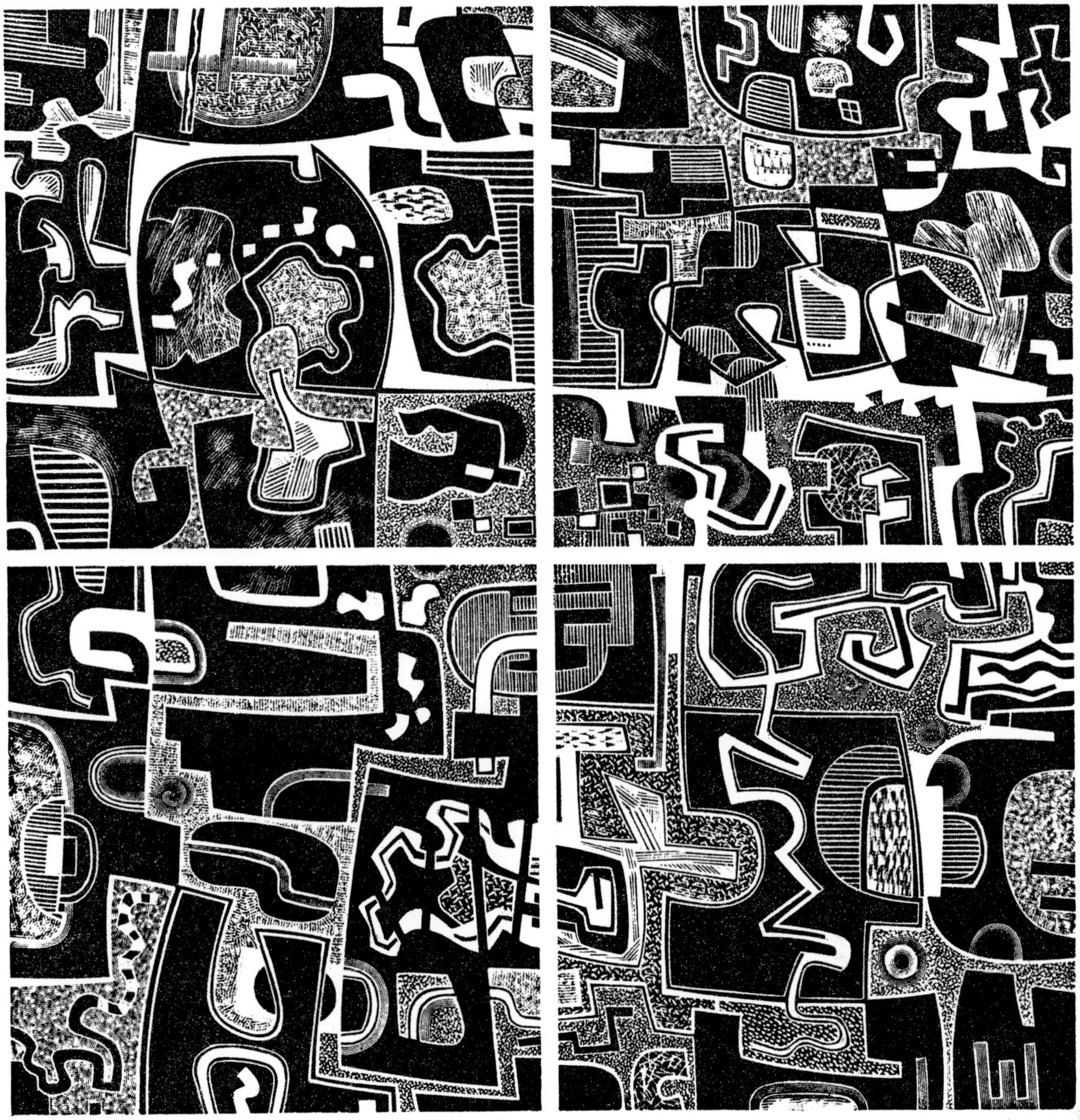

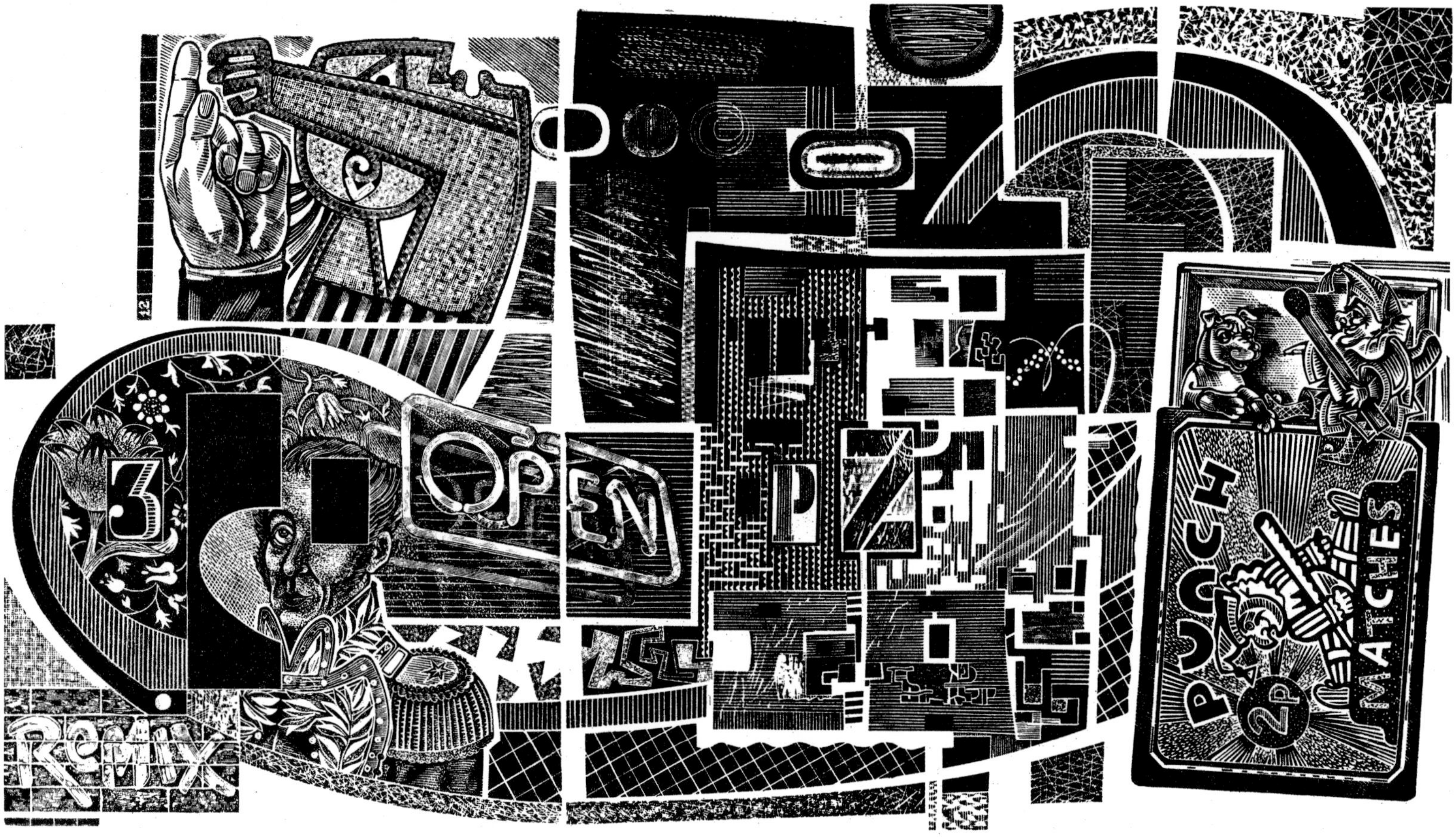

Creative Review, 2003, 160 × 270 mm